COLLEGE OUTLINE SERIES

A. W. LITTLEFIELD, *General Editor*

[*Continued on next page*]

[Continued from preceding page]

AN OUTLINE-HISTORY OF MUSIC

By HUGH MILTON MILLER, Ph.D.

Professor of Music, The University of New Mexico

Revised

New York

BARNES & NOBLE, INC.

Printed in the United States of America

To Jeanne

Preface

THE acquisition of historical information about music is of little value unless that information is applied directly to the literature of music. In any study of the history of music there is, inevitably, a considerable quantity of factual material that is of purely historical interest. However, in the present outline, nonessentials, such as biographical detail, have been minimized or else eliminated altogether. The present emphasis is upon the organization and presentation of essential historical information that has a direct bearing upon the actual music of any given period, or else upon the development of musical trends. The outline deals primarily with the characteristics of form and style as they apply to music of broad and specific periods, to nationalities or schools, and to the most important composers. This outline, then, is intended to be a substantial guide to the intelligent study of music by the amateur as well as by the advanced student of music. It can be applied equally well to the occupation of listening to records and to detailed analysis of musical scores.

Furthermore, the present work is more than a mere review outline. It is a functional work which can be used as the basic textbook in a college course in the history of music. This does not preclude collateral reading in the many excellent textbooks in general music history which are indeed valuable. But the present outline should be the core of the study.

At the end of each chapter through baroque music, record lists have been provided. These are selected from available recordings principally by Columbia and Victor, and from the valuable Anthologie Sonore. As more and more representative works are issued, especially recordings of music prior to 1600, the lists should be considerably supplemented.

Score lists, also, have been provided for representative music up to 1750, music for later periods being much more easily accessible. These lists are primarily based upon two musical anthologies: *Historical Anthology of Music,* edited by Dr. Willi Apel and Dr. Archibald T. Davison, and scheduled for publication in 1947 by the Harvard University Press; and Arnold Schering's *Geschichte der Musik in Beispielen* ("History of Music in Examples") published by Breitkopf & Härtel, Leipzig, 1931.

The author here wishes to express his deep gratitude to Dr. Lloyd Hibberd, North Texas State College, Denton, Texas, for reading of the entire manuscript and for numerous invaluable suggestions and criticisms and to Mr. Walter Robert for reading proof.

HUGH M. MILLER

Denton, Texas

CONTENTS

ILLUSTRATIONS AND CHARTS

TABULATED BIBLIOGRAPHY
OF
STANDARD TEXTBOOKS ON THE HISTORY OF MUSIC
(See next two pages.)

The following list gives the author, title, date, and publisher of the standard textbooks referred to in the table on the two succeeding pages.

Einstein, *A Short History of Music,* 1938, Knopf.
Ferguson, *A History of Musical Thought,* 1935, Crofts.
Ferguson, *A Short History of Music,* 1943, Crofts.
Finney, *A History of Music,* 1935, Harcourt, Brace.
Láng, *Music in Western Civilization,* 1941, Norton.
Leichtentritt, *Music, History, and Ideas,* 1938, Harvard.
McKinney and Anderson, *Music in History,* 1940, American Book Company.
Moore, *From Madrigal to Modern Music,* 1942, Norton.
Nef, *An Outline of the History of Music,* 1935, Columbia University.
Oxford History of Music (7 vols.), 1929–34, Oxford.
Pratt, *The History of Music,* 1935, Schirmer.
Reese, *Music in the Middle Ages,* 1940, Norton.

Tabulated Bibliographies are exclusive features of the College Outline Series and are fully protected by copyright.

QUICK REFERENCE TABLE TO STANDARD TEXTBOOKS

Light-faced type indicates pages. Bold-faced type indicates chapters.

CHAPTER	TOPIC	EINSTEIN	FERGUSON (Musical Thought)	FERGUSON (Short History)	FINNEY	LANG	LEICHTEN-TRITT	McKINNEY & ANDERSON	MOORE	NEF	OXFORD HISTORY	PRATT	REESE
I	Antiquity to about 200 A.D.	3-13	1, 2, 3	1	1, 2, 3	1, 2, 3	1	33-110		1		1, 2, 3	1, 2
II	The Christian Era	14-25 33-39	4	2	31-46 77-85	4, 5, 6	2	113-140 170-189		2	II: 5	4 85-92	3, 4, 5, 6, 7, 8
III	Early Stages of Polyphony	25-29	5	3	5, 6	7	3	141-153		53-57	I: Int. 1, 4, 5	77-85	9
IV	The Ars Antiqua	29-33	6	4	8	7	3	153-168		57-62	I: 6		10, 11
V	The Ars Nova	39-44	7.	5	9	8	3	189-203		62-66	I: 7 II: 305-327		12, 13
VI	The Netherlands Schools	44-56	9	7.	10, 11	9	4	203-210		66-80	II: 2 336-317	93-102	14
VII	The Sixteenth Century	57-78	10	8	12, 13	9	4, 5	221-305	2	4 80-86, 91-129	II: 3, 4	8, 147-150 159-162	
VIII	Instrumental Music to 1600		11, 12	9	85-87 14, 15	9		168-169 211-220	33-36	129-145 187-190	II: 6	75-76, 106-107 152-155	
IX	Musical Notation to 1600		8	6	46-52, 110-111 155-156			123-124 164-165		86-90		71-73 108	
X	THE BAROQUE PERIOD		8		209-210 24	10, 11	6	307-320	37-45		III: 1, 2	244-246 329-332	
XI	Nuove Musiche	79-97	176-183	154-161	215-224			324, 340, 348		146-150	III: 1, 2, 3	151 165-170	
XII	Dramatic Music	97-105 123-130	183-192 15, 17	161-169 11, 13	224-226, 17, 18, 19, 22, 297-305		6	320-348	78-96	150-187, 206-230, 235-243	III: 4, 5, 6, 7, 9, 10; IV: 1, 2, 3, 4, 5, 10	170-179, 11, 261-272, 273-285, 255-296	
XIII	Church Music	123-130								166-173 222-230	IV: 1, 2, 3, 4, 5	12	
XIV	Instrumental Music	105-123	16 250	12 228-229	20 305-314		6	348-360	45-78	187-205 230-235	III: 8 IV: 7, 8, 9	13, 14, 17, 18	
XV	Bach and Handel	131-141	18	14	23		7	407-448		218-227		249-261 289-295	

No.	Subject											
XVI	THE CLASSICAL PERIOD	142-148			354	12, 13, 14	8	361-371	97-102,		V: 1, 2, 3	335-336 406-408
XVII	Instrumental Music	148-178	20, 21	16, 17	361-369 26		8, 9	384-394, 427-435 449-470, 481-493	102-135 150-153	245-255	V: 7, 8, 9, 10, 11	336-354 371-378
XVIII	Opera	142-148 165-178	19	15 344-356	355-361			373-384, 394-405 439-446, 493-506		240-244 255-259	V: 4, 5	20, 21
XIX	Religious Music							407-427 471-472		282-283	V: 6	394-399
XX	THE ROMANTIC PERIOD	187-202	308-311	287-290	417-418	15, 16	10	507-523	163-167		VI: 1	411-413 495-498, 37
XXI	Beethoven	178-187	22	18	27		183-191	523-543	135-149	260-266		24
XXII	Opera—Italian	207-212	388-392 428-431	364-368 402-406	411-412, 422-423, 499-504			590-606	239 245-249	266-268	VI: 4	26 546-550
	Opera—French	207-212	386-387 392-394	362-363 368-370	412-415, 420-422, 504-506			606-618 622-623	240 249-253	268-274	VI: 3	26 550-556
	Opera—German	202-207 222-235	380-386 27	357-362 23	415-420 32		11	618-622, 624-648 664-666	240-245	274-282	VI: 2, 5, 14 VII: 8	424-431, 24 635-639
	Opera—Of Other Countries										VI: 13	
XXIII	Oratorio and Choral Music							525-564 656-658	233-239	282-288	VI: 8, 9 VII: 12	28 599-607
XXIV	Solo Song		312-319	290-298	29			562-564 573-583	167-171	288-296	VI: 12 VII: 10, 11	432-437 608-610
XXV	Piano Music		337-346	316-326	447-451				171-183	300-306	VI: 11	385-394, 457-461 536-545
XXVI	Instrumental Ensemble							564-572, 649-656 659-698	183-233	296-306 317-320	VI: 7, 8, 9 VII: 4, 5, 6, 7	35 533-536
XXVII	Summary of Principal Composers		312-324, 24, 25 415-428, 29, 30	287-302, 390-402 20, 21, 25, 26	30, 31, 33 35, 36, 37			699-810	167	307-317 321-344		30, 31, 32 639-654
XXVIII	MODERN MUSIC	244-253	31	27		17, 18, 19	12	813-832	254-262			
XXIX	Specific Aspects of Style	244-253	32	28	42		12	813-832	6	8		
XXX	20th Century Composers		480-506	448-482	40, 41			832-872				

See preceding page for complete list of titles

Abbreviations

AS   Anthologie Sonore
C   Columbia
CHM   Columbia History of Music
CM   Columbia Masterwork Set
D   Decca
G   Gramophone (His Master's Voice)
HAM   *Historical Anthology of Music* (to be published c. 1946)
MC   Musicraft
PM   Pro Musica
SB   Schering, *Geschichte der Musik in Beispielen*
SEMS   Société Edition de Musique Sacrée
WS   Wolf, *Sing- und Spielmusik aus älterer Zeit*
V   Victor
VM   Victor Masterpiece Set

PART ONE

Monodic Music to about 1300

CHAPTER I

Antiquity to about 200 A.D.

THE history of music until about 200 A.D. is shrouded in darkness. The limitations of the study are attributable to the fact that there is virtually no extant music because of the absence or inadequacies of early notation systems. Furthermore, except in the rather extensive Greek literature, little about music was written by ancient contemporaries.

Limited Knowledge of Ancient Music

Methods of Studying Musical Antiquity. Some knowledge of antiquity has been gained, however, through certain methods applied by modern scholars. (1) The study of musical systems of old civilizations of today (India, China, etc.) affords some insight into early practices. (2) The study of primitive tribes of today likewise provides some information about music's past. (3) Reconstruction of ancient systems from pictures, drawings, a few actual specimens of instruments, and a few fragments of old musical notation have provided some enlightenment.

Theories about Origins of Music. From the above methods, certain theories about the origin of music have been evolved. (1) Music may have developed from primitive communications: tribal drums, calls, etc. (2) It may have been associated with work rhythms at a very early time. (3) It seems to have been associated almost instinctively with emotional expression.

Ancient Uses of Music. Music probably did not exist as a separate art until the Middle Ages or later. Before then it was undoubtedly used in connection with various functions. Probably the most important of these were religious rituals, mystic ceremonies, festivals, etc.

3

It was probably used with war dances and other ceremonial dances. Work songs were very likely employed.

The Music of Ancient Civilizations

Despite our limitations of knowledge concerning musical antiquity, a few general facts are known about the music. It was not developed as a separate art, and it always existed in primitive simplicity.

Chinese Music. Chinese music made considerable use of a five-tone scale (*pentatonic*). Music was an important part of Oriental mysticism.

Egyptian Music. Egyptian music was very likely quite extensive. It had considerable influence upon later Greek music and musical theory of the 7th century B.C. The Egyptians were largely responsible for the development of the harp and lyre family of instruments.

Early Hebrew Music. Among the Hebrews music was important, judging from numerous Biblical references. It was probably of a ritual nature. The Hebrews employed unison singing, chanting, and considerable melodic embellishment. They also employed *antiphonal singing* (one choir or group of singers answered by another). The historical significance of early Hebrew music lies in the great influence it had upon Christian music, particularly upon plainsong.

Greek Music. The music of the Greeks is the most important in all antiquity for several reasons. (1) Greek theory had a marked influence upon theory in the Middle Ages. Such terms as *perfect consonance* (fourths, fifths, octaves) and *imperfect consonance* (thirds and sixths) come from Greek theory and are still used today. (2) Throughout history there have been recurrences of Greek ideals in music as, for example, the revival of Greek tragedy in the late 16th century which gave rise to opera. (3) The doctrine of *ethos* (see page 6) has been manifest in various ways.

GREEK CULTS. There were two cults that dominated musical concepts in general: (1) The Apollonian cult made use of the *cithara* (a plucked stringed instrument), and was characterized by clarity of form, purity, and objectivity of expression. (2) The Dionysian cult, on the other hand, used the *aulos* (a double-reed wind instru-

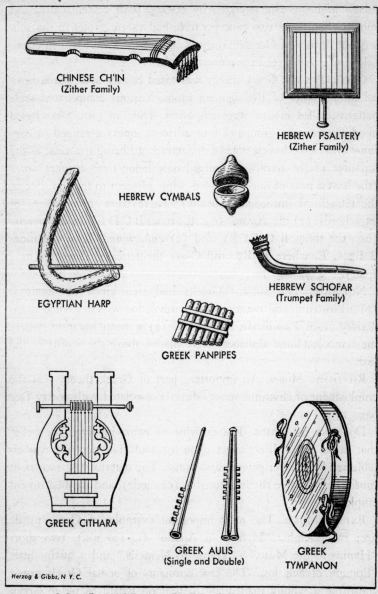

CHINESE CH'IN
(Zither Family)

HEBREW PSALTERY
(Zither Family)

HEBREW CYMBALS

HEBREW SCHOFAR
(Trumpet Family)

EGYPTIAN HARP

GREEK PANPIPES

GREEK CITHARA

GREEK AULIS
(Single and Double)

GREEK
TYMPANON

Herzog & Gibbs, N.Y.C.

SOME INSTRUMENTS OF ANTIQUITY

ment) and was characterized by ecstasy, passion, sensuality, and subjectivity. These two concepts have had varying roles in the subsequent history of Occidental music, the former embodied in classical trends, the latter in romantic trends.

GREEK THEORY. Greek theory was based largely upon the acoustical mathematics of Pythagorean ratios. Various complicated scale patterns, called *modes,* were employed. They, in turn, were based upon *tetrachords* (groups of four adjacent tones) arranged in *conjunct order* (the lowest note of one tetrachord being the same as the top note of the tetrachord immediately below) or *disjunct order* (the lowest note of one tetrachord being adjacent to the top note of the tetrachord immediately below). There were three genera of tetrachords: (1) the *diatonic* (e.g., the tones B C D E), (2) *chromatic* (e.g., the tones B C C♯ E), and (3) *enharmonic* (e.g., the tones B B♯ C E, where B, B♯, and C are theoretically a quarter tone apart).

NOTATION. The ancient Greeks had two kinds of notation: (1) an instrumental notation, the symbols for which were perhaps derived from Phoenician letters, and (2) a vocal notation, where the symbols (Ionic alphabet) were placed above the words of the text.

RHYTHMIC MODES. An important part of Greek theory was the employment of rhythmic modes directly associated with poetry (see page 12).

DOCTRINE OF ETHOS. The doctrine of *ethos* involved the belief that music has a direct effect upon the soul. The doctrine was established by the Peripatetics and Stoics. The determining factors in musical ethos were rhythm, tonality (or mode), and the instrument employed.

EXTANT MUSIC. The most important examples of Greek music are: two Delphic "Hymns to Apollo" (c. 130 B.C.), two short "Hymns to the Muse," a "Hymn to Nemesis," and a quaint little "Epitaph of Seikilos." The few remnants of actual Greek music constitute a wholly inadequate basis upon which to judge Greek music.

WRITERS. Although most of the Greek philosophers dealt in some measure with the subject of music, Aristoxenos is considered the most important Greek writer and theorist.

In general it should be kept in mind that music to the Greeks was not an individual art but was inseparably bound up with poetry and drama.

Roman Music. Very little is known about Roman music. In general, the Romans were imitators of Greek culture. Music did not develop extensively in their hands. It is likely that they were responsible for separation of music and poetry. They developed brass instruments largely for military purposes. Music was also used for enhancing sensual pleasure.

RECORDS
Hymn to Apollo. V 3529A.
Skolion of Seikilos. No. 1 in "2000 Years of Music."
Hymn to the Sun. No. 1 in "2000 Years of Music."
Jewish music. No. 2 in "2000 Years of Music."

SCORES
Skolion of Seikilos. SB 1, HAM 7c.
First Delphic Hymn. HAM 7a.
Hymn to the Sun. HAM 7b.
Jewish music. HAM 6.

CHAPTER II

The Christian Era

THE Christian Era in music encompasses the development of monodic music from about 200 A.D. to about 1300. Sacred and secular monody continued to develop long after the advent of polyphony (c. 800 A.D.).

Sacred Monody: Plainsong

Religious monody is referred to variously as *plainsong, plain chant, Gregorian chant,* and *cantus planus.* These terms may all be used synonymously; Gregorian chant usually implies a special branch of plainsong (see page 10). Catholic plainsong constitutes the greatest body of pure monody known to man, even greater in extent and beauty than folk song.

General Characteristics of Plainsong. Plainsong (1) is monodic, (2) is *modal* (i.e., it is based upon the eight church modes), (3) is unaccompanied, (4) is nonmetric, (5) uses a free prose rhythm, following that of the text, (6) has a limited range, (7) uses a Latin text, and (8) makes use of a special neumatic notation (see page 60).

The Eight Church Modes. The church modes are divided into two classes: (1) *authentic modes* which have an approximate melodic range (called *ambitus*) of an octave above the *final* (the plainsong tonic, i.e., the tone on which the melody ends), and which have Greek names, and (2) *plagal* modes which have an approximate melodic range of a fifth above and a fourth below the final, and which use the prefix *hypo-* with the Greek name. The eight church modes are: (1) Dorian, range D to D (scale as on the white keys of a piano), final D; (2) Hypodorian, range A to A, final D; (3) Phrygian, range E to E, final E; (4) Hypophrygian, range B

8

to B, final E; (5) Lydian, range F to F, final F; (6) Hypolydian, range C to C, final F; (7) Mixolydian, range G to G, final G; (8) Hypomixolydian, range D to D, final G. Four additional modes are infrequently used in Catholic church music: the Aeolian and Hypoaeolian modes on A (the same as the natural minor scale), and the Ionian and Hypoionian modes on C (the same as the major scale).

Styles of Text Setting. There are four styles of text setting of plainsong: (1) *syllabic,* where one note of the melody is set to one syllable of the text; typical of hymns and tropes (see page 10), (2) *neumatic,* a few notes to one syllable, the most common style, (3) *psalmodic,* numerous syllables to one note or pitch; used in psalms and gospel readings, and (4) *melismatic,* numerous notes to one syllable; used in settings of the Alleluia.

Early Chant Cultures. Sacred monody of the pre-Christian eras had an important influence upon later Christian chant. There are four principal pre-Christian chant cultures. (1) Syria, a part of the Roman Empire near the Holy Land, was the scene of much religious activity. The Syrians employed *antiphonal* chant (one choir answered by another) and *responsorial* chant (a solo voice answered by a choir). (2) Byzantine culture contributed hymn writing. It influenced Greek Orthodox Church chant. (3) Armenian chant was developed in connection with an alphabetic notation and later with a system of neumatic notation (see page 60). Armenian chant was in the style of hymns. (4) Hebrew chant was perhaps the most important early chant culture because much early Christian plainsong was taken directly from Hebrew chants.

Branches of Christian Chant. There are five branches of Christian chant: (1) Russian chant is derived from Byzantine chant and is used in the Greek Orthodox Church. (2) Ambrosian chant, named for Ambrose, Bishop of Milan in the 4th century A.D., is characterized by development of hymnody and antiphonal singing. (3) Gallican chant flourished in France until Charlemagne ordered substitution of Roman rites around 800 A.D. A few of these Gallican tunes were carried over into Roman service. (4) Mozarabic chant stems from the Moorish invasion of the Spanish peninsula where Christianity was allowed to continue. The earliest Mozarabic chant manuscripts date from the end of the 9th century. (5) Gregorian chant is the most important branch of plainsong. It begins with the liturgical organization effected by Pope Gregory the Great in the 6th century A.D. He collected and organized liturgical chant.

Catholic Liturgy. Plainsong is used in the Catholic Mass and in some of the smaller services known as Canonical Hours. The Mass includes two types of liturgy: (1) the *Ordinary of the Mass,* including the Kyrie, Gloria, Credo, Sanctus, and Agnus Dei, the texts of which do not vary, and (2) the *Proper of the Mass,* including the Introitus, Graduale, Alleluia, Offertorium, and Communio, the texts of which vary from day to day according to the season or the saint. The Ordinary of the Mass is a later development than the plainsongs of the Proper, which gradually became standardized from about the 7th century.

Tropes and Sequences. From the 9th to the 12th centuries a new development in plainsong took place. This originated with the practice of interpolating plainsong melody and text phrases (syllabic style) between the words of an already existing plainsong, or between the verses of a hymn. These additions were called *tropes.* A special kind of trope, called *sequela* or *sequence,* originated with the practice of adding prose texts syllabically to the *jubilus* (long melismatic passages occurring at the end of the Alleluia). Sequences became detached from the original plainsong. Tuotilo (10th century) is considered the father of the trope. Notker Balbulus (9th century) and Adam of St. Victor (12th century) are important writers of sequences.

Secular Monody

Lacking the organization and systematic dissemination that plainsong received in the hands of the Church, secular music, though doubtless extensive, was not preserved. Little secular music has been recorded earlier than the 10th century. The "Song of the Sibyl" is one of the earliest known secular songs.

General Characteristics of Secular Monody. Secular monody differs from plainsong in various respects: (1) It usually has a metrical basis and is more strongly rhythmic than is plainsong. (2) It often has a wider range. (3) The phrases of secular melody are usually more regular. (4) Secular melody is not strictly modal. (5) It is usually nationalistic in character as opposed to the more universal nature of plainsong. (6) It is now more often harmonized and sung to accompaniment. (7) Secular texts are usually in the vernacular language.

Latin Songs. An exception to characteristic (7) above is a body of songs with Latin texts. From the late 10th to the early 13th centuries vagrant students and men in minor ecclesiastic orders, known as *goliards,* roamed over Europe composing and singing Latin songs on various subjects—love songs, drinking songs, spring songs, ribald songs, and humorous paraphrases of plainsong. *Conductus* is a term loosely applied to all sorts of Latin songs from the 11th to the 13th centuries. These were normally based upon metrical texts and the music was original. However, conductus probably originated as a trope sung during processions in the liturgy.

Jongleurs and Gaukler. In the Middle Ages there was an important class of minstrel entertainers called *jongleurs* in France and *Gaukler* in Germany. They were performers and entertainers rather than poets or composers. They were musically important in that they kept alive a large body of secular melody.

Troubadours and Trouvères. The most important body of secular monody comes from two minstrel groups in France: the *troubadours* and the *trouvères.* Unlike the jongleurs they were persons of rank. The troubadours flourished in Provence in southern France from the end of the 11th century to the end of the 13th. Of this group some 264 melodies are preserved and about 2600 poems. The most important names of this group are Marcabru of Gascony, Bernart de Ventadorn, Guiraut de Bornelh, Guiraut de Riquier, and Bertran de Born. The trouvères, located in northern France, reached a peak of development slightly later than did the troubadours. There are about 1400 extant melodies and roughly 4000 poems of the trouvères. The most important trouvères are Quesnes de Béthune, Blondel de Nesle, Thibaut IV (King of Navarre), and Adam de la Halle, the latter famous for a medieval play with music, *Robin et Marion.*

Characteristics of Style. Troubadour and trouvère songs have virtually the same characteristics. The melodic range is usually within an octave. There is some use of the church modes, but the tendency is toward major and minor. The songs are based upon *rhythmic modes* derived from the Greeks, and are usually thought to be in some form of triple meter. The basic modes are: (1) *trochaeus* — ∪ ♩♪ , (2) *iambus* ∪ — ♩♪ , (3) *dactylus* — ∪∪ ♩.♩♪ , (4) *anapaest* ∪∪ — ♪♪♩ , (5) *spondeus* — — ♩.♩. and (6) *tribrachys* ∪∪∪ ♩♪♪. Another characteristic of troubadour and trouvère music is the great variety of forms employed. Apparently it was common practice among the minstrels to improvise accompaniments to their songs with the *vielle* (the most important string instrument of the Middle Ages; four strings, one drone string, bowed) or some form of lyre.

Poetic Types. The main poetic types, according to subject, used by the medieval minstrels were: (1) *canso,* a love song, (2) *sirventes,* a satirical poem sung to a known melody, (3) *planh,* a lament on the death of a great personage, (4) *pastourell,* where a knight woos a shepherdess, (5) *chanson de toile,* a spinning song, (6) *enueg,* a satire, (7) *aube,* the song of a friend watching over lovers until dawn, (8) *tenso* or *jeu-parti,* dialogue between two or three people, and (9) *chanson de geste,* an epic chronicle of the deeds of a hero.

Song Forms. A great wealth of diversified musical forms was employed by the troubadours and trouvères. These forms may be divided into four main classes: those derived from (1) *litany,* (2) *rondel,* (3) *sequence,* and (4) *hymn.*

LITANY TYPES. Musical forms derived from the litany are the *chanson de geste,* the *rotrouenge,* the *strophic laisse,* and the *chanson with refrains.*

a. *Chanson de Geste.* The chanson de geste consists of numerous unequal paragraph-like sections called *laisses,* each of which consists of two short melodic patterns repeated over and over until the end of a thought is reached, at which point a cadential formula is sung or played. The plan of the laisse, then, is: *ab ab ab ab . . . c.*

b. *Rotrouenge.* The rotrouenge form makes use of a refrain, apparently intended for participation by an audience. It consists of a

SATAN PLAYING A VIELLE
(13th Century)

ANGEL PLAYING A REBEC
(13th Century)

**JONGLEUR PLAYING
A VIELLE**
(15th Century)

**A PLAYER ON THE
TROMBA MARINA**

Adapted from A History of Music by Emil Naumann

Herzog & Gibbs, N. Y. C.

SOME INSTRUMENTS OF THE MIDDLE AGES

strophe and a closing formula presented by a soloist, and a refrain which is the same melodic pattern as the close of the strophe. It may be represented by the formula: *a a a . . . b B*. (Lower-case letters stand for soloist performance, capitals for chorus refrain.)

c. *Strophic Laisse*. A shorter lyric form growing out of the chanson de geste is the strophic laisse in which a single laisse pattern is used over and over again with each stanza.

d. *Chanson with Refrains*. A fourth litany type is the chanson with refrains. This includes several different refrains borrowed from well-known songs, each being chosen for its appropriateness to the foregoing strophe.

RONDEL TYPES. The rondel types include the *rondeau, virelai,* and *ballade.* These were often dance songs for leader and chorus.

a. *Rondeau*. The rondeau has the musical form: *a A ab AB*. If the text has eight or more lines the complete refrain (*AB*) appears at the beginning as well as at the end. The rondeau continued to be a popular form for several centuries.

b. *Virelai*. When a two-part refrain (*AB*) is used at the beginning and at the end, but different material is used by the soloist, the form is called a virelai and is represented by the formula: *AB cc ab AB*.

c. *Ballade*. Three principal ballade forms are represented by the following formulas: (1) *AB cd cd ef AB,* (2) *AB cd cd e ab AB,* and (3) *ab ab cd E* (which drops the introductory refrain).

SEQUENCE TYPES. The various forms derived from the plainsong sequence are various forms of the *lai* and the *estampie.* They are characterized by melodic phrases immediately repeated to new words.

a. *Lai*. The lai may be represented in general by the formula: *aa bb cc dd ee,* etc., or by $aa_1 \ bb_1 \ cc_1 \ dd_1$, etc., in which the repetition is a slight variation of the preceding phrase.

b. *Reinforced Lai*. A group of phrase pairs repeated together is called reinforced lai. For example it might be represented by the formula: *aa bb   cc dd ee ff   cc dd ee ff   gg hh.*

c. *Strophic Lai*. A shortened version of the lai plan includes fewer phrase units (single phrases or phrase pairs), and it may be represented by the typical pattern: *a bb cc d.* The pattern might be further reduced to the formula: *aa b a,* which is the familiar plan of later song form and the da capo aria. Other shortened versions of the lai form are called *lai segments.*

d. *Estampie.* A dance form, known as the estampie (see page 52), employs the general sequence construction, but is characterized by grouping of the pairs (called *puncta*) as follows: ab_1 ab_2 cb_1 cb_2 db_1 db_2 eb_1 eb_2. (This would be an estampie with four puncta.)

HYMN TYPES. Forms derived from plainsong hymns are the *vers, chanson* (without refrain), and *rounded chanson.*

a. *Vers.* Each strophe or stanza of the vers, as with the plainsong hymn, consists of different musical phrases (*a b c d e f g*).

b. *Chanson.* The chanson without refrain is represented by a repeated section and an unrepeated one: *ab ab cd,* in which the unrepeated section (*cd*) is longer than the repeated section.

c. *Rounded Chanson.* The rounded chanson resembles the chanson but with the addition of the second phrase of the opening section heard again at the end: *ab ab cdb.*

Minnesingers. The *Minnesingers* (singers of chivalrous love) flourished in Germany in the 12th and 13th centuries, largely as an outgrowth of the troubadour movement in France. Their songs closely resemble the style of the troubadour and trouvère music. They used duple as well as triple meter and employed the Ionian (major) mode as well as the older church modes.

NAMES. The most important names of this class are Walther von der Vogelweide, Neithart von Reuenthal, Heinrich von Meissen (called "Frauenlob"), and Heinrich von Müglin (14th century).

FORMS. The principal types employed by the Minnesingers are: the *Lied,* the *Tagelied* (similar to the French aube), the *Leich* (similar to the French lai), and the *Spruch,* a proverb.

Meistersingers. The *Meistersingers* of the 14th to 16th centuries, unlike the aristocratic Minnesingers of an earlier period, were of the burgher class, and were resident members of the typical guild organizations of the Renaissance. Characteristic of the Meistersinger music are the numerous pedantic rules governing musical creation, the recurrent use of standard melodies, and a certain amount of crudity and lack of inspiration. The principal Meistersingers were Conrad

Nachtigall, Sebastian Wilde, Adam Puschmann, and Hans Sachs (immortalized, along with the whole Meistersinger movement, in Richard Wagner's *Die Meistersinger von Nürnberg*).

English Secular Monody. The extant music of the British Isles prior to the 15th century is not extensive, but it indicates a high degree of artistic development. In the Anglo-Saxon period two classes of minstrels existed: *scops,* who were resident minstrels, and *gleemen,* traveling minstrels. Both classes seem to have practiced the recitation of long poems to harp accompaniment. One name is associated with early English monody: St. Godric (12th century), a half-legendary hermit of northern England from whom numerous songs are supposed to have come.

RECORDS

 Plainsong

  Ordinary of the Mass: Kyrie, Agnus Dei, Gloria, and Sanctus from the Mass "Lux et origo." V M87 1–2.

  Examples from the Proper of the Mass. V M87 1–2. AS 34.

  Alleluia ascendit Deus; Alleluia Dominus in sina. C 9088M.

  Requiem aeternam. C 9088M.

  Hymn in honor of St. John the Baptist (1st half only); Hymn: Veni Creator Spiritus; Te Deum. V 20896B.

 Secular Monody

  Blondel de Nesle, Perrin d'Agincourt, Richard Coeur de Léon, Walther von der Vogelweide, Rumelant. AS 18a, 18b.

  Thibaut of Navarre, Adam de la Halle. V 17760.

SCORES

 Plainsong

  Ordinary of the Mass: Gloria and Sanctus from the Mass "In festis duplicibus." SB 2a.

  Gradual verse: "Qui sedes." Roman and Milan versions. SB 2b.

  Gradual verse: "Haec dies." HAM 12.

  Responsorium: "Libera me." HAM 14.

  Byzantine chant. HAM 8.

  Ambrosian hymns. HAM 9.

  Psalm 146 with antiphon. HAM 11.

  Alleluia: Angelus Domini. HAM 13.

Alleluia: Dominus in sina, with sequence "Christus hunc diem."
HAM 16.

Tropes. Tuotilo, "Omnipotens." SB 3. Kyrie, Kyrie trope.
HAM 15.

Sequence: SB 4, 5, 6. HAM 16.

Secular Monody

Troubadour and trouvère songs. SB 11, 13, 14. HAM 18, 19.

Minnesingers. SB 12, 21. HAM 20.

Meistersingers. HAM 24.

Latin songs (conductus). HAM 17.

Latin songs (religious laudi). HAM 21.

Spanish songs. HAM 22.

English song: St. Godric, "Sainte Marie." HAM 23.

PART TWO

The Polyphonic Period (800–1600)

CHAPTER III

Early Stages of Polyphonic Music

THE most significant innovation in the entire history of music is
the advent of polyphony in the 9th century. The polyphonic concept
—more than one single melodic line at a time—dominates the artistic
development of all Occidental music. The early stages of its development (800–1200) take place in the late Carolingian period and the
early Middle Ages.

Organum. The term *organum* is applied to various types of early
polyphony. The terms *organum, discant,* and *diaphony* were used
interchangeably at first. Organum began about the 9th century with
the practice of singing plainsong melody in two parts simultaneously a fourth or fifth apart. In other words, the organum moved
in parallel motion without melodic or rhythmic independence of
the parts.

Theories concerning the Origin of Parallel Organum. (1) Belaiev,
a Russian musicologist, holds that the practice of singing in parallel
fourths and fifths appears in secular music before it does in sacred.
(2) One explanation of parallel organum is based upon the physical
series of overtones: octave, fifth, fourth, third, etc. Beginning with
the much earlier practice of singing melodies in octaves (called
magadizing), this is also the order in which these intervals appear
chronologically in parallel organum. (3) Another theory relates
early organum to the fact that the natural pitch ranges of the human
voice lie approximately a fifth apart, hence it would be natural for
tenors and bases to sing the same melody a fifth apart. (4) It is
believed that two-part music was played on an organ at an early
time, leading to the practice of doubling the voice part at the interval

of a fourth or fifth, and in general experimenting with parallel polyphony. (5) Finally, parallel organum may have originated from the practice of repeating a sequence phrase a fifth higher by a second chorus, which was only a step from both choruses singing the same phrase simultaneously.

Types of Organum. The following types of organum are presented in approximate chronological order, although no dates can be affixed to the beginning or end of any one practice. There are two factors in the development of polyphony: (1) melodic independence, departure from strict parallel motion of two or more voice parts, and (2) rhythmic independence, where two or more notes in one voice part are sung to one note in the other parts.

STRICT SIMPLE ORGANUM. The most primitive stage of polyphony is called *strict simple organum*. It consists of two voice parts moving in parallel motion a fourth or a fifth apart. It is based upon a plainsong melody, called *vox principalis*. The added part, the same melody sung simultaneously a fourth or a fifth below the principalis, is called *vox organalis*.

COMPOSITE ORGANUM. For polyphony of more than two parts the vox principalis was doubled an octave below and/or the vox organalis doubled an octave above. This is called *composite organum*, which is simply a manner of adding parts without departing from strict parallel motion.

FREE ORGANUM. Melodic independence began with the practice of beginning two-part organum in unison (both parts on the same note); then while the vox organalis remains stationary the vox principalis moves until the interval of a fourth is reached. Both voices then move in parallel motion until the close of the melody (called *occursus*) where they again move to unison. This form was preferred by Guido d'Arezzo (11th century). Strict organum was probably still used in the 11th century, although the interval of a fifth was no longer permitted in parallel motion.

SUSTAINED-TONE STYLE, ORGANUM PURUM. Free organum gave melodic independence to polyphony. The next step was toward rhythmic independence, gained in the *sustained-tone style,* sometimes called *organum purum*. Here each tone of the plainsong melody was sustained, or held out (hence the term *tenor*), while added counterpoint moved in free melismatic style. The tenor part may have been played by an instrument.

GYMEL. The practice of singing a given melody in thirds was called *gymel* or *cantus gemellus* (i.e., "twin song"). This practice seems to have had no connection with ecclesiastical developments in organum and it may have existed prior to organum. It was probably of Welsh or English origin.

Writers and Documents Pertaining to Organum. The first distinct reference to part singing was by Bishop Aldhelm (c. 640–709). The first detailed description of organum is in an anonymous work entitled *Musica Enchiriadis* of the 9th century or earlier. An early mention of organum is found in the treatise *De Harmonica Institutione* by Hucbald. The *Winchester Troper* is an important 11th-century manuscript collection of tropes with organum. John Cotton, an English theorist in the early 12th century, prescribed the use of fourths, fifths, and octaves in parallel and contrary motion, the crossing of voices, and two or three notes of the organalis against one note of the plainsong cantus firmus. These writings of Cotton show that polyphony had achieved some degree of melodic and rhythmic independence by the early 12th century.

RECORDS
    Organum. V 20897, examples 2 and 3.
    Veni Sancte Spiritus. CHM Vol. 1.
    Mira lege. CHM Vol. 1.
    Alleluia: Angelus Domini. V M739–2.
    Organum purum. Easter Gradual: "Haec dies." V M739–2.

SCORES
    Organum: "Cunctipotens genitor." SB 9.
    Parallel organum. HAM 25.
    Free organum. HAM 26.
    Melismatic organum. HAM 27.

CHAPTER IV

The Ars Antiqua

The music of the 12th and 13th centuries (the Middle Ages or the Gothic period) is referred to as the *ars antiqua*.

General Characteristics of the Period. In the Middle Ages Paris became the cultural center of the world. This was the time of the troubadours and trouvères, the late crusades, and the building of the great Gothic cathedrals of Europe. Important developments in polyphonic music took place at St. Martial in Limoges and at Chartres in the 12th century, and at Notre Dame in Paris in the late 12th and 13th centuries.

General Characteristics of the Music. (1) Complete melodic and rhythmic independence was established. (2) All intervals were employed in various combinations. Octaves, unisons, fifths predominated as perfect consonances. Thirds and sixths were more frequently used than before. Seconds, sevenths, ninths, and fourths were treated as dissonances. (3) Frequent sharp, dissonant clashes of the voice parts characterize the harmony of the period. (4) Triple time (*tempus perfectum*) was used almost exclusively. (5) Adherence to the rhythmic modes often resulted in rhythmic monotony. (6) Three-voice polyphony prevailed. Two-part polyphony continued to be used and four-part polyphony began. (7) A device known as *hocket* or *hoquetus* was used. It consists of frequent arbitrary interruptions in the melodic line of one part alternating with similar interruptions in another part.

Forms. Various styles of free organum were employed, particularly the sustained-tone style. In addition to these, new forms were created.

CLAUSULA. At the beginning of the 13th century there arose a new polyphonic form called *clausula*. As opposed to organum, which used an entire plainsong as the cantus firmus basis, the clausula used a short melisma from an Alleluia for the cantus firmus tenor. To this were added two contrapuntal parts in faster-moving note values. All the parts were sung without text or possibly played by instruments. In the manuscripts only a word or two or sometimes just a syllable were used to indicate the plainsong from which the tenor was borrowed.

POLYPHONIC CONDUCTUS. Another important form of the period is the *polyphonic conductus*. Here a freely composed tenor is used, rather than a plainsong. All the parts move in more or less uniform rhythm and use the same text throughout in all parts.

PARIS MOTET. The most important form of the period is the *motet*. This is usually called the *Paris motet* or the *13th-century motet* to distinguish it from the very different style of the later Renaissance motet. The lowest part, the tenor, is a plainsong broken up into one of the rhythmic modes, usually the slower-moving spondeus. Two upper-voice parts with different rhythms usually move in faster values than the tenor. The upper voices were set to different religious texts in Latin. Late in the 13th century secular texts in French were used for the two upper voices, and eventually for all three parts. The tenor part has a Latin text, but it was probably often performed instrumentally. Harmonic clashes of the voice parts are particularly characteristic of the motet.

RONDEL. A less important form of the *ars antiqua* is the *rondel* or *rondellus*. It is a polyphonic form that makes use of the principle of *exchange*, which means that different melodic motives or phrases are exchanged between two or more voices. For example, the lowest of three voices might sing the melodic phrases *a*, *b*, and *c*, while a second voice at the same time would sing the same phrases in the order *c*, *a*, and *b*, and the top voice would sing the same phrases in the order *b*, *c*, and *a*. This practice is important because it opened the way to the contrapuntal devices of imitation and canon.

Important Names and Manuscripts. Perhaps the first important composer in music history is Léonin, connected with the Notre

Dame school in the middle 12th century. His successor was Pérotin in the late 12th and early 13th centuries. An important writer and composer of the late 13th century is Franco of Cologne. Pierre de la Croix (or Petrus de Cruce) in the late 13th and early 14th centuries represents a transition from the 13th- to the 14th-century styles. The largest manuscript collection of 13th-century motets is the *Montpellier Codex*. The famous *rota* or round, "Sumer Is Icumen In," was formerly thought to belong to the 13th century, but recent evidence established by Dr. Manfred Bukofzer shows it to be a product of the early 14th century.

RECORDS
"O Miranda Dei caritas." "Puellare gremium." V M739-3.
Pérotin, "Difusa est gratia." Léonin, "Deum time." AS 65.
Pérotin, conductus: "Beata viscera." Lumen 32012.

SCORES
Organa. HAM 29, 31.
Motets. WS 3. HAM 32, 33–35. SB 18, 19, 20.
Clausulae. HAM 30. SB 15.
Conductus. HAM 38, 39. SB 16.

CHAPTER V

The Ars Nova

T HE music of the 14th century was referred to as the *ars nova* ("the new art") by contemporaries to distinguish it from the older practices of the 13th century which they referred to as ars antiqua.

General Characteristics of the Period. In general, the 14th century is marked by great literary activity with such names as Petrarch, Dante, Boccaccio, and Chaucer. The most important painter of the period is the Florentine Giotto. It was also a period of trouble in the Church, resulting in a dual papacy (Avignon and Rome) between 1378 and 1418. Two additional historical events belong to the 14th century: the "Hundred Years' War" between France and England (1337–1453) and the Great Plague of the black death (1349). Italy shares musical leadership with France in the ars nova.

General Characteristics of the Music. (1) Predominance of secular music in the ars nova is attributable to trouble in the Church. (2) New polyphonic forms were added to the old ones. (3) Imitation and canon were employed rather extensively for the first time. (4) An important characteristic of the ars nova was the development of a new rhythmic freedom. *Tempus imperfectum* (duple time) now predominated over tempus perfectum (triple time). Strict adherence to the rhythmic modes disappeared, along with the monotonous, short, recurrent patterns characteristic of the ars antiqua music. (5) There was a predominance of two-part writing (especially in Italy). Three- and four-part polyphony was used mainly in France and England. (6) Melodic style was generally more florid. This was especially true in Italy. (7) Harmonic style was characterized by a more extensive use of thirds and by a bold treatment of dissonance. There was little parallelism.

Important Names. Philippe de Vitry (c. 1290–1361), a French theorist and composer, is noted primarily for a treatise entitled *Ars Nova* which deals with expansion of systems of notation. The first prohibition of parallel fifths appears in this work. De Vitry was probably a great composer as well, but not much of his music has been preserved. Guillaume de Machaut (c. 1300–1377) is the foremost French composer of the 14th century. Francesco Landini (c. 1325–1397), a blind organist, is the greatest Italian composer of the 14th century.

French Ars Nova Forms. Most of the forms used by French composers in the 14th century are a continuation of earlier forms of the Middle Ages.

ISORHYTHMIC MOTET. The most important 14th-century liturgical form is the *isorhythmic motet,* developed from the Paris motet of the 13th century. It is a polyphonic composition of three or four parts, based upon a liturgical cantus firmus in the tenor. Instead of the short modal patterns of the Paris motet tenor, however, longer patterns are employed. These are called *talea* (i.e., "cutting" where a rhythmic pattern begins again). There is also repetition of melodic units, called *color,* which do not coincide with talea. This isorhythmic plan was applied less strictly to the upper parts of the motet, than to the tenor.

BALLADE. In the secular field perhaps the most important form was the *ballade,* a polyphonic form derived from the troubadour type of the same name.

OTHER FORMS. Other forms employed in the French ars nova music are the *lai, chanson ballade* or *virelai,* and the *rondeau.* Credit for the first complete polyphonic setting of the Mass by one composer goes to Machaut.

Italian Ars Nova Forms. In Italy new forms were developed. These were largely secular forms. Little sacred music was produced in Italy in this period.

MADRIGAL. An important form of the early 14th century is the Italian *madrigal.* The origin of the term has been explained variously as being derived from *mandriali* (a pastoral poem), *matricale* (a rustic song in the mother tongue), and *madriale* (a hymn to the

Virgin). The ars nova madrigal was usually a two-part composition, the upper part characteristically florid and the lower part in slower-moving values, often played on an instrument. The formal plan of the madrigal consists of two or three strophes of three lines each and a final strophe of two lines called *ritornello*. The musical setting was usually the same for the strophes but different for the ritornello. Frequent use of imitation and a free rhythmic style are typical of the madrigal.

CACCIA. A second important form of the period is the *caccia,* a hunting song. It was most often a three-part composition with two parts in strict canon, while the lowest part (tenor) did not imitate the melody of the other voices but was free. It was probably performed instrumentally. The caccia was a lengthy composition.

BALLATA. The third most important form of the Italian ars nova is the *ballata.* It corresponds to the French virelai and not to ballade. The poetic form consists of several six-line stanzas, each preceded and followed by a refrain. Landini made two- and three-voice settings of ballatas.

RECORDS
Machaut, "Douce dame jolie." V 45083B, first part.
Machaut, Mass. AS 31, 32.
Vincenzo da Rimini, "Ita se n'era." AS 8a.
Giovanni da Cascia, "Io son un pellegrin." AS 8a.
Religious songs of the 14th century. AS 8b.
14th-century canons. AS 59.

SCORES
French Ars Nova
Isorhythmic motet. WS 5. SB 27. HAM 44.
Ballade. HAM 45, 47. SB 26a.
Virelai. HAM 46. SB 26b.
Rondeau. HAM 48.

Italian Ars Nova
Madrigals. HAM 49, 50, 54. SB 22.
Ballata. HAM 51, 53. SB 23, 24.
Caccia. HAM 52. WS 7.
Mass: Movements from the Ordinary. HAM 56, 57.

CHAPTER VI

The Netherlands Schools

In the 15th century leadership in polyphonic development shifted from France and Italy to the Netherlands area. This includes the activities of two schools: the Burgundian in the first part of the 15th century, and the Flemish in the second half. The techniques of the latter dominated the 16th century, and spread over all of continental Europe.

General Historical Background. The 15th century represents the transition from the Middle Ages to the Renaissance. There is a general breakdown of feudalism, and in its place the rise of the bourgeois class, particularly in the new commercial cities. France and England rise as national powers. Of particular significance to the history of music is the important cultural influence of Burgundian courts under Philip the Good (1419–1467) and Charles the Bold (1467–1477). Their patronage of music, both sacred and secular, gave great impetus to the art. In painting, this is the period of Leonardo da Vinci, Van Eyck, and Raphael. The invention of movable type (1454) does not directly affect music until the 16th century.

The Burgundian School

There is a marked difference of style between the music of the first half of the 15th century represented by the Burgundian school and that of the later 15th century referred to as the Flemish school.

Characteristics of the Music. The following characteristics distinguish the music of the Burgundian school from that of the Flemish school. (1) Three-voice polyphony prevails. (2) Melodic and rhythmic interest centers on the upper voice. (3) The melodic interval of a third becomes the chief characteristic of melodic style in general. (4) Harmony is characterized by many incomplete triads (without thirds), but open fifths and octaves are not used in parallel motion. (5) Parallelism does occur in sections of polyphonic compositions in the form of a device known as *fauxbourdon* or *English discant*. This consists of progressions of first inversion triads (triads arranged so that the third of the chord is the lowest-sounding member; e.g., the chord C–E–G with E in the bass). (6) Contrapuntal imitation is infrequent. (7) The *7–6–1 cadence* (sometimes mistakenly called the "Landini cadence") is commonly employed. This cadential formula, employed at ends of phrases and in final cadences, consists of the melodic progression of the scale degrees 7, 6, and 1 (e.g., the tones B, A, and C in the key of C). (8) Polytextuality disappears. (9) The use of a cantus firmus, or "borrowed tenor," is less frequently employed than before or after the first half of the 15th century.

Principal Composers. In the early 15th century there is an important group of English composers. They are Roy Henry (Henry V, King of England), Cooke, Pycard, Damett, Lionel Power, and, the most important, John Dunstable (c. 1370–1453). Power and Dunstable were well known on the Continent and are directly connected with the Burgundian school proper. The two most important names of the Burgundian group are Guillaume Dufay (c. 1400–1474) and Gilles Binchois (c. 1400–1460).

The Flemish School

The Flemish School is perhaps the more important because the techniques of polyphony established by its composers were the basis of style and form for the entire 16th century in sacred vocal po-. lyphony.

Characteristics of the Music. A comparison between the corresponding elements of style of the two schools will show the marked differences in the respective music. (1) Four-voice polyphony predominates. (2) There is more equality of parts. (3) A bass part is added, giving a lower register to the music. (4) There are more complete triads, and more sonority. (5) Sections using *chordal style* (sometimes called *familiar style*) alternate with sections more rhythmically independent. The latter are often *fugal* (i.e., employing imitative counterpoint). (6) There is a technical mastery of counterpoint revealed in this period. This does not mean that technical facility in counterpoint was featured at the expense of real artistry. The following contrapuntal devices were established: canon, imitation, *augmentation* (increasing the time value of each note of a melody or theme), *inversion* (turning the theme upside down), and *retrograde* (the theme or melody read backwards). A composition consistently using the latter device is called a *cancrizans,* or "crab canon." (7) Duet style is frequently found in the late 15th century, particularly in the motets of Josquin. This consists of passages during which only two voice parts at a time are performing. (8) Fauxbourdon and the 7–6–1 cadence disappear. The latter is replaced by *authentic* (V I), *plagal* (IV I), and *modal cadences* of various kinds. (9) In general, expressive beauty is achieved by the Flemish composers. This quality was later referred to as *musica reservata.*

Principal Composers. The composers of this school did not for the most part remain in the Low Countries but established themselves in courts all over Europe, thus broadly disseminating their art. The principal composers of this group in the late 15th century are Jean Ockeghem (d. 1495), Jacob Obrecht (d. 1505), Josquin Desprez (d. 1521), Pierre de la Rue (c. 1460–1518), Jean Mouton (d. 1522), and Heinrich Isaac (c. 1450–1517).

15th-Century Forms, Manuscripts

Throughout the 15th century the same forms of musical composition were employed. Sacred polyphony was more important in the period than secular polyphony. The latter developed more prominently in the second half of the century.

Religious Forms. The forms which dominated the religious music of the 15th century are liturgical, i.e., composed for definite functions in the Catholic service. There are two principal forms: the Mass and the motet.

POLYPHONIC SETTINGS OF THE MASS. From the time of Machaut polyphonic settings of the Ordinary of the Mass became more prevalent until they constituted a major part of polyphonic literature of the 15th and 16th centuries. Settings of the Mass naturally conform to the five main sections of the Ordinary (Kyrie, Gloria, Credo, Sanctus, and Agnus Dei). The cantus firmus for each part of the Mass was borrowed either from plainsong or, strangely enough, from secular song. One of the most popular of these was a French tune, "L'Homme armé," used as a cantus firmus by all the principal composers through Palestrina. The cantus firmus was almost always in the tenor part and in longer note values than those of the other voices. The text was invariably in Latin.

MOTET. The *motet* of the 15th and 16th centuries may be defined as a sacred polyphonic composition composed to Latin text (usually Biblical). It is a shorter composition than the complete Mass setting, and it is used in the Proper of the service or at certain canonic offices, principally Vespers. It differs further from the Mass in that it makes more use of imitation, less use of cantus firmus. In all other respects its musical style is identical with that of the Mass. In other words, an excerpt from a motet would sound exactly the same as an excerpt from a Mass, except, of course, for the text which is standardized for the Mass.

Secular Forms. Developments in secular form lagged somewhat behind those in religious music. Secular forms, on the whole, were less conventionalized than religious forms. Also, they were less sophisticated and less scholarly. Much of the secular music of the 15th century was still monodic. Some 14th-century forms were still employed in the 15th century (ballades, rondeaus, virelais, etc.). However, some forms that became highly sophisticated in the 16th century found their inception in the 15th century.

FRENCH CHANSON. The French *chanson,* either polyphonic or homophonic, is characterized principally by its lively dance rhythm. The Flemish masters contributed considerably to this type of secular music.

ITALIAN SECULAR FORMS. In Italy an important body of secular music was created. Here again, it is mostly of an unpretentious folk-like nature. The *villota, canzonetta,* and *balletto* are secular forms mostly derived from dances. In the late 15th and early 16th centuries *carnival songs* were developed in the Medici court in Florence. These are simple, chordal part songs. Heinrich Isaac composed a number of these.

POLYPHONIC LIED. In Germany the *polyphonic lied* had its origin in the late 15th century. Folk songs were given polyphonic settings. Isaac was one of the most important composers of polyphonic lieder in the 15th century.

Important Collections. The *Old Hall MS.* is a collection of Mass compositions and hymns written by prominent composers of the 15th century. The most important manuscript collection of 15th-century music is contained in the seven volumes of the *Trent Codices.* About 75 composers are represented in this collection. The *Odhecaton* is historically significant as the earliest publication of polyphonic music (printed in 1501 by Petrucci). It is a collection of late 15th-century compositions, mostly secular. The first complete cycle of motets for the entire church year is the *Choralis Constantinus* by Heinrich Isaac. Important collections of secular music, including monophonic as well as polyphonic songs, are the *Lochamer,* the *Münchner,* and the *Glogauer Liederbücher.*

RECORDS
   Dunstable, "Quam pulchra es." V M739–4.
   Dufay, "Christe Redemptor." "Conditor alme siderum." CHM
      Vol. 1.
   Dufay, "Flos florum." V M739–5.
   Dufay, "Le Jour s'endort." "Pourrai-je avoir." AS 1a, 1b.
   Obrecht, Kyrie, Agnus Dei, Credo, from Mass "Sine nomine."
      V M739 7–10.
   Obrecht, "Qui cum patre." V M739–6b, No. 3.
   Josquin, "Ave verum." "Ave coelorum domina." V 1167.
   15th-century rondeaus. AS 39, 43.

SCORES
Religious Music
   Mass movements. HAM 63, 66, 73, 77, 89, 92. SB 29, 39, 55, 59,
      65.

Motets. HAM 62, 64, 65, 76, 90. SB 30, 31, 34, 37, 38, 43, 52, 54, 60, 66, 76. WS 9, 11, 12, 13, 15.

Secular Music
Accompanied song. HAM 61.
"L'Homme armé." HAM 66a.
Ballade. HAM 67.
Rondeau. HAM 68, 69, 71, 72, 79. SB 42.
Chanson. HAM 70, 91. SB 35, 40, 41. WS 14.
Virelai. HAM 74, 75.
From *Lochamer Liederbuch*. HAM 81a.
Lieder. HAM 87, 93. SB 44–47, 85, 87, 88. WS 16.
Canto carnascialesco. HAM 96. WS 18.
English part songs. HAM 85, 86. SB 32.
Canon. SB 61.
Frottola. SB 69–72. WS 20, 21, 22, 23.

CHAPTER VII

The Sixteenth Century

THE 16th century witnesses the full flower of the Renaissance. In music it sees the culmination of a vocal polyphony that has never been surpassed. For this reason the period is sometimes referred to as "The Golden Age of Polyphony."

General Considerations

General Historical Background. In the 16th century European politics were dominated by Charles V and Philip II of the Holy Roman Empire. The predominant philosophy of the period was humanism, a philosophy away from medieval theology and toward man's interests on earth. The Renaissance spirit is most clearly manifest in the arts and in literature. In painting some of the greatest artists belong to the 16th century: da Vinci (d. 1519), Michelangelo, Titian, Dürer, Holbein. Literature claims the following great names: Machiavelli in Italy, Rabelais, Montaigne, and Ronsard in France, Cervantes in Spain, and Shakespeare, Spenser, Bacon, and Ben Jonson in England. Copernicus and Galileo lead the field of science. 16th-century religion is dominated by the name of Luther, the Protestant Reformation, and the Catholic Counter Reformation. The Protestant Reformation perhaps had more direct influence upon music—certainly upon religious music—than any other historical event of the period.

General Characteristics of the Music. The broad characteristics of 16th-century music may be stated as follows: (1) Vocal polyphonic style, developing almost continuously from the 9th century, reaches an ultimate degree of perfection in the 16th century. (2) Secular music greatly increases in importance. (3) Religious music is fostered by the Catholic Church; secular music is primarily fostered by nobility. (4) An independent instrumental style emerges in the late 16th century. (5) Modality still prevails in both sacred and secular music; but definite signs of its breakdown appear in the second half of the 16th century. (6) Music printing contributes greatly to the dissemination of musical literature throughout Europe. The first printing of music was accomplished by Ottaviano Petrucci in a collection of 15th-century vocal polyphony entitled *Odhecaton* (1501). (7) Italy takes musical leadership from the Flemish school. France and England also become important musical powers.

Sacred Polyphony of the Catholic Church

General Characteristics of Style. Among all schools of sacred polyphony in the 16th century there is a high degree of uniformity of style. This is because of the widespread influence of the Flemish school, the masters of which established their technique everywhere on the Continent. This does not apply to Reformation music, to which a separate section will be devoted (see page 40). (1) There is complete mastery of counterpoint: melodic and rhythmic freedom of voice parts, and at the same time a beautiful, euphonious texture of the whole. (2) Tranquillity of mood prevails in the liturgical music of the Renaissance. Because of the sacred atmosphere of the music, which does not attract attention to itself, 16th-century sacred polyphony is the perfect religious vehicle for worship. (3) The number of voice parts ranges from four to eight or more parts, five-part polyphony being the most usual. (4) Fugal style and chordal style are often employed in the same composition. (5) The complete triad becomes the basis of the harmony. No unprepared seventh chords are employed until the 17th century. (6) Universally strict treatment of dissonance is characteristic of sacred polyphony of the 16th century. The non-chordal dissonances employed are: passing tones, neighboring tones, suspensions (particularly prominent in polyphonic texture), and changing-note groups. (7) Diatonic modality still prevails, but there are marked tendencies toward a feeling for major and minor. In a treatise entitled *Dodecachordon* (1547) the theorist Glareanus established modes on A and C. (8) The beginning of chromaticism (the extensive use of altered tones, e.g., C, C♯, D, E♭), which eventually undermined modality, is to be found in the late 16th century in the works of Lasso and the late Roman school. (9) Archaic effects such as parallelism, open fifths, etc., completely disappear. (10) Liturgical music of the Renaissance was probably performed *a cappella* (for voices alone without instrumental accompaniment). At least there was no separate instrumental accompaniment, although it is likely that instruments were employed to double voice parts or occasionally to carry voice parts by themselves. Instruments undoubtedly played a more important part in the secular music of the Renaissance.

Forms. The two liturgical forms, the Mass and the motet, constitute the main body of Catholic Church music of the Renaissance. A body of nonliturgical music called *laudi spirituali* (religious songs of praise) were used outside the auspices of the Catholic Church. Such pieces were employed mainly in Italy. They were written in a simple chordal and rhythmic style, often resembling secular music, and they used Italian rather than Latin texts. Nonliturgical music in other countries was less significant.

Schools and Composers. Despite the general universality of style in religious music of the Renaissance there were several different schools of development that in varying degrees and extent have special characteristics.

FLEMISH SCHOOL. Flemish composers held important musical posts all over Europe, continuing the traditions and styles established in the 15th century by such composers as Josquin. The most important Flemish composer of the 16th century is Orlando di Lasso (or Orlandus Lassus) (c. 1532-1594), who ranks with Palestrina in his contributions to Catholic Church music. Other important Flemish composers of the period are Philippe de Monte (c. 1521-1603) and Clemens non Papa (c. 1510-c. 1558).

ROMAN SCHOOL. It was natural that the composers working in Rome directly with the mother church would constitute the most significant school of sacred polyphony. This school continued the traditions of *a cappella* style through later periods when other composers had turned to operatic styles and forms. At the head of the Roman school stands Giovanni Pierluigi da Palestrina (c. 1525–1594), whose complete mastery of his art has made his name synonymous with the perfection of sacred vocal polyphony. Other composers of this school are Ingegneri (c. 1545–1592), Nanino (c. 1545–1607), and F. Anerio (c. 1560–1614), all of whose styles show increased use of chromaticism in the late Renaissance.

SPANISH SCHOOL. The contributions of two Spaniards, Cristobal Morales (c. 1500–1553) and Tomas Ludovico da Victoria (c. 1540–1611), are sufficient to establish a Spanish school. Their styles are essentially those of the Roman school, with the possible addition of a certain starkness of expression reminding one of the later canvases of El Greco.

VENETIAN SCHOOL. Perhaps the most outstanding style in sacred polyphony of the 16th century is that developed by the Venetians. There are two contributions of this school that differentiate its style from that of other schools. (1) The Venetians made extensive use of *polychoric music* (music written for two or more complete choirs of voices), and antiphonal effects created by various choirs situated in different parts of the church. (2) Magnificence characterizes the music of the Venetians. This is partly because of the polychoric technique developed and also because of bold harmonies and rich textures. The most important composers of this school are Adrian Willaert (a Flemish composer, d. 1562), Andrea Gabrieli (c. 1510–1586), and his nephew, Giovanni Gabrieli (1557–1612).

ENGLISH SCHOOL. A great and extensive literature of Catholic Church music was created in England in the 16th century, despite religious conflicts and the rise of Anglicanism. Many fine Masses and motets were written by English composers. The Anglican Church retained most of the practices of the Catholic Church. In its music it used motets and a modified motet style of polyphony but with English texts. These motets were called *cathedral anthems* or *full anthems*. Late in the 16th century a new form and style came into being. This was the *verse anthem* which makes use of soloists and instrumental accompaniment as well as chorus. Soloist and choir alternate by sections. The principal composers of English church music are: Thomas Tallis (c. 1505–1585), who wrote both Catholic and Anglican Church music; William Byrd (1543–1623), the greatest English composer of the 16th century, who also wrote Catholic and Anglican Church music, although he remained a staunch Catholic throughout his life; and Orlando Gibbons (1583–1625), who wrote only for the Anglican services.

GERMAN SCHOOL. Catholic Church music did not flourish in Germany in the 16th century because of the Lutheran Reformation. Hence there is really no German school of sacred polyphony. Jacobus Gallus (Handl) (1550–1591) is the only German name of real significance in this field. Ludwig Senfl (c. 1492–c. 1555), a Swiss, wrote fine Catholic and Protestant church music.

Reformation Music

Perhaps the most cataclysmic event in the history of Christian religion is the Reformation of the 16th century. The rise of Protestantism had great effects upon music, which effects were manifest principally in Germany, to a lesser extent in France and England, and not at all in Italy. However, not until after the 16th century did Protestant music rival the great art of Catholic Church music of the Renaissance.

Martin Luther and Protestantism. The principal figure of the Protestant Reformation is Martin Luther (1483–1546), whose *Ninety-five Theses* (1517) and political and theological attack on the Church (1520) brought open conflict on matters of long standing pertaining to Church authority and to certain Church abuses. The Protestant revolt spread to Switzerland under the leadership of Zwingli and Calvin, who, however, were not favorably disposed toward music in religion. In France, the Huguenots (part of the Calvinist movement) developed an important Protestant music. Protestantism in England under Henry VIII, involving a somewhat different situation, gave rise to the Anglican Church, also fostering some important musical developments (see pages 39 and 42).

Luther's Influence upon Music. Luther had strong convictions about the importance of music in religion. He retained some of the music of the Catholic service (Mass and motet) but modified it to meet the needs of the German Reformation. There was a general tendency to substitute the German language for Latin, even before Luther's time. He encouraged congregational participation in the Protestant service, a practice abandoned by the Catholic Church with Gregorian reforms at the end of the 6th century. Congregational participation brought about the birth of a great body of religious song, called *chorale,* comparable in importance to Catholic plainsong. Johann Walter (1496–1570) was Luther's principal collaborator in this musical development. Chorales were sung in unison by the congregation, sung in parts by the choir, and at a later time they were played on the organ.

Protestant Chorale Melody. Chorale melody is of great importance to church music of the late Renaissance and Baroque periods.

CHARACTERISTICS OF CHORALE MELODY. The style of chorale melody differs considerably from that of Catholic plainsong. (1) It is definitely metric. (2) The rhythm is characterized by a slow, even, plodding pulse. (3) The phraseology of the chorale melody is clearer and more regular than that of plainsong. (4) Chorale melody is more major or minor than modal. (5) Because of its limited range, evenness of rhythm, and melodic progression, it is easily singable. (6) Chorale melody is more often harmonized than is plainsong. The chorale harmonizations by Bach in the 18th century are the most famous. (7) Chorale melodies are sung in the vernacular language (German) as opposed to the Latin of plainsong.

SOURCES OF CHORALE MELODY. There are three main sources of chorale melody: (1) Plainsong was modified and set to German texts. (2) Secular melody was also employed with religious texts. For example, Isaac's "Innsbruck, ich muss dich lassen" ("Innsbruck, I must leave thee") becomes "O Welt, ich muss dich lassen" ("O World, I must leave thee"). The famous "Passion" chorale, "O Sacred Head now wounded," that Bach uses in the *St. Matthew Passion,* comes from an old German love song, the first line of which runs, "Mein G'muth ist mir verwirret, das macht ein Jungfrau zart" ("Confused are all my feelings; a tender maid's the cause"). (3) Finally, original chorale melodies were composed by Protestant

musicians. Perhaps the most famous of these is Luther's "Ein' feste
Burg" ("A Mighty Fortress").

USES OF THE CHORALE. The significance of the chorale can be seen
in the fact that it soon became the very backbone of the Lutheran
musical service. Not only did it constitute a superb body of melody
for congregational singing and use in the home, but it was extensively employed as cantus firmus in various polyphonic forms: (1) in
the organ chorale prelude, (2) in vocal polyphonic settings, and
(3) in sacred cantata choruses and instrumental parts of the cantata
(see page 82).

French Reformation Music. In France the Huguenot movement
gave rise to a comparatively modest body of religious music.
Clément Marot and Théodore de Bèze versified Psalms. These were
set to music by Claude Goudimel (c. 1505–1572), Claude Lejeune
(1528–c. 1600), and Jacques Mauduit (1557–1627). The French
Huguenot Psalter was completed in 1561. These Psalms were probably intended for use in the home rather than for congregational
singing.

CHARACTERISTICS OF HUGUENOT PSALTER MUSIC. The Psalm settings
resemble the German chorale harmonizations. In general they have
the following characteristics: (1) They have a simplicity of style.
(2) Although they are usually set in a simple, chordal style, a free
polyphonic style is not entirely excluded. (3) The principal melody
is in the soprano voice, the uppermost part in a four-voice setting.
(4) The Psalms employ a straightforward rhythm, somewhat more
varied and animated than the German chorale. Rhythm and meter
follow the accentuation of the text.

Anglican Church Music. The most important aspects of English
Reformation music have been discussed in connection with the
English school of sacred polyphony (see page 39). One additional
feature of English church music is *Anglican chant*. It is a method of
singing psalms, canticles, etc., differing from that of the Catholic
Church in that: (1) it is sung in English, (2) it is harmonized in
simple, four-part chordal style, and (3) it is more strictly metrical.
16th-century composers who made settings of Anglican chant are
Tallis, Byrd, Morley, and Gibbons.

Secular Polyphony

In the 16th century great developments in secular vocal polyphony took place, and for the first time the secular art rivaled that of religious polyphony.

General Characteristics of Style. Secular polyphony differs from sacred polyphony in the following ways: (1) It has a tendency toward a stronger and more lively rhythm than is usually employed in sacred polyphonic music. (2) It has a tendency toward major tonality and has less modal flavor. (3) It consistently employs secular texts in the vernacular tongue. (4) It is usually limited to four or five voices. (5) Cantus firmus is less often and less strictly employed as the basis of secular polyphony.

Italian Secular Music. The Italian Renaissance not only produced great literature, painting, and sacred music, but it also contributed a great wealth of secular music in various forms.

FROTTOLA. One of the first important secular forms to develop in the 16th century is the *frottola*. It originated in northern Italy in the early 16th century from a dance form. It is definitely secular and popular in style. The melody is in the soprano voice. Usually four voice parts in chordal style are employed. The lower voices probably were played on instruments. The principal composers of this form are Marco Cara and Bartolommeo Tromboncino.

VILLANELLA. A form related to the frottola is the *villanella* or *canzona villanesca*. It comes from southern Italy and flourishes about the middle of the century. It is similar in style to the frottola, but its texts are generally more refined and the music somewhat more sophisticated. It may also be parodistic. The principal composers of this form are Adrian Willaert, Baldassare Donati, Giovanni Gastoldi, and Luca Marenzio, all of whom are also important madrigal composers.

MADRIGAL. The *madrigal* of the Italian Renaissance is not to be confused with that of the ars nova, where the term first appears. The 16th-century Italian madrigal is a more highly developed form and a more sophisticated style than either the 14th-century madrigal or the 16th-century frottola and villanella. The madrigal as a form continues its development well into the 17th century. There are three broad periods of its development.

a. *The Early Period.* The first period (roughly from 1525 to 1560) is characterized by homophonic style, the melody in the uppermost of three or four voices, and a general quiet sentiment somewhat resembling sacred polyphony. Composers in this period are Adrian Willaert, Jacques Arcadelt (c. 1514–c. 1570), Philippe Verdelot (d. before 1567), and Costanzo Festa (d. 1545).

b. *The Middle Period.* The madrigal of the second period (roughly 1560 to 1590) usually employs five parts and is more polyphonic in style. It is further characterized by breaking of the text by rests for emotional expression and by considerable naïve tone painting (i.e., expressing simple pictorial ideas of the text in the music). The composers of madrigals in this period are Lasso, Palestrina, Andrea Gabrieli, Cyprian de Rore (1516–1565), and Philippe de Monte.

c. *The Late Period.* The third period of development (1590–1640) reveals a transition from polyphonic to homophonic treatment with more use of solo voices. It is further characterized by a new dramatic expression and a certain amount of *virtuosity* (display of technical facility). There is also an extensive use of chromaticism. The principal composers of late Italian madrigals are Luca Marenzio, Baldassare Donati, Orazio Vecchi (c. 1550–1605), Don Carlo Gesualdo (c. 1560–1614), Giovanni Gastoldi, and Claudio Monteverdi (1567–1643).

MADRIGAL COMEDY. An interesting forerunner of early 17th-century opera is the *madrigal comedy.* These were quasi-dramatic forms consisting of a chain of madrigals in dialogue centered around pastoral themes. An example of a madrigal comedy is *L'Amfiparnasso* (1594) by Vecchi.

MADRIGALE SPIRITUALE. A madrigal of religious and moral content was called a *madrigale spirituale* ("spiritual madrigal"). These madrigal-style religious pieces are related to the laudi spirituali, and do not belong to the category of secular music.

English Secular Music. The flowering of English secular music in the Renaissance is coeval with the Elizabethan period and its great achievements in drama and verse. It reaches a peak of development somewhat later than the Italian madrigal.

ENGLISH MADRIGAL. The *English madrigal* was influenced by secular developments in Italy. However, it was definitely developed along individual lines and bears unmistakable qualities of English treatment of melancholy and merriment. The English madrigal is characterized by these factors: (1) The excellence of English verse contributed no little to its artistic value. (2) It was undoubtedly intended for solo voices singing in small groups. (3) From four to six voice parts were used. (4) On the whole, English madrigals are more chordal and more rhythmic than the Italian madrigals. (5) They are characteristically diatonic, in contrast to Italian chromaticism. (6) Use of the *fa-la-la chorus* is fairly common. Nonsense syllables (such as "fa-la-la") were employed in a recurrent chorus or refrain, a practice probably borrowed from the Italian balletto or villanella. (7) It is not uncommon to find changes of meter in the madrigal (i.e., the use of three-four and four-four time in the same composition). The principal composers are William Byrd, Thomas Morley (c. 1557–1603), John Wilbye (c. 1574–1638), Thomas Weelkes (c. 1575–1623), John Ward (d. c. 1640), John Bennet (fl. 1600–1620), Thomas Bateson (c. 1570–1630), Orlando Gibbons (1583–1625), John Farmer (fl. 1591–1601), and Francis Pilkington (d. 1638). The most important collection of English madrigals is the *Triumphs of Oriana* (1603), composed by the leading madrigalists of the time and dedicated to Queen Elizabeth. Each madrigal ends with the line, "Long live fair Oriana." The idea imitates a similar collection of Italian madrigals entitled *Il trionfo di Dori* (1592).

CANZONET. The *canzonet* is similar to the madrigal in general style. It is written for only two or three voice parts and has characteristically lively rhythms and merry texts, usually of a pastoral nature. Thomas Morley was the principal writer of canzonets.

AYRE. A form developing somewhat later than the madrigal, the *ayre,* is a strophic song in homophonic style. The melody is supported by other voices or by instruments, sometimes by both. The lute was a favorite accompanying instrument for English ayres. The principal composers of this form are John Dowland (1563–1626), Thomas Campion (1567–1620), Francis Pilkington (d. 1638), Philip Rosseter (c. 1575–1623), and Robert Jones (fl. c. 1597–1617).

The French Polyphonic Chanson. The most important French contribution to Renaissance music lies in the field of the *polyphonic chanson.* As in the case of the English madrigal, much of the excellence of the French chanson is attributable to the high quality of verse of such poets as Ronsard. The characteristics of the French chanson are: (1) They were usually written for four voices, the upper most prominent. (2) A lively rhythm characterizes most of the chansons. (3) Two metric styles were employed. The first, called *chanson rimée,* employed regular meters. The second, *chanson mesurée* (or *vers mesuré*), was a later 16th-century development. In this type strongly accented syllables were given twice the note value ($\downarrow$) of the unaccented syllables ($\backsim$), resulting in irregular metric effects. (4) There is frequent use of repeated-note motives at the beginning of the chansons. (5) The French polyphonic chansons were freely composed (i.e., not based upon a cantus firmus). (6) There are three general styles of chanson. The first is the fugal style which makes use of imitation among the voices. The second is a chordal style in which there is vertical alignment of text syllables for all voices. The third is the solo chanson usually with a polyphonic instrumental accompaniment.

Composers. The composers of French chansons are numerous. The principal ones are: Pierre de la Rue (c. 1460–1518), Clément Jannequin (c. 1485–1560), who is particularly noted for the "portraiture chanson" which makes use of naïve, realistic effects; Lasso, Jacques Mauduit (1557–1627), William Costeley (1531–1606), Claude de Sermisy (c. 1490–1562), Nicolas Gombert, Jacques Arcadelt, Claude Lejeune (1528–1600), Claude Goudimel (c. 1505–1572), Bertrand, and Jacob Regnard (c. 1540–1599). Bertrand and Regnard are especially noted for chanson settings of Ronsard poems.

The German Polyphonic Lied. German polyphonic secular music was invariably based upon an already extant folk song melody. Some of these melodies were given simple chordal settings. But a fine polyphonic literature developed in the form of the *polyphonic* *lied.* Between about 1450 and 1550 the polyphonic lieder utilized imitation of the principal motives of the secular melody in all voices, of which there were usually four. There were numerous organ arrangements of these vocal compositions. In the second half of the 16th century the style of the secular polyphonic music in Germany is definitely derived from Italian models.

COMPOSERS. The composers of the first period are Adam von Fulda (c. 1440–1506), Heinrich Finck (1445–1527), Heinrich Isaac, Paul Hofhaimer (1459–1537), and Ludwig Senfl (c. 1492–c. 1555). In the second half of the 16th century the principal composers are Hans Leo Hassler (1564–1612), Lasso, and Johannes Eccard (1553–1611). Ludwig Senfl was particularly noted for compositions called *quodlibets,* which are humorous pieces incongruously and simultaneously combining different folk songs. Quodlibets were popular in the 15th and 16th centuries.

RECORDS

Sacred Polyphony
Palestrina, Missa "Papae Marcelli." V 35941/4.
Palestrina, "O bone Jesu." V 15731.
Palestrina, "Improperium." V 7183.
Byrd, "Agnus Dei." "Justorum animae." C 4137M.
Lasso, Benedictus from "Missa pro defunctis." V M739–11.
Victoria, "O vos omnes." SEMS 8.

Reformation Music
Goudimel and Lejeune, Psalm settings. AS 12.
Chorales: See numerous chorales in Bach's *St. Matthew Passion.* VM 411–413. See also CHM, Vol. 2.

Italian Secular Polyphony
Arcadelt, "Il bianco e dolce cigno." V 1964. MC 213.
Vecchi, "Il bianco e dolce cigno." V 1964. MC 213.
Lasso, "Matona mia cara." MC 214.
Lasso, "Olà! O che bon eccho." V 4326.
Gesualdo, "Dolcissima mia vita." MC 20.
Marenzio, "Già torna." MC 20.
Monteverdi, "Ecco mormorar l'onde." V M496.
Palestrina madrigals. AS 47.

English Secular Polyphony

Byrd, "I thought that love." V 4316.

Morley, "Now is the month of Maying." "My bonnie lass." V 4316.

Farmer, "Fair Phyllis." Gibbons, "The silver swan." C 5717. CHM, Vol. 1.

Gibbons, "Ah, dear heart." Wilbye, "Sweet honey sucking bees." V 4317.

Dowland, "Awake, sweet love." CHM, Vol. 1.

Madrigals by Morley, Jones, Dowland. AS 58.

French Secular Polyphony

Chansons by Jannequin, Garnier, Sermisy, Costeley, and others. AS 6, 15, and 45.

Jannequin, "Petit nymphe folastre." Lasso, "Fuyons tous d'amour le jeu." MC 214 (in album 20).

German Secular Polyphony

Isaac, "Zwischen Berg." AS 1.

Isaac, "O Welt, ich muss dich lassen." Hofhaimer, "Mein einigs." V 1960.

Finck, "Wach auf." "Ach herzigs Herz." Senfl, "Also heilig." AS 51.

Hassler, "Feinslieb, du hast mich g'fangen." V 1963.

SCORES

Sacred Polyphony

SB 53, 97, 102, 104, 107, 120 (laude), 121, 122, 126–131, 163.

HAM 109, 112, 113, 114, 125, 127, 128, 139, 140, 141, 143, 144, 146b, 149, 150, 156, 157, 164, 166.

WS 30, 37 (laude), 41.

Reformation Music

SB 77, 80, 84, 108, 109, 110, 123, 142, 143, 159, 160, 161, 162, 285.

HAM 108, 110, 111, 126, 132, 151, 167a, 169, 171, 172.

WS 35, 36.

Italian Secular Music

SB 69–72, 98–101, 106, 132, 140, 164, 165–167.

HAM 95, 129–131, 142, 146a, 155, 158, 160, 161, 186, 188.

WS 20–23, 33, 38, 45–48, 56.

English Secular Music
SB 145, 146.
HAM 159, 162, 163, 170.
WS 50, 51, 66.

French Secular Music
SB 116–118, 133, 144. HAM 91, 107, 138, 145a, 147. WS 27.

German Secular Music
SB 85, 87, 88, 111, 124, 125, 141, 152.
HAM 87, 93, 165, 168. WS 16, 25, 28, 31, 42, 62, 63, 64.

CHAPTER VIII

Instrumental Music to 1600

U NTIL about 1600 the principal developments in music took place almost entirely in vocal music. But the Renaissance saw an awakening of interest in instrumental music that continued to grow until in the 18th century its importance surpassed that of vocal music.

General Considerations

Characteristics of Instrumental Style. A growing awareness of the fact that musical instruments have certain special properties eventually led to an independent instrumental style. The presence of any one, or a combination, of the following properties implies the use of instrumental idiom as opposed to vocal idiom: (1) angularity of melodic line, the use of skips, (2) wide range of melodic line, (3) long sustained notes, long phrases, (4) sharp rhythm, strong accents, syncopation, (5) a freer treatment of dissonance than practiced in vocal music, (6) rapid, repeated notes and figures, (7) rapid scales, (8) freely added parts and chords filled in (called *Freistimmigkeit*), particularly in lute and keyboard music, (9) melodic ornamentation, including *figuration* (repeated figures or patterns on each note of the basic melody), *embellishment* (mordents, turns, trills, etc.), and *coloration* (free melismatic material added to the basic notes of the melody). The latter is not exclusively instrumental.

Instruments and Instrumental Music before 1600. In general, it should be kept in mind that a completely instrumental style was not evolved until the 17th century, although lute and keyboard music of the 16th century shows unmistakable signs of instrumental idiom.

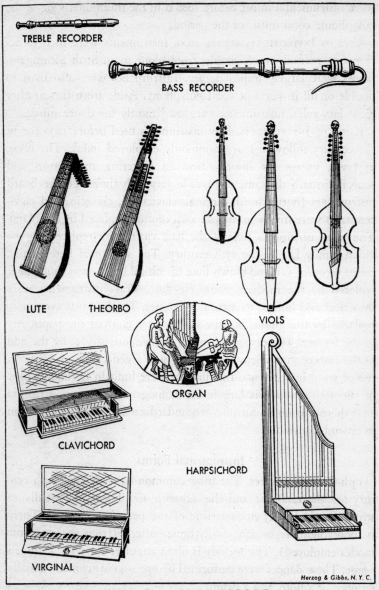

TREBLE RECORDER

BASS RECORDER

LUTE

THEORBO

VIOLS

ORGAN

CLAVICHORD

HARPSICHORD

VIRGINAL

Herzog & Gibbs, N. Y. C.

SOME INSTRUMENTS BEFORE 1600

Most instrumental music before 1600 is in the traditional style of the polyphonic vocal music of the period.

USES OF INSTRUMENTS BEFORE 1600. Instruments were used to accompany monody, for example, troubadour song. Such accompaniments were largely improvisatory. Instruments were also used to double or fill in parts in vocal polyphony. Aside from these rather secondary roles, instruments were used mostly for dance music.

KINDS OF INSTRUMENTS. Few instruments used before 1600 (or in the century following) are commonly employed today. The oboe, however, except for improvement in fingering mechanism and tone, is virtually the same as it was in very early times. The keyboard instruments (harpsichord, virginal, clavichord, clavecin, and clavicembalo) were finally in the late 18th century replaced by the piano. The viol instruments (except the bass viol) were replaced by the violin family late in the 17th century. The soft-toned flute family, called *recorder* (an end-blown flute of conical bore), was much later replaced by the modern transverse flute. Brass instruments were imperfect and limited to natural overtones. The lute was eventually replaced by the guitar, but the latter never enjoyed the popularity of the former. The organ had made tremendous strides by the end of the 16th century. Before 1600 there was a general emphasis upon use of wind instruments. Instruments were built in families. Music of the 16th century is largely for homogeneous groups. Prior to 1600 there was no uniformity or standardization of instrumentation in ensemble music.

Instrumental Forms

13th-Century Dances. The most common dances of the 13th century are the *estampie* and the *danse-royale*. These are usually in strong, triple meter, characteristic of the period in general. There is monotonous repetition of rhythmic pattern (from the rhythmic modes employed). The melody is often angular, but with a limited range. These dances were performed by one solo instrument, usually an oboe or a flute, and a drum.

14th-Century Dances. The *rota* and the *saltarello* are the two most common dances of the 14th century. They frequently employ duple as well as triple meter and the rhythmic patterns are more varied than those of the 13th century. They were played by bowed string instruments or woodwind instruments and drums.

Instrumental Forms of the Renaissance. In the 15th and 16th centuries, instrumental forms became more varied.

RENAISSANCE DANCES. In the 15th and 16th centuries dance forms were commonly in pairs, both employing the same melody, but contrasting in tempo and meter. Their combination was the result of the prevalent way of dancing. This pairing of dance forms was the prototype of the baroque dance suite. The *basse-danse* is a slow dance in three-four time, and it is followed by the *tourdion,* a lively dance in four-four time. Another dance pair is the *pavane,* slow, four-four time, followed by the *galliard* (Fr. *gaillarde*) in fast, triple time. An Italian dance pair is the *ronde* and *saltarello* which follow the general plan of the pavane and galliard. The German dance pairs were called *Tanz* and *Nach-Tanz.* These dances were written for lute, for keyboard instruments, and for instrumental ensemble.

FANTASIA. Pieces called *fantasias* were written for lute, keyboard instruments, and instrumental ensemble. They are usually polyphonic with imitative counterpoint used extensively. They have no basic structural form and are less strict in contrapuntal treatment than the ricercare (see below). In English keyboard music of the late 16th century the *fantasia* (or *fancy*) often includes display passages and figuration as well as polyphonic treatment. Fantasias are often based on folk song.

TOCCATA AND PRELUDE. In the Renaissance, free structural forms in an improvisatory style were called variously *toccata, praeludium,* or *praeambulum.* Such pieces, written for organ, harpsichord, or lute, are often characterized by virtuosity (rapid scale passages, arpeggios, etc.). They also employ polyphonic and chordal material as well.

CANTUS FIRMUS COMPOSITIONS. Instrumental compositions based upon a borrowed melody were written chiefly for the organ. The *cantus firmi* were taken variously from plainsong melody, German chorale melody, and secular melody. Such compositions, employing the title of the borrowed melody, are consistently polyphonic in character. The cantus firmus is often given prominence by long sustained notes. But coloration of the original melody is also very common.

RICERCARE. In the 16th and 17th centuries the term *ricercare* was used for various kinds of instrumental pieces. Of these the most important type is the polyphonic ricercare, primarily a church form for organ. It is virtually an instrumental motet in style, usually in a slow, dignified tempo. Like the motet, it makes use of several short themes or motives which are introduced successively and contrapuntally imitated in all voices. It is further characterized by display of contrapuntal skill: inversion, augmentation, and retrograde treatment of the thematic material. The polyphonic ricercare reveals no virtuosity and no real instrumental idiom.

CANZONA. The *canzona* is the secular counterpart of the ricercare. It is virtually an instrumental chanson. It differs from the ricercare in that it employs longer fugue-like themes which are likewise imitated in all voices. It is usually more lively than the ricercare. Various sections of the canzona in contrasting tempi and meters often employ the same melody. The ricercare and the canzona are prototypes of the fugue which gradually emerges in the 17th century.

VARIATION. The *variation* form is of special significance in that it has remained an important basis of composition down to the present day. The variation form is one of the most important contributions of the Spanish lutenists and the English virginal school of the late 16th century. The variations are usually based upon a popular melody which is repeated a number of times, each time with different figuration. Virtuosity is a notable characteristic of this form. The English *ground* is a special variation type on a composed bass theme, constantly reiterated while different figuration appears above it. Other variations on a bass theme are called *passacaglia* and *chaconne* (see page 92). These are more common in the Baroque period.

Instrumental Classes
Styles, Forms, Schools, Composers

Lute Music. From about 1450 to about 1650 the lute (a fretted, guitar-like instrument, with six strings and a long neck) was as universal as the piano is today. It was an accompanying instrument as well as a solo and ensemble instrument.

STYLE IN GENERAL. Most lute music displays some degree of virtuosity in the form of rapid scales and figuration. Polyphonic style was generally attempted. Although the nature of the instrument prevented a strict polyphonic texture, implied lines by jumping from one voice to another were used. The third and most idiomatic style to be found in lute music is the use of straight chordal material.

FORMS. The principal forms of lute music are the fantasia, preamble or prelude, dances, variations, and arrangements of vocal music (motets and chansons).

LUTE TABLATURE

SCHOOLS AND COMPOSERS. The principal composer of Spanish lute music was Luis Milan (c. 1500–after 1561). In Italy Francesco Spinaccino and Ambrosio Dalza were the leading lute composers. In Germany the principal names in lute music were Arnold Schlick (d. after 1527), Hans Judenkunig (c. 1460–1526), Hans Gerl, and Hans Neusiedler (c. 1508–1563). In France, Pierre Attaingnant published a considerable amount of French lute music (c. 1530 ff.). In England John Dowland (1563–1626) was the principal lutenist composer. In Poland an important lute school was led by Albert Dlugorai.

TABLATURE. A special notation called *tablature* was used for lute music. It consists of letters or numbers placed on six horizontal lines corresponding to the six strings of the lute. The letters or numbers indicate the fret or finger position of each note to be played. Rhythm is indicated above the tablature.

Organ Music. The organ was definitely and almost exclusively associated with church service, a fact which largely determines the style of organ music.

STYLE. For the most part organ music of the Renaissance duplicates the style of vocal polyphony. Little virtuosity appears in organ music before the Baroque period, except for some toccatas (Merulo). Ornamentation and coloration are extensively employed. Organ music is mostly polyphonic.

FORMS. The principal forms of organ music are the fantasia, praeambulum, toccata, ricercare, canzona, cantus firmus compositions based upon Catholic plainsong and Protestant chorale melodies, and *verses* or *versets,* usually short pieces played by the organist between verses of a hymn sung by the congregation or choir.

SCHOOLS AND COMPOSERS. The first important composer in the German school is Conrad Paumann (c. 1410–1473), who wrote an "organ method" in 1452 entitled *Fundamentum Organisandi.* This work consists of two-part pieces in organ tablature and instructions. Other German composers, following Paumann, are Hans Buchner (1483–1538), Hans Kotter (c. 1485–1541), Leonhard Kleber (c. 1490–1556), Paul Hofhaimer (1459–1537), and Arnold Schlick (d. after 1527). The publisher Attaingnant represents the only significant contributions to organ literature in France with publications of anonymous composers around 1531. The principal name in Spain is that of Antonio Cabezon (1510–1566). In Italy a notable school of organ composition is associated with the names Claudio Merulo (1533–1604), Girolamo Cavazzoni, Annibale Padovano, and Andrea and Giovanni Gabrieli. There seems to have been little creative activity in organ music in England, where the virginal school overshadowed almost all other instrumental activity. John Redford in the early 16th century and John Bull in the late 16th century are the only names of any significance in English organ music.

Harpsichord Music. The most extensive literature for harpsichord before 1600 appears in England in the second half of the 16th century. Here the first truly independent instrumental style is extensively developed. On the Continent, harpsichord music still has little differentiation of style from that of vocal polyphony and organ music. The keyboard instrument used in Elizabethan England is called a *virginal,* a small, one-manual instrument of the harpsichord type (see page 89).

STYLE. One of the most prominent features of the English virginal school is a sheer delight in instrumental virtuosity. Musicians apparently enjoyed playing rapid scales up and down the keyboard, and using figures, arpeggios, fast repeated chords, etc. Figuration is extensively used: repeated patterns of broken chords, thirds, rapid scales, etc., ornamenting the notes of a borrowed melody. Embellishment (trills, mordents, etc.) is also employed. The English virginal music is more or less contrapuntal, but comparatively little use of imitation is to be found.

FORMS. The English virginal school was not only the first to exploit a truly instrumental style but it also was the first (along with the Spanish lutenists) to develop the variation form. These variations are usually on popular tunes of the day. The English were also fond of writing variations on a ground bass, usually an originally composed theme. A third type of variation, *hexachord variation,* is based upon six ascending or descending scale tones. These were usually given such titles as "Ut re mi fa sol la." Dances were popular forms in harpsichord music: pavanes, galliards, allemandes, etc. Cantus firmus compositions were employed. These were invariably based upon plainsong melodies and they may have been intended for performance on the organ. Pieces with descriptive titles, battle pieces, etc., and preludes are to be found among the large collections of English virginal music.

COMPOSERS AND COLLECTIONS. The principal composers of English virginal music are Hugh Aston (early 16th century), Giles Farnaby (c. 1560–c. 1600), William Byrd, John Bull (c. 1562–1628), and Orlando Gibbons. The principal collections of virginal music are the *Fitzwilliam Virginal Book, Parthenia,* and *My Ladye Nevells Booke,* the latter containing 42 pieces by William Byrd. In France Pierre Attaingnant published a collection of keyboard dances. Cabezon in Spain wrote *diferencias* (variations) for harpsichord and for lute. Elsewhere there seems to have been no distinction between harpsichord and organ music.

Ensemble Music. The problems of *Aufführungspraxis* (how early music was intended to be performed) are not yet entirely solved. This is particularly true in the field of instrumental ensemble, where there was little standardization of instrumental combinations, and where actual instrumentation was seldom indicated in manuscripts. This is because in general before 1600 it was felt that any medium of performance for a given composition would be satisfactory.

INSTRUMENTAL MEDIA. Three general classes of instruments were employed for instrumental ensemble before 1600. Ensemble music for strings employed various members of the viol family. A combination of viols was called a *consort of viols*. Members of the flute family (recorders) were frequently employed in ensemble music. In combination with viols the ensemble was called a *mixed consort*. The use of brass ensembles was particularly characteristic of the Venetian school. In Germany wind ensembles were used to sound the hours of the day by playing chorales from municipal towers or churches.

STYLE. In instrumental ensemble music there is little independent instrumental style. The pieces for ensemble are generally polyphonic and use imitation. In ensemble dance music the style is more chordal and rhythmic.

FORMS. The three principal forms in ensemble music are the fantasia, various dances, and canzonas. The latter were employed by the Venetian composers.

SCHOOLS AND COMPOSERS. In England the principal composers are Gibbons and Matthew Locke. In Germany, Melchior Franck, Valentin Hausmann, and Erasmus Widmann are the principal composers. In Italy Giovanni Gabrieli composed canzonas for brass ensembles. All these composers belong to the late 16th and the 17th centuries.

RECORDS
Lute Music
Spanish songs with lute accompaniment. AS 17.

16th-century lute music. AS 36.

Luis Milan, Three pavanes. AS 40.

Organ Music

Giovanni Gabrieli, Ricercare. AS 4.

Palestrina, Ricercare. Landini, "Questa fanciulla." Pathé 63.

Virginal Music (Harpsichord)

English virginal pieces. AS 14.

Byrd, Pavane and galliard. CHM, Vol. 1.

Bull, "King's hunt." Farnaby, "A toye." CHM, Vol. 1.

Ensemble Music

Dances of the 13th and 14th centuries. AS 16.

French dances of the 16th century. AS 5.

Giovanni Gabrieli, "Sonata pian e forte." (Six-part canzona.) AS 25.

Franck, Pavana, tanz, intrada. AS 57.

Norcome, Divisions on a ground. Wellkes, Fantasy for a chest of viols. CHM, Vol. 1.

Vocal pieces with ensemble accompaniment. AS 27, 39, 43.

SCORES

Lute Music

SB 90, 91, 93–95, 114, 115, 138, 150, 181. HAM 97–99, 105, 121–124, 160, 162. WS 29, 32, 34.

Organ Music

SB 48, 56, 57, 82, 83, 92, 103, 105, 113, 149, 158. HAM 84, 100, 101, 116–118, 120, 133–135, 153, 154, 157, 174, 180, 181. WS 43, 57.

Harpsichord Music

SB 112, 135–137, 147, 158, 174, 181. HAM 102, 104, 134, 145b, 177, 178, 179. WS 24, 57.

Ensemble Music

SB 61, 62, 67, 75, 81, 105, 109, 119, 134, 148, 151, 153–157. HAM 88, 136, 137, 157, 162, 167b, 173, 175, 176. WS 17, 26, 39, 40, 48, 54, 55, 56, 58–60, 63.

CHAPTER IX

Musical Notation to 1600

Our modern system of musical notation dates from the early 17th century. Prior to about 1600 various systems had been used in man's attempt to record graphically the music he heard. The evolution of musical notation is the progress toward accurate symbolic representation of two general musical factors: the pitch and the duration of a musical tone.

Neumatic Notation

Neumes. The term *neume* comes from the Greek *neuma,* meaning a nod or a sign. Neumes were probably first used about 680 A.D. At this time they did not indicate exact pitch or time value; they were merely "reminders" of melodic contour of already known plainsong melody. Neumes are derived from three basic accents: **(1)** grave (\), a descending inflection, (2) acute (/), ascending inflection, and (3) circumflex (∧), ascending-descending. Later they were combined to form various compound neumes, called *ligatures.* At first these signs were placed above the lines of the text, a practice known as *in campo aperto,* i.e., notes "in the open field" without staff lines.

Origin of the Staff. Scribes began placing neumes above the text relative to highness and lowness of the melody. Then they used a ruled line for guidance. Gradually the line assumed meaning of actual pitch. Colored lines were later used (11th century): red for F, and yellow for C. Neumes thus began to record exact pitch.

More and more lines were added, up to ten or eleven lines. Eventually the middle C line was omitted, separating the treble from the bass registers and making the reading easier. Modern plainsong notation uses conventionalized neumes on a four-line staff.

Mensural Notation

Polyphonic music requires a system of notation conveying time values, so that various parts can keep together. This need gave rise to *mensural* (or measured) notation, which began around 1250 and was used until about 1600.

13th-Century Notation. In the 13th century, notation was dependent upon the rhythm of the text and upon the rhythmic modes (see page 12). Ternary rhythm prevailed. The system of notes employed is called *black mensural notation,* because the notes were all filled in. There were four kinds of notes used: (1) the *maxima* (▬◗), equal to two *longae* (◖◗), (2) the *longa* (◖), equal to three *breves* (■ ■ ■), and (3) the *breve* (or brevis) (■), equal to three *semibreves* (◆◆◆).

14th-Century Notation. The period from 1300 to about 1450 is characterized by great complexity in systems of notation, the rules of which varied with different localities and at different times. In this period duple and triple division of notes were recognized as equally important. Black notes, as before, indicated triple division (*perfect time*), while notes colored red indicated duple division (*imperfect time*). The relation of longa to breve was called *modus;* the relation of breve to semibreve was called *tempus;* and the relation of semibreve to minim was called *prolatio.* Each mensural relationship, then, could be either perfect (triple division of the larger note) or imperfect (duple division of the larger note).

15th- and 16th-Century Notation. The period from about 1450 to 1600 is characterized by the use of white instead of black notes. In most other respects the systems were essentially the same. In the 15th and 16th centuries only the tempus and prolatio relationships were used. Each of these was represented by a sign as shown in the following table.

Tempus perfectum: ⊙ means □ ‧ ◊◊◊   (1 breve equals 3 semibreves).

Tempus imperfectum: ℭ means □ ‧ ◊◊   (1 breve equals 2 semibreves)

Prolatio major: ● means ◊ ‧ ◊◊◊   (1 semibreve equals 3 minims).

Prolatio minor: no dot means ◊ ‧ ◊◊   (1 semibreve equals 2 minims).

Thus, tempus and prolatio could be combined in the four following ways:

(1) ⊙ means □ ‧ ◊◊◊ ◊◊◊ ◊◊◊ (the equivalent of modern 9/8 time).

(2) ◯ means □ ‧ ◊◊ ◊◊ ◊◊ (the equivalent of modern 3/4 time).

(3) ℭ means □ ‧ ◊◊◊ ◊◊◊ (the equivalent of modern 6/8 time).

(4) ℭ means □ ‧ ◊◊ ◊◊ (the equivalent of modern 4/4 time).

It will be observed that the last sign (C) is still employed today to indicate four-four time. Sometimes different signs were used simultaneously in different voices of a polyphonic composition. Mensural notation was further complicated by *ligatures* (combination of two or more notes into a single graph) which were subject to highly intricate rules, and by the use of *proportions* diminishing normal note values in arithmetic ratios. For example, the sign $\frac{3}{2}$ introduced in a part would mean that three notes of the following passage equal two notes of the preceding passage.

Musical Score

A musical score means the writing of music for an ensemble so that all the parts are represented in vertical alignment. Simple scores were used in polyphonic music prior to 1225. Hence, organum, conductus, etc., were written down in this logical fashion. This practice was abandoned, however, with the advent of the 13th-century motet. In place of the score, the *choir-book* arrangement was adopted. This consisted of the parts being notated separately on one page or, more commonly, on two opposite pages. The following diagram illustrates the usual plan for a four-part polyphonic composition; the letters standing for soprano, tenor, alto, and bass, respectively:

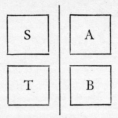

Choir books were used until about the middle of the 16th century. These were replaced by *part books*. This meant separate books for each individual part. Hence four-part polyphonic music would require four books, each including the particular part for several compositions. Finally, around the turn of the century, ensemble music again began to be written in score form. One of the first printed scores is a collection of madrigals by Cyprien de Rore (1577). Probably the earliest extant instrumental score is that of the *Ballet comique de la reine* (1581) (see page 77).

PART THREE

The Baroque Period (1600-1750)

CHAPTER X

General Considerations

General Historical Background. The century and a half between 1600 and 1750 was a period of colonization. The first half of the 17th century was dominated in Germany by religious, political wars known as the "Thirty Years' War" (1618–1648). The second half of the 17th century was dominated by the culture of Louis XIV of France (1643–1715) and his lavish court at Versailles. The principal names in science are Newton, Harvey, Galileo, Bacon, and Leibnitz. The leading thinker in the field of civil government is John Locke. The leading philosophers of the period are Descartes, Pascal, and Spinoza. In the field of literature there is an important array of English names: Milton, Dryden, Defoe, Addison, Swift, Pope, and Samuel Johnson. In France the principal literary names are Corneille, Racine, and Molière. The great names of baroque painting are Rembrandt, Rubens, Van Dyck, El Greco, and Velasquez.

THE MEANING OF BAROQUE. The painting, architecture, and music of this period are in general characterized by a certain spirit of theatricalism, of grandiose concepts, and by a rather heavy elaboration of design and magnificence of effect. Baroque spirit in general began in Italy as a result of the Catholic Counter Reformation which sought to impress the world and to re-establish the influence of the Church. Baroque style in the arts and music soon spread over all Europe and dominated the spirit of cultural creations.

General Characteristics of Baroque Music. The baroque spirit pervades the music of the period in the same ways it pervades the arts. It is manifest in large-scale productions, spectacular music, contrasts, and an over-all grandeur.

RELATIVE IMPORTANCE OF SACRED AND SECULAR MUSIC. Musical art, which in the polyphonic period had been developed largely by the Church, was in the Baroque period influenced more by nonecclesiastical bodies. The nobility and the upper classes everywhere took the greatest interest in music. Hence, secular music takes precedence over sacred music in the Baroque.

RELATIVE IMPORTANCE OF INSTRUMENTAL AND VOCAL MUSIC. Before 1600 vocal music predominates. In the Baroque period instrumental music comes into its own and may be said to be on a par with vocal music. An independent instrumental style is generally developed in this period.

NATIONAL SCHOOLS. Although not until the 19th century was there a conscious attempt to nationalize music, there was, nevertheless, in the Baroque period, a demarkation of national styles and schools more evident than before.

DRAMATIC ELEMENT. An important attribute of the baroque spirit, the dramatic element, is characteristic of much of the music of this period. It is manifest in the tremendous developments in opera, oratorio, and cantata. It even invaded and dominated the style of much church music.

HOMOPHONIC STYLE. In the early 17th century a new importance was attached to homophonic music. It dominated the whole period but it did not completely replace polyphonic music, which continued to develop to a new height, reached at the hands of J. S. Bach at the end of the period.

TONALITY. Clearer concepts of key feeling are apparent in the music of the Baroque. Major and minor as we know it today replace the old church modes. However, influence of the latter was to be felt throughout the period.

HARMONY. For the first time in music history attention to chord structure and chord progressions is evident. The harmonic or vertical approach to music tends to overshadow the older contrapuntal or horizontal approach. Chromaticism, the extensive use of altered tones, plays an important role in baroque harmony. It furnished a means of harmonic experimentation; it provided increased harmonic color, and, more than any other factor, it broke down modality.

FIGURED BASS. The characteristic importance of harmony in the Baroque period is reflected in an entirely new device, the *figured bass,* which is generally employed throughout the period. In fact, the entire Baroque period is sometimes referred to as the Figured Bass period. Figured bass is a sort of musical shorthand in which chords are indicated by placing numbers below the bass part played by a keyboard instrument. Its origin and development will be discussed in the following chapter.

NEW FORMS. Clarification of formal structure and more clearly defined formal concepts characterize the music of the Baroque period in comparison with that of the Renaissance. New forms are developed. The new instrumental forms of the Baroque are: the dance suite, the solo sonata, the trio sonata, the solo concerto, the concerto grosso, the overture, and the fugue. The latter is also a choral form. In vocal music the new forms are the aria, arioso, and accompanied solo song. Recitative, an innovation of the early 17th century, should be mentioned here, although it is more a style of dramatic declamation than a structural form. Three large vocal forms come into being in the Baroque: the opera, the oratorio, and the cantata. All three make use of the new ideas of the period: dramatic declamation (recitative), accompanied solo song (arias and ariosos), chorus and orchestra.

Important Composers. Further evidence of the growth of musical art is to be seen in the enormous increase in the number of first-rank composers.

ITALY. Claudio Monteverdi (1567–1643) wrote madrigals and operas. Alessandro Scarlatti (1659–1725) was the chief figure in Neapolitan opera. Domenico Scarlatti (1685–1757) wrote sonatas for keyboard. Arcangelo Corelli (1653–1713) and Antonio Vivaldi (c. 1680–1743) wrote chamber and concert music for strings.

FRANCE. Jean Baptiste Lully (c. 1632–1687) wrote opera and ballet. François Couperin (1668–1733) worked principally in the field of keyboard music. Jean Philippe Rameau (1683–1764) wrote operas, ballets, keyboard music, and he was the most important theorist of the period.

ENGLAND. Only one name of first rank belongs to England in this period. It is that of Henry Purcell (1658–1695), who wrote much fine dramatic music and instrumental music of various kinds. Because of his many years of creative activity in England, George Frederick Handel (Georg Friedrich Händel) is said to belong to the English school, although he was German by birth and Italian by training.

GERMANY. A long list of illustrious names comes from Germany, chiefly in the fields of instrumental and church music. Johann Hermann Schein (1586–1630) wrote keyboard music, as did Samuel Scheidt (1587–1654). The most important German composer of vocal music in the 17th century is Heinrich Schütz (1585–1672), who wrote choral music, cantatas, oratorios, and Passion music. Johann Jakob Froberger (1616–1667) wrote keyboard music. Michael Praetorius (1571–1621) wrote choral music in renaissance and baroque styles. Dietrich Buxtehude (1637–1707) and Johann Pachelbel (1653–1706) were the immediate predecessors of J. S. Bach in the fields of organ music and church cantatas. Finally, J. S. Bach (1685–1750) and George Frederick Handel (1685–1759) are the culminating figures of baroque music. Bach worked in the fields of church music and instrumental music, while Handel contributed principally to opera and oratorio (see Chapter XV).

CHAPTER XI

Nuove Musiche

THE term *nuove musiche,* meaning "new music," is used to apply to the revolutionary aspects of early 17th-century music that show a radical departure from the practices of the polyphonic period. The term originated from a collection of accompanied solo songs by Giulio Caccini, entitled *Nuove Musiche,* published in 1602.

Three Essentials of Nuove Musiche. The basic innovations of the early 17th-century revolt against polyphony dominated the entire period. (1) Perhaps the most revolutionary of the three innovations is the use of dramatic declamation in music, called *recitative.* Recitative follows the free rhythm of prose text. Its melodic line and accompaniment are of secondary importance. (2) The *solo song* (in connection with opera, called *aria*) is a homophonic vocal composition with accompaniment intended for performance by a lute or keyboard instrument, with or without additional instruments. In the nuove musiche period the solo songs, arias, and especially the recitatives had the simplest kind of chordal accompaniments. (3) The third essential innovation of the early 17 century is the *figured bass* (see page 72). It was used throughout the entire Baroque period for accompanied song and recitative, and for vocal and instrumental ensemble.

The Origin of Nuove Musiche. The "new music" of the early 17th century was a natural reaction against the old polyphonic art which had reached its culmination in the Renaissance. It represents a desire for new dramatic expressions.

THE FLORENTINE SCHOOL. Shortly before 1600 a group of noblemen in Florence, Italy, calling themselves the *Camerata,* began meeting for the purpose of reviving the art of Greek tragedy. But the result of their activities was the emergence of a new concept in music: opera and dramatic music. The Camerata was chiefly concerned with problems of appropriate dramatic declamation. The Florentine school avoided polyphonic treatment of any sort, made little use of the aria as such, and little use of the chorus. The important names connected with the Florentine movement are Giovanni Bardi, the patron and sponsor of the group; Vincenzo Galilei (the father of Galileo, the scientist), who made an early case against polyphony (1581), upholding the ideals of homophonic simplicity; Ottavio Rinuccini, a poet and librettist of the earliest extant opera, *Euridice;* Peri, a musician and the composer of *Euridice;* Giulio Caccini, the composer of *Nuove Musiche* and of operas; and Jacopo Corsi, nobleman and later patron of the Camerata.

The Figured Bass. The practice of using figures below the bass line to indicate harmony probably originated from a similar practice in the late 16th century known as *organ bass.* When an organ was used to accompany a polyphonic vocal composition it was necessary for the organist to make some sort of improvised score. To do this he used the bass or lowest-sounding part and inscribed numbers to indicate the harmonies produced by the other parts. It was only a step from this practice to the idea of originally indicating the harmonies of a composition by using figures (i.e., numerals, with sharp, flat, and natural signs to indicate alterations). The part in ensemble music which carries the figures is called *basso continuo* or *thorough-bass.* The basso continuo part was almost invariably performed by at least two instruments. A string bass instrument or a group of string basses would play the bass melody as written. A keyboard instrument, usually organ or harpsichord, would also play the same bass melody with the left hand, and with the right hand fill in the implied harmonies of the figured bass. This allowed considerable latitude to the keyboard artist, although there were elaborate rules as to how the figured bass should be *realized* (i.e., performed by filling in the parts). The improvisatory art of realizing a figured bass was highly developed in the baroque period and has since been lost.

"FLY WITH BEN"

THE HOLDER OF THIS TICKET

M Edward M Gregores

Has made an Air Voyage in 14-Passenger

Tri-Motored Ford Plane from

Fairfax Airport, Kansas City, Kansas

BEN F. GREGORY, Pilot

Aug. 23, 1936

Important Works of Nuove Musiche. An early opera, probably the earliest prototype of real opera, *Dafne,* written in 1597 by Rinuccini and Peri, has been lost. The work usually referred to as the earliest opera is *Euridice,* produced in 1600 by Rinuccini, Caccini, and Peri on the occasion of a festival for the wedding of Maria de' Medici and Henry IV of France. In the same year, 1600, an allegorical play by Cavalieri and Guidicioni called *La Rappresentazione di anima e di corpo* was presented. It is related to the origin of Roman oratorio and opera. Two additional operas of the period should be mentioned: *Orfeo* by Monteverdi (1607), and *Dafne* (1608), a lyrical tragedy by Gagliano. The most important early use of figured bass belongs to a collection of church pieces for from one to four voice parts with basso continuo, entitled *Cento concerti ecclesiastici* (1602) by Viadana. Finally, the collection of solo songs with figured bass accompaniment entitled *Nuove Musiche* by Caccini has been mentioned as one of the important works of the early 17th century.

RECORDS
  Italian monodies (Monteverdi, Manzoli). AS 21.
  Peri, *Euridice:* "Funeste piaggie." "Non piango." V 21752.
  Peri, "Bellissima regina." "Cante d'Orfeo." Caccini, "Amarilli."
    "Fere selvagge."

SCORES
  SB 168–173, 175–177. HAM 182–185, 187, 189.

CHAPTER XII

Dramatic Music of the Baroque Period

THE forms and styles of nuove musiche were first conceived in Florence, where opera and other dramatic forms were born. These new ideas were soon taken up in other Italian cities and eventually spread over all of Europe.

Italian Opera Schools

Roman Opera. The innovations of the Florentine school (see page 71) were soon taken up by musicians in Rome, which was the second city to develop opera. Special features of opera in the Roman school are (1) the more extensive use of choruses, and (2) the use of comic scenes, called *intermezzi,* interpolated among the scenes of the serious drama. The latter feature is important in that it later led to Italian comic opera, called *opera buffa.*

COMPOSERS AND OPERAS. The principal composers and operas of the Roman School are Domenico Mazzochi, who wrote *La Catena d'Adone* (1626); Michel Angelo Rossi, who wrote *Erminia sul Giordano* (1637); Loreto Vittori, who wrote *La Galatea* (1639); Steffano Landi, who wrote *Santo Alessio* (an oratorio); and Luigi Rossi, who wrote another *Orfeo.*

Venetian Opera. The Venetian school, following the Roman school, flourished around the middle of the 17th century. It was in Venice that the first public opera was established (Teatro San Cassiano) in 1637. Venetian opera is characterized by considerable use of canzonas and popular tunes. There are short, singable melodies and fewer endless arias. The Venetian composers made use of instrumental pieces and instrumental sections within arias called *ritor-nelli*. They also wrote short overtures to operas in the style of fanfares. In the Venetian school recitative and aria became completely distinct.

COMPOSERS AND OPERAS. The principal composers of the Venetian school are Francesco Cavalli (1602–1676), who wrote *Giasone;* Marc Antonio Cesti (1623–1669), who wrote *La Dori* and *Il Pomo d'oro;* and Giovanni Legrenzi (1626–1690), who wrote operas but was more important in church music and instrumental music.

MONTEVERDI. The greatest Italian musician of the first half of the 17th century is Claudio Monteverdi (1567–1643). He may be said to belong to the Venetian school of opera, but his contributions to music are such that special consideration needs to be given him. Monteverdi took up the innovations of the Florentines and developed them, adding his own genius of dramatic expression. Monteverdi had what may be called a dual style: (1) He retained the old contrapuntal styles of which he was a master throughout his life. He wrote many madrigals. (2) He also became a master of the new homophonic, dramatic style which he mastered equally well. His specific innovations in the instrumental field are the violin tremolo and the string pizzicato. Monteverdi's harmonies are radical and expressive. His important operas are *Orfeo* (1607); *Arianna* (1608), now lost except for the famous aria, "Lament"; *Il Combattimento di Tancredi e Clorinda* (1624), in which he made the first use of tremolo and pizzicato; *Il Ritorno d'Ulisse* (1641); and his last great opera, *L'Incoronazione di Poppea* (1642).

Neapolitan Opera. Naples was the last of the Italian cities to develop opera, late in the 17th century, but this school came to dominate opera not only in Italy but everywhere in Europe. The Neapolitan school developed a sense of musical form rather than dramatic truth. The principal musical form of the school is the *da capo aria* which follows a simple ternary plan, represented by the structural formula, *A B A,* i.e., a section, a contrasting section, and a return to the first section with embellishment. The melodic style of the Neapolitan school is characterized by vocal embellishment, florid writing, and coloratura, much of which was improvised by the singer. In addition to the ornamental melodic style, virtuosity was of great importance to the Neapolitans. Excess of display of technique over dramatic truth led to a decline of operatic art and to the reforms of Gluck in the 18th century. Hand-in-hand with the love for virtuosity were the *castrati* (male altos and sopranos), who were the stars of the day and whose vocal pyrotechnics were of more interest to the public than the opera itself. The Neapolitans made little use of the chorus.

ITALIAN OVERTURE. A final contribution of the Neapolitan school was the new form of overture, called *sinfonia*. It consists of three movements, the first fast, with strong rhythm, and in canzona style. The second movement is slow, short, and usually chordal in style. The third movement is again fast, usually fugal and dance-like.

COMPOSERS AND OPERAS. Francesco Provenzale (d. 1704) is considered the founder of the Neapolitan school. The greatest figure is Alessandro Scarlatti (1659–1725), whose principal operas are *La Rosaura* (c. 1690), *Teodora* (1693), *Tigrane* (1715), and *Griselda* (1721). In addition to operas Scarlatti wrote some six hundred cantatas, a hundred and fifty oratorios, and a great quantity of church music.

French Opera and Ballet

Italian opera spread to France and flourished there before an indigenous French opera appeared. Luigi Rossi's *Orfeo* was one of the first to be performed in Paris (1647). In the second half of the 17th century French opera came into its own with the works of Cambert and Lully.

Characteristics of French Opera. French opera was dominated by the classical tragedy of Corneille and Racine. The high quality of poetry and the greater importance of the drama are considerable features of French opera. There is more importance of melody and of dramatic expression in recitative as well as in aria. French opera made more use of short airs than of extended and elaborate arias. The French predilection for the dance is shown in the use of chaconnes, bourées, menuets, gavottes, etc. In the 17th century there was much use of fantastic stage machinery. In general the French made greater use of instrumental music in their operas. Five-part string orchestration characterizes the instrumental music of the French baroque opera.

FRENCH OVERTURE. French opera under Lully developed a special overture. The first movement is in a slow, stately style and is especially characterized by the use of dotted rhythms. The second movement is fast, lively, and fugal. The third movement, which was not always used, returns to the plan of the first movement. This form was employed outside of France, and even as a form separate from opera. Bach used it extensively, as did Handel (e.g., the overture to the *Messiah*).

BALLET. Court dances with costume and scenery but without singing or spoken dialogue were common in the Burgundian and French courts of the 15th century. The earliest extant music for ballet is that of the *Ballet comique de la reine* (1581). The highest development of ballet was reached in the Baroque period in the Versailles Court of Louis XIV. Royalty often participated in these, as did Louis XIV. One of the most important court ballets (*ballet de cour*) was the *Ballet de la nuit* (1653) by Lully. Later, Lully and Molière collaborated to create the *comédie-ballet*, a combination of play and ballet. *Le Bourgeois gentilhomme* (1670) is perhaps the most famous of these. Later, Lully introduced ballets into his operas and called these productions *tragédies*, or *opéra-ballets*. *Armide* and *Cadmus et Hermione* are examples of this type of opera.

COMPOSERS AND LIBRETTISTS. The first opera in the French language was called *Pastorale*, written by Abbé Pierre Perrin (librettist) and Robert Cambert (composer) in 1659. This is of additional interest because it marks the opening of the Académie Royale de Musique, an institution in Paris that still lives as the Grand Opera. Jean Baptiste Lully (1632–1687) is the most important composer of French opera in the 17th century. His librettist was Philippe Quinault. Jean Philippe Rameau (1683–1764) carried on the great traditions of ballet and opera established by Lully. His principal operas are *Hippolyte et Aricie* (1733) and *Castor et Pollux* (1737).

Opera in Germany

During the baroque period there was very little indigenous opera in Germany. This was principally because of the tremendous impact of Italian opera, but in part also because of the disruption of the Thirty Years' War. Furthermore, there was a dearth of libretto literature of any quality.

Italian Opera in Germany. Aside from an early opera by Heinrich Schütz, *Daphne* (1627), now lost, nearly all operatic activity in Germany consisted of Italian operas performed by Italian companies. Even German composers were content to write in the Italian style and to Italian texts. Some of these composers are Fux, Hasse, and, later, Gluck and Mozart. The principal cities in Germany where opera flourished were Vienna, Munich, and Dresden. In Hamburg the first German opera began. An opera house opened in 1678 with Johann Theile's *Adam und Eva*. The most important names connected with Hamburg are Georg Philipp Telemann (1681-1767) and Reinhard Keiser (1674-1739).

Opera and Dramatic Music in England

Similar to the situation in Germany, there was very little real English opera in the Baroque period. The first genuine opera in English is John Blow's *Venus and Adonis* (c. 1685). The only great figure in English opera is Henry Purcell who wrote *Dido and Aeneas* (c. 1689).

Types of Dramatic Music in England. In addition to Italian opera which flourished in England as it did on the Continent, there were certain types of dramatic production that tended to take the place of opera.

MASQUE. The *masque* is a dramatic form of entertainment produced for the nobility, based upon an allegorical or mythological subject, and consisting of poetry, vocal and instrumental music, scenery, stage machinery, costumes, and dancing. Famous literary names connected with writing of masques are Ben Jonson and John Milton. Henry Lawes wrote the music to Milton's masque *Comus*. Other composers of masques are John Blow, Matthew Locke, William Lawes, and Henry Purcell. *Acis and Galatea* (c. 1720) is a famous masque by Handel.

BALLAD OPERA. In the second quarter of the 18th century there arose in England a type of comic opera, known as *ballard opera*. These were parody operas burlesquing the mannerisms of Italian grand opera. They were composed by setting words to already existing popular tunes or folk songs. Heroic characters of grand opera were replaced by beggars, thieves, pickpockets, prostitutes, etc. The best-known example of ballad opera is *The Beggar's Opera* by Gay and Pepusch (1728). The popularity of ballad opera in England, lasting throughout the century, had much to do with Handel's failures in his productions of Italian opera in England.

INCIDENTAL AND ENTR'ACTE MUSIC. English composers were fond of writing music to go with already existing plays. *Incidental music* was composed as background or atmosphere music used during the action of a play. Examples of incidental music are Purcell's *The Fairy Queen* and *King Arthur*. *Entr'acte music* was composed for performance between the scenes and acts of a play. Examples of entr'acte music (often called *act-tunes* or *curtain tunes*) are Matthew Locke's *Instrumental Musick Used in "The Tempest,"* Henry Purcell's *Dioclesian* and *Collection of Ayres Composed for the Theatre*.

Comic Opera

Early in the 18th century a new type of opera began to appear in various forms in Europe and England. The type is referred to generally as comic opera, although it should be noted that the humorous element is not necessarily prominent.

General Characteristics of Comic Opera. Comic opera in general differs from serious opera in several respects. (1) Light, frivolous, often humorous subjects are used. (2) Commonplace characters replace exalted personages of serious opera. (3) Spoken dialogue replaces lengthy recitatives of serious opera. (4) Light, popular melody instead of heavy dramatic arias is characteristic. (5) On the whole the use of chorus is more important in comic opera. Choral finales are usually employed. (6) Comic opera often takes on the nature of parody: parody of character, or frivolous tunes set to words of a well known serious aria, or frivolous words set to the melody of a well-known aria of a serious opera.

Types of Comic Opera. In Italy, France, Germany, and England comic opera had somewhat different origins and developed along somewhat different lines.

ITALIAN OPERA BUFFA. Comic opera in Italy is called *opera buffa.* Its origin was in the comic intermezzi used between acts of serious opera. Early in the 18th century it emerged as a separate form in Naples. Its popularity as entertainment increased throughout the century. It is generally characterized by full chorus finales, popular tunes, lively action, and witty dialogue. An example of opera buffa is *La Serva padrona* by Pergolesi (1733). Other composers of buffa opera are Logroscino, Paisiello, Cimarosa, Piccini, Galuppi, and Mozart.

FRENCH OPÉRA-COMIQUE. In France comic opera originated in the early 18th century as a farce, satire, parody on serious opera. Short satirical poems sung to already existing popular airs, called *vaudevilles,* were commonly employed. Poets of early parody opera in France are Lesage and Favart. Composers of opéra-comique are Duni, Jean Jacques Rousseau (*Le Devin du village*), Philidor, Monsigny, and Grétry.

BALLAD OPERA. The English counterpart of comic opera on the Continent is the ballad opera (discussed on page 79).

GERMAN SINGSPIEL. The term *Singspiel* (drama with music) was at first used for serious and comic opera alike. Later it came to designate comic opera. Singspiel began as an offshoot of English ballad opera. Coffey's ballad opera *The Devil to Pay* was translated into German and set to new music by Standfuss about 1750. Principal developments of Singspiel took place in the second half of the 18th century. The most important composers are Johann Adam Hiller (1728–1804) and Mozart.

Oratorio, Cantata, Passion

Along with opera, other important dramatic forms developed from the innovations of nuove musiche. They are oratorio, cantata, and Passion.

Definitions. *Oratorio* is a dramatic production on a large scale, usually dealing with a Biblical subject, and produced without staging, costuming, or scenery. Oratorio makes use of a narrator, vocal soloists, chorus, and orchestra. The forms used in oratorio are overture, aria, recitative, and diverse choral ensembles. The *cantata* is similar to the oratorio except that it is a short, lyric form. It deals with varied subject matter, either religious or secular. Cantatas are written for a small number of performers, often limited to soloists with few accompanying instruments. A special dramatic form is the *Passion* which is a dramatic presentation of the story of Easter (see page 82).

Oratorio. Early prototypes of the oratorio are to be found in the liturgical dramas of the late Middle Ages and in the miracle plays and mystery plays of the 14th and 15th centuries. Music in some form was usually employed in these early religious dramas, which were based upon scenes from the Bible, hagiology, and allegory. Late in the 16th century, under the leadership of Saint Philip Neri (d. 1595), a group of Romans, calling themselves *Oratorians,* congregated for quasi-evangelical meetings. Among other things they sang laudi spirituali and performed religious allegorical or morality plays which included dialogue-laudi performed by different groups of singers. This movement gave rise to the oratorio proper. One of these allegorical plays is *La Rappresentazione di anima e di corpo* (1600) by Emilio Cavalieri (c. 1550–1602). It makes use of all the innovations of nuove musiche.

Two Types of Oratorio. In the 17th century there were two types of oratorio: (1) *Oratorio Latino* was based upon a Biblical text and was sung in Latin. Oratorio Latino was real church music. (2) *Oratorio volgare* was based upon a free text, was sung in Italian, and tended toward a more secular approach. The distinction between these two types disappeared in the late Baroque.

Composers and Oratorios. Steffano Landi wrote *Il Santo Alessio* (1632). Giacomo Carissimi (1605–1674) wrote *Jephtha.* Carissimi may be said to have established the true oratorio form and style in the Roman oratorio of the 17th century. One of Alessandro Scarlatti's important oratorios is *I Dolori di Maria sempre vergine* (1693). The most important contributions to German oratorio in the 17th century are Heinrich Schütz's *Historia der Auferstehung* ("Story of Resurrection," 1623) and *Die sieben Worte Jesu Christi am Kreuz* ("Seven Last Words," c. 1645), both in the nature of Passion music. Undoubtedly the most important composer of oratorio in the entire Baroque period is Handel. The following are the characteristics of his oratorios: (1) They have an "earthy" quality, less worshipful than similar works by Schütz and Bach. (2) Handel wrote imposing choruses. (3) Biblical history and decorous love interest are to be found in most of Handel's oratorios. (4) Operatic influence on Handel's oratorios is to be found in his use of three acts instead of the conventional two acts of oratorio. The famous *Messiah* (1741) is a special case in that it is reflective rather than narrative. Some of Handel's oratorios are *Athalia, Semele, Samson, Israel in Egypt, Belshazzar, Judas Maccabaeus,* and *Solomon.*

Cantata. The cantata, a third product of nuove musiche, in its earliest form was a musical recitative or short drama in verse, without action, and with a simple accompaniment of one instrument.

SECULAR CANTATA. Secular cantata (*cantata da camera* in Italy, *Kammerkantate* in Germany) was developed before sacred cantata. It predominates in the 17th century, especially in Italy. The most important composers in Italy are: Carissimi, Cesti, A. Scarlatti, and Stradella. In France the leading composers are Charpentier, Campra, Bernier, Clérambault, and Rameau.

CHURCH CANTATA. The church cantata (called *cantata da chiesa* in Italy, *Kirchenkantate* in Germany) developed later than the secular cantata and mostly in Germany. It had an important function in connection with the Lutheran service. It makes use of soloists and instrumental sections and sometimes chorus. Also important to the church cantata is the use of chorale melody and text. This type of cantata, then, belongs to the category of church music. The principal composers of church cantatas are Schütz, Buxtehude, Telemann, Kuhnau, and J. S. Bach.

Passion Music. Presentation of the story of Easter according to the gospels of St. Matthew, St. Mark, St. Luke, and St. John has a long history, going back into the early Christian era. Five stages in its development can be traced.

GOSPEL RECITATION. From about 300 A.D. to 1100 it was common practice in the Church to have the gospels of the Evangelists recited during Holy Week.

PLAINSONG PASSION. In the 12th century the Passion story was presented as a sort of play in which the part of Christ was sung in a low register by a priest, the part of the Evangelist or narrator was sung in a middle register by another priest, and the part of the crowd (*turba*) was sung in a high register by still another priest. Most of this was done in a psalmodic style, except for the words of Christ, "Eli, Eli, lama asabthani," which were given a more expressive melody.

POLYPHONIC PASSION. In the Renaissance period composers began using polyphonic settings of the story, at first setting only the exclamations of the turba, in a motet style. One of the earliest of these was a setting of the St. Matthew gospel by Jacob Obrecht in the late 15th century. Polyphonic Passions were composed by most of the 16th-century masters, including Palestrina.

ORATORIO PASSION. With the advent of the 17th century and the nuove musiche styles the presentation of the Passion story was inevitably affected. Recitative for the Evangelist and other principal characters was then employed, as were also chorus, orchestra, and arias. The basic gospel story was adhered to but free texts were also interpolated.

CHORALE PASSION. The importance of the chorale in the Lutheran service was bound to affect settings of the Passion. Early in the 18th century Protestant chorales were added as reflective elements in the narrative of the Easter story. In Bach's *St. Matthew Passion,* four-part harmonizations of chorales are used reflectively throughout the work, especially the famous "Passion Chorale" by Hassler ("O Sacred Head").

RECORDS
  Italian Opera
  Steffani, "Occhi, perchè piangete." AS 29.
  Monteverdi, Air from *L'Incoronazione di Poppea.* CHM, Vol. 2.
  Monteverdi, "Lagrime d'amante al sepolcro." CM 218.
  Collection of airs and madrigals. VM 496.

Cavalli, *Serse:* "Beato chi può."

Cesti, *Orontea:* "Intorno all' idol mio." A. Scarlatti, "Cessate ti piagarmi." V 21747.

Cesti, *Il Pomo d'oro:* "Air de Venus." AS 82.

A. Scarlatti, "Chi vuole innamorarsi." V 17914.

Pergolesi, vocal selections from *La Serva padrona* (sung in French). Decca LY6014.

French Opera

J. J. Rousseau, airs from *Le Devin du village.* AS 54.

Lully, orchestral excerpts from four operas. CM 376, CM X117.

Lully, *Alceste:* Prelude. V 7424.

Lully, opera airs. AS 20.

Lully, *Le Bourgeois gentilhomme* (incidental music). G P809.

Rameau, *Hippolyte et Aricie:* March. AS 81.

Rameau, *Castor et Pollux:* "Tristes apprêts." *Thésée:* "Revenez, amours." C 214M.

English Dramatic Music

Gay-Pepusch, *Beggar's Opera:* selections. VM 722. G C3166.

Purcell, *Dido and Aeneas* (complete). D 25573/9.

Purcell, *Dido and Aeneas:* "When I am laid in earth." V 17257.

Purcell, *Fairy Queen* (incidental music). C 69407D.

Purcell, *Ayres for the Theatre* (entr'acte music). D 25570.

Handel, "Dank sei dir, Herr" (from cantata). V 15365.

Handel, *Atalanta* (opera): "Care selve." V 15182.

Oratorio, Cantata, Passion

Handel, "Look down, look down, harmonious Saints" (cantata). AS 70.

Handel, *Messiah* (complete). CM 271.

Handel, *Judas Maccabaeus:* "We come in bright array" (chorus). C 9724.

Carissimi, *Ezechias* (oratorio): "Air d'Ezechias."

Bach, *Weichet nur, betruebte Schatten* (secular cantata). VM 664.

Bach, *Schweigt stille* ("Coffee Cantata"). Musicraft 5.

Bach, *Meine Seele ruehmt und preist* (church cantata). AS 23.

Bach, *Christ lag in Todesbanden* (church cantata). V 11178–82.

Bach, *St. Matthew Passion.* VM 411, 412, 413.

SCORES

Italian Opera

SB 171, 175, 177, 178, 199–204, 223, 224, 226, 227, 231, 258, 259, 278, 298. HAM, 187, 189, 206, 208, 209, 221, 222, 223, 259, 286, 298, 300.

French Opera

SB 222, 232–234, 261, 296, 298. HAM 223–225, 276, 277, 291, 304.

English Dramatic Music

SB 247, 281. HAM 203, 243, 255, 263.

German Singspiel and Opera

SB 195, 236, 250, 266, 268, 269, 293, 309. HAM 228, 267, 282, 292, 303.

Oratorio, Cantata, Passion

SB 169, 170, 180, 191, 192, 197, 198, 212, 225, 230, 242, 260, 267, 280, 284, 308. HAM 182, 207, 214, 218, 226, 235, 254, 258, 266, 272, 279, 281.

CHAPTER XIII

Church Music of the Baroque Period

Pᴿᴵᴼᴿ to 1600 church music was largely vocal. In the Baroque, however, the use of instruments became important and separate instrumental forms for church performance, such as the church sonata for strings and organ and the chorale prelude for organ, were used. These will be considered separately in the chapter on baroque instrumental music. The distinction between religious music and liturgical church music should also be pointed out: the oratorio was usually based upon religious subjects but it was not generally intended for performance in church services. The German cantatas, on the other hand, were expressly written for performance in the Lutheran service and are therefore real church music.

General Characteristics of Baroque Church Music. The nuove musiche styles permeated nearly all church music. There was a general abandonment of the renaissance *a cappella* choral style. In its place we find the use of soloists, figured bass accompaniment (basso continuo) and a large use of independent instrumental material: introductions, interludes, ritornelli, etc. Furthermore, there was a general prevalence of the characteristic dramatic style of the new music. The church music of the Baroque was more generally in the vernacular language (French, Italian, German, etc.), replacing the almost universal use of Latin in the Renaissance. The old church modes were abandoned for major and minor keys. Chromaticism was widely used. The pure *a cappella* style of the Renaissance was not completely abandoned, however. The Roman school continued the traditions of Palestrina well into the 17th century. The Sistine

Chapel in Rome was particularly strict in keeping alive the worshipful, nondramatic style of church polyphony.

Principal Schools and Composers. Whereas in the Renaissance, church music had an almost universal style, in the Baroque there is a sharper distinction of nationalistic styles.

ITALIAN CHURCH MUSIC. It has been pointed out above that much of the renaissance tradition was kept alive in Italy. But Italy was also the birthplace of nuove musiche, and so this naturally affected much of the church music written there. Viadana's *Cento concerti ecclesiastici* was the first important collection of church music in the Baroque. Church music was composed by most of the operatic composers of the period: Carissimi, Monteverdi, Cavalli, Legrenzi, A. Scarlatti, etc. Francesco Durante (1684–1755) was almost exclusively a church composer. Mention should be made of a cantata-like work by Pergolesi, *Stabat Mater* (c. 1730), sung to a Latin text. This work may be taken as an example of the fine church music written in Italy in the Baroque. Another work, a fifty-three-voice Mass (1628) by Orazio Benevoli, which makes use of vocal and instrumental choirs, is a continuation and expansion of the Venetian technique, and it represents very well the baroque ideals of the grandiose and magnificent.

FRENCH CHURCH MUSIC. French church music of the Baroque is on the whole rather superficial. It, too, conformed to the new styles in music. Cantata-like forms, called "motets," were written. These used soloists, chorus, and orchestral accompaniment. The most important French church composers of the Baroque are Lully, who retained the *a cappella* style of writing, Charpentier, Campra, Lalande, and Rameau.

GERMAN CHURCH MUSIC. The nuove musiche techniques were employed in Germany in various forms in the 17th century. There was a general tendency, however, toward a crystallization in the church cantata, which was fairly standardized by Bach's time. The German church cantatas make extensive use of chorale melodies, and employ soloists, chorus, and orchestral accompaniments with basso continuo. The most important figure in German church music in the 17th century is Heinrich Schütz. His music incorporates the old Venetian style and the new dramatic forms of the period; in this respect Schütz resembles Monteverdi. He wrote many cantata-like forms called *Cantiones sacrae, Geistliche Gesaenge, Symphoniae sacrae,* and *Geistliche Konzerte.* The most important composers between Schütz and Bach are Tunder, Weckmann, Fux, Buxtehude, Telemann, and Kuhnau.

ENGLISH CHURCH MUSIC. The English composers of the Restoration continued to use the verse anthem as the principal form in the Anglican Church. It became more lengthy and more cantata-like, taking on the general aspects of nuove musiche. The hallelujah chorus, usually as the finale, was quite common. The principal composers are John Blow and Henry Purcell.

RECORDS

Italian Church Music
Pergolesi, *Stabat Mater.* VM 545.
Durante, "Misericordias Domini." V 17633.

German Church Music
Schütz, *Geistliche Konzerte.* AS 28.
Schütz, motet: "Selig sind die Toten." AS 60.
Schütz, *Geistliche Gesänge:* "Dank sagen wir alle Gott." G EJ 130.
Buxtehude, solo cantata: "O fröhliche Stunden." MC 1008.
Bach, motet: "Singet dem Herrn." V 14613.
Bach, *B Minor Mass.* VM 104.
Bach, Cantata No. 189: "Meine Seele rühmt und preist." AS 23.

English Church Music
Purcell, "Bell Anthem": "Rejoice in the Lord." CHM, Vol. 2.
Handel, "Vouchsafe, O Lord." V 1767.

SCORES

Italian
SB 159, 168, 273, 275. HAM 185, 301.

French
HAM 226, 257, 266.

German
SB 161–163, 189, 190, 212, 271, 284. HAM 200, 201, 213, 218, 235, 272.

English
SB 246. HAM 242, 268, 279.

CHAPTER XIV

Instrumental Music of the Baroque Period

INSTRUMENTAL music rivals vocal music for the first time in the Baroque. Its importance is seen in the development of new instrumental forms and new independent instrumental styles, in the improvement of instruments, and in the greater amount of instrumental music written.

General Considerations

Instruments of the Baroque Period. With a few exceptions, most of the instruments used in the Renaissance period were still used throughout the Baroque; there were some important improvements in instruments but no new instruments were invented.

KEYBOARD INSTRUMENTS. The harpsichord was the most important keyboard instrument of the period. It usually had two *manuals* (i.e., two keyboards). Its basis of tone production is the string plucked mechanically by a quill when the key is depressed. The harpsichord was used for basso continuo parts as well as for solo forms. The clavichord has a weak, delicate tone, and was used only in small rooms. Its tone is produced by a string struck by a tangent when the key is depressed. The organ was still inseparably connected with church music. In the Baroque period its mechanism was greatly improved, and the literature for organ increased proportionately.

STRING INSTRUMENTS. In the late Baroque the violin was added to, but did not replace, the older viol instruments. A distinct violin idiom was developed, particularly by the Italians. The bowed instruments were used for both solo and ensemble music. The lute became less important as an instrumental medium in the late 17th century, but production of lute literature continued throughout the Baroque period.

WIND INSTRUMENTS. The oboe and the bassoon (double-reed woodwinds) were the standard wind instruments in the Baroque. The clarinet and the English horn did not appear in general orchestral usage until about the 19th century. The French horn, or hunting horn, was commonly employed. It was without valves until the 19th century. Instruments of the trumpet and trombone class were not yet standardized in the Baroque, and the former were also limited to the natural overtones. In the late Baroque the transverse flute superseded the recorder type of instruments.

General Characteristics of Baroque Instrumental Music. (1) A distinct instrumental style was developed. (2) Many new instrumental forms appeared. (3) Instrumental virtuosity was an important feature of style. (4) On the whole, instrumental music tended to be more polyphonic than homophonic. (5) Instrumentation for ensemble music was still far from becoming standardized, but strings predominated and the harpsichord or organ was consistently employed for the basso continuo part. (6) The bass is more prominent in instrumental music of the Baroque than in any other period. It functions both as harmonic bass and contrapuntal (i.e., melodic) bass. (7) Late in the Baroque period *equal-tempered tuning* of keyboard instruments (i.e., division of the octave into twelve equi-distant tones—the modern system) replaced the older *just intonation* (i.e., tuning in perfect fifths, resulting in unequal half-steps in the octave).

Lute Music

Lute music in the Baroque was less extensive and less important on the whole than it had been in the Renaissance. It persisted mainly in France and Germany. In Italy and Spain popular guitar music took the place of the sophisticated art music for the lute. The lute literature of the 17th century consists mainly of preludes and stylized dances and dance suites. The most important composers of

17th-century lute music are Denis Gaultier (d. 1672) in France, and Reusner and Weiss in Germany. J. S. Bach wrote a few pieces for lute.

Harpsichord Music

Forms. The distinction between harpsichord forms and styles on the one hand and those of the organ on the other became more marked in the 17th century, but there was still a good deal of overlapping. In general, harpsichord music was secular, whereas organ music was largely in the realm of church music.

DANCE SUITE. Groups of stylized dances (i.e., nonfunctional dance music), called *suites,* began to be written around the middle of the 17th century. They evolved from the 16th-century dance pairs (basse-danse and tourdion, pavane and galliard, etc.). The style of the baroque suite in general is contrapuntal, usually limited to two or three parts. Ornamentation is particularly characteristic of harpsichord dances. There are four standard dances of the suite: *allemande, courante, sarabande,* and *gigue.* In addition to these, various optional dances are included in the suite.

a. *Allemande.* The allemande is usually moderately fast, in duple time. It usually begins with an eighth-note or sixteenth-note pickup.

b. *Courante.* The courante of the dance suite is in triple meter, a combination of three-two and six-four meter. It also uses the pickup note and frequent dotted rhythms.

c. *Sarabande.* The third basic movement of the suite, the sarabande, is in slow, triple time. It makes use of the dotted rhythms: ♩.♪♩ and ♩♩.♪.

d. *Gigue.* The last movement of the dance suite is the gigue. It is in lively six-eight or nine-eight time and in a fugal style (i.e., making use of imitation). Often the theme in the second half is an inversion of the opening thematic material.

e. *Optional Dances.* Most of the optional dances employed in the baroque suite originated in the French ballets of the late 17th century. In the Bach suites they usually appear between the sarabande and the gigue. The suite of the late Baroque often begins with a prelude. The optional dances are: *gavotte,* a dance in four-four time, beginning phrases on the third beat of the measure; *bourrée,* a dance in four-four time, as a rule beginning on the fourth beat; *menuet* in three-four time; *loure, air, polonaise, rigaudon,* and *passepied.*

f. *Structure of Dance Movements.* The conventional structure of the dance movements is *binary,* i.e., in two sections. The first section, ending with a double bar and repeat sign, modulates to the dominant key (a fifth above the tonic key) or if the suite is in a minor key it modulates to the relative major key (a minor third above the tonic key). The second half of the dance movement modulates from the contrasting key back to the tonic key, and it also concludes with a double-bar repeat.

SONATA. In the Baroque period the term "sonata" was used for various keyboard pieces as well as for other instrumental music. This term should not be confused with the later classical sonata form. No clear or consistent structural principles were established. The principal composer of baroque keyboard sonatas is Domenico Scarlatti (1685–1757), who wrote virtuosic pieces called *esercizii* (exercises), as well as sonatas and suites.

VARIATION FORMS. Different types of variations continued to be popular in baroque keyboard music. These are the *partita* (a term also applied to the dance suite), the *chaconne,* the *passacaglia,* and the *ground.*

DESCRIPTIVE PIECES. The use of descriptive titles for various kinds of music was commonly employed. Such music attempts some sort of word painting, or imitation of sounds. The "Combat between David and Goliath" in Kuhnau's *Biblical Sonatas,* and Rameau's "La Poule" ("The Hen") are examples of descriptive keyboard music. In baroque keyboard and lute music one often runs across the title *Tombeau* (Fr. "Tombstone"). Such pieces, intended as eulogy for some famous deceased person, are of a decidedly expressive character.

PRELUDE AND FUGUE. Pieces in various free styles and forms, called preludes, were often combined with the strict fugue in the late 17th and first half of the 18th centuries. The prelude-fugue combination was more common in organ literature than in harpsichord music. The most important collection of preludes and fugues for the harpsichord is J. S. Bach's *Well-Tempered Clavichord (Das wohltempe-*

rierte Clavier). It consists of two sets of 24 preludes and fugues in all keys, major and minor, illustrating the advantages of the new equal-tempered tuning. The term "clavichord" in this case was probably meant to imply any keyboard instrument.

MISCELLANEOUS FORMS. In addition to the principal forms of keyboard music listed above, such terms as "toccata," "prelude," and "fantasia," and various dance forms are to be found.

Schools and Composers. The most important schools of harpsichord music were in Italy, France, and Germany.

ITALY. In the first half of the 17th century the most important names in Italian keyboard music are Trabaci, Valente, and Girolamo Frescobaldi (1583–1643). The latter wrote outstanding variations (called "partitas") for the *cembalo* (Italian harpsichord). In the second half of the 17th century Bernardo Pasquini composed toccatas, suites, and sonatas. The most important Italian keyboard composer of the Baroque is Domenico Scarlatti (1685–1757), a contemporary of J. S. Bach. He wrote virtuosic, one-movement sonatas, usually binary in form, and displaying all sorts of scale and arpeggio figuration with characteristic repetition of short phrases or figures. Figuration is more important than counterpoint in Scarlatti's sonatas.

FRANCE. Jacques Champion de Chambonnières (c. 1602–1672) was the first important composer in the French school of *clavecin* music (French harpsichord). Henri d'Anglebert (1635–1691) was a pupil of Chambonnières. François Couperin (1668–1733) is perhaps the most important composer of baroque harpsichord music. He wrote suites (called *ordres*) and many descriptive pieces. The French school reaches its culmination with Jean Philippe Rameau (1683–1764). In general, the French clavecin school is characterized by a fondness for dance pieces and descriptive music, for rich ornamentation, characterization, and dramatic surprise. The French school considerably influenced the harpsichord style of the German school, particularly that of Bach's keyboard music.

GERMANY. Johann Jakob Froberger (1616–1667), a pupil of Frescobaldi, was largely instrumental in establishing the order of the suite movements. His keyboard music shows further development of the Frescobaldi trait of freely adding or taking away contrapuntal parts and filling in chords (*Freistimmigkeit*). J. K. F. Fischer (1650–1746) wrote a collection of preludes and fugues in all keys, called *Ariadne musica* (1715), possibly for organ. Johann Kuhnau (1660–1722) wrote keyboard sonatas of a descriptive nature. J. S. Bach wrote suites (sometimes called partitas), preludes and fugues for the harpsichord.

ENGLAND. The two principal composers of baroque harpsichord music in England are Henry Purcell (1658–1695), who wrote numerous suites and single dance pieces and grounds, and Handel, who wrote suites and a few fugues for harpsichord.

Organ Music

Forms. Organ music, which is generally vocal in style in the Renaissance, becomes more idiomatic and more instrumental in the Baroque. Four main categories of organ forms are: (1) free forms, (2) fugal forms, (3) chorale prelude forms, and (4) variation forms.

FREE FORMS. This classification includes a wide variety of styles and involves no standard structural principles. The baroque *toccata* is characterized by a display of virtuosic material (rapid scales, arpeggios, broken chords, etc.), the use of full chordal sections, and the use of polyphonic sections or *fughettas*. The toccata is usually in a free rhythm and has a rhapsodic character, especially in North Germany (Buxtehude and Bach). Special types of toccatas are to be found in the *perpetuum mobile* style, which consists of rapid, consistent, étude-like material, and in the *liturgical toccata,* which is a short prelude in a restrained, dignified style. The *fantasia* or *fantasy* is similar to the toccata in its indeterminate, free, improvisatory style. It is usually less virtuosic than the toccata, often more polyphonic. The *prelude* also includes a wide range of styles and structures. It is usually shorter than the fantasia and the toccata, and frequently precedes a fugue. The *capriccio* in the 17th century is more contrapuntal, more fugal than the others. It is often based on a pre-existing theme. Because of its decidedly contrapuntal nature, the capriccio is sometimes considered as one of the ancestors of the fugue.

FUGAL FORMS. Although imitative counterpoint is employed in many forms in the Baroque, there are three forms which are primarily based upon imitation: the *ricercare* (see page 54), the *canzona* (see page 54), and the *fugue*. The fugue emerges in the second half of the 17th century. It differs from the ricercare and canzona chiefly in its monothematic basis and its economy of material derived from the subject. A fugue subject may resemble the lively canzona style or the slow ricercare style. The fugue gradually replaced the canzona and the ricercare in the late Baroque period.

CHORALE PRELUDE. The chorale prelude is essentially a cantus firmus type of composition, based upon a chorale melody or sometimes a plainsong. Six types of chorale prelude can be distinguished.

a. *Simple Cantus Firmus Treatment*. When the chorale melody is stated in long notes against a faster-moving counterpoint the chorale prelude belongs to the simple cantus firmus type.

b. *Coloration*. When the original chorale melody is highly ornamented by melismatic treatment this is called coloration and constitutes an important style in chorale prelude writing.

c. *Fugal Chorale*. When fragments of the chorale melody are used imitatively the chorale prelude belongs to the fugal type.

d. *Trio Chorale*. When three distinct polyphonic parts are used (one for each of two hands and pedals), this is designated as a trio type of chorale prelude. The material is derived from the original chorale melody.

e. *Chorale Variations*. This type consists of polyphonic variations on the chorale melody, which is then somewhat altered.

f. *Chorale Fantasy*. Free, rhapsodic use of material derived from the chorale melody is sometimes made. This type, as well as the fugal and trio types, is not strictly a cantus firmus composition because the chorale melody is not continuous throughout.

VARIATIONS FOR ORGAN. In addition to chorale variations, other terms indiscriminately applied to variations are *passacaglia, chaconne,* and *ground* (English). These are all continuous variations based either upon a recurrent bass theme (ostinato bass) or else upon a recurrent harmonic progression.

Schools and Composers. Germany led in the field of baroque organ music. Less important contributions were made by Italy, France, and England.

GERMANY. A continuous line of German organ composers and

organ music extends from Paumann in the 15th century to Bach in the 18th century. German organ music expanded enormously in the 17th century and eclipsed that of all other schools. The German school of organ music of the 17th century begins with the Dutchman, Jan Pieters Sweelinck (1562–1621), who applied English virginalist technique to his organ chorale variations. Samuel Scheidt (1587–1654), a pupil of Sweelinck, was perhaps the most important German organ composer in the first half of the 17th century. Dietrich Buxtehude (1637–1707) and Georg Böhm (1661–1735) are the most significant predecessors of Bach in North Germany. They developed particularly the free forms of organ music and the fugue. Heinrich Bach (J. S. Bach's grandfather), Johann Krieger, Johann Pachelbel, and Johann Kuhnau, all Middle-German composers, contributed to the development of the chorale prelude and the variation forms. From South Germany the composers Hassler, Erbach, Steigleder, and Froberger developed the Italian contrapuntal styles of organ music, particularly the ricercare and the fugue. The achievements of the German organ school are summed up in the crowning works of J. S. Bach, who, writing in all the forms and styles, wrote the greatest organ music of all time.

ITALY. The Italian organ school flourished chiefly in the first half of the 17th century. After 1650 there is a marked decline in the quality and quantity of its organ music. Its traditions were largely passed on to the South German school, from Frescobaldi to Froberger. Girolamo Frescobaldi (1583–1643), a famous organist at St. Peter's in Rome, was undoubtedly the greatest of Italian organ composers. He wrote toccatas, canzonas, ricercares, capriccios, and a collection of church pieces for organ entitled *Fiori musicali*. His style is notable for its daring harmony and chromaticism, for virtuosity and contrapuntal ingenuity.

FRANCE AND ENGLAND. Organ music in France and England was of little consequence. The French are noted for contributions to organ registration and colorful stops. Jean Titelouze (1563–1633) wrote liturgical organ music (mostly cantus firmus compositions on plainsong) in Renaissance style. Other names connected with French baroque organ music are Dumont, Nivers, Gigault, Le Bègue,

Raison, Marchand, Couperin, and Daquin. Organ music in England is even less significant than that in France. *Voluntaries* and similar short pieces to be used in the church service were composed by John Blow, Purcell, Clark, and Croft. Special mention should be made of Handel's 12 organ concertos intended for performance between the acts of oratorios.

Chamber Music

Music designated as chamber music is written for small combinations of instruments, and usually one instrument to a part.

Media. Although, as has been pointed out, there was little or no standardization of instrumentation in ensemble music in the Baroque, still there was a growing tendency toward certain chamber music media. There were two of these: the *solo sonata* and the *trio sonata*.

SOLO SONATA. The solo sonata of the Baroque was a composition in several movements for a solo instrument, usually with a figured bass accompaniment. The violin was by far the most common solo instrument, but solo sonatas were also written for the viol, viola da gamba, flute, and oboe. Somewhat less common was the unaccompanied solo sonata for some bowed string instrument which, in lieu of a keyboard accompaniment, filled in harmonies by double and triple stopping.

TRIO SONATA. Like the solo sonata, the trio sonata is a composition in several movements. But it was written for two solo instruments, usually violins, and a basso continuo part. The trio sonata, then, was usually performed by four instruments: two violins, a low string instrument (cello or viola da gamba) playing the continuo part, and a keyboard instrument (harpsichord or organ) also playing the continuo part and filling in the indicated harmonies of the figured bass.

Forms. In addition to renaissance ensemble forms such as the fantasia for viols which continued to be written in the 17th century, two new forms arose in the second half of the 17th century: the *chamber sonata* and the *church sonata*. Both forms were written for solo sonata and trio sonata media.

CHAMBER SONATA. The chamber sonata (*sonata da camera* in Italy, *Kammersonate* in Germany) is a dance suite usually consisting of the conventional four dance movements (allemande, courante, sarabande, and gigue) and one or more optional dances.

CHURCH SONATA. The church sonata (*sonata da chiesa* in Italy, *Kirchensonate* in Germany) is a more dignified and more abstract form than the chamber sonata, because it was actually used in the church. It is usually in four movements following the plan of tempo contrast: slow, fast, slow, and fast. The fast movements are usually fugal, the slow movements more cantabile in style, or sometimes chordal. Although not so labeled, the last movement is very often a lively gigue. There is no definite plan of key contrasts between the movements, although occasionally the third movement is in a relative key. It is not uncommon for one movement to end on the dominant, leading directly into the following movement.

Style. It should be kept in mind that the term "sonata" in the Baroque period designates an entirely different form and style from that of the 18th-century classical sonatas of Haydn, Mozart, and Beethoven. The conventional thematic material, the "tune element," is not present in the baroque sonata. Nor is there any thematic development, so important to the classical sonata. Furthermore, the movements are generally in a binary form similar to that of the dance suite movements. A definitely instrumental violin idiom is developed in the baroque sonata. This is shown by the extensive use of violin figuration and double stopping.

Schools and Composers. Chamber music in the Baroque period was developed chiefly in Italy and Germany.

ITALY. The Italian school was the first to develop the baroque sonata forms and styles, principally for strings. Perhaps the first important composer to be named is Giovanni Vitali (c. 1644–1692). He was followed by Giuseppe Torelli (c. 1650–1708). The greatest figure in the 17th century is Arcangelo Corelli (1653–1713), who wrote solo and trio sonatas of the church and chamber types, as well as much fine orchestral music for strings. Antonio Vivaldi (c. 1680–1743), a contemporary of Bach, is noted for his strength and vigor which undoubtedly had considerable influence upon Bach.

Giuseppe Tartini (1692–1770) was particularly noted for advances in bow technique and for virtuosity of style. Less important composers of the Italian school are: Marcello, Pergolesi, Veracini, Pugnani, Nardini, and Locatelli.

GERMANY. In Germany Johann Rosenmüller (1620–1684) wrote solo and trio sonatas. A special feature of the sonatas of Heinrich von Biber (1644–1704) was the use of *scordatura* (different tuning of the violin strings for the purpose of obtaining special effects in double stopping). Georg Philipp Telemann (1681–1767) wrote trio sonatas, solo sonatas, and ensemble music called *Tafelmusik*, i.e., "table music" to be performed at a banquet. Again, in the field of chamber music, the works of J. S. Bach reveal the assimilation of forms and styles, and the highest peak of baroque music. He wrote 6 sonatas and suites for unaccompanied violin, 6 sonatas and suites for unaccompanied cello, 6 solo sonatas for violin and figured bass, 6 suites for violin and figured bass, 6 flute sonatas, and 2 trio sonatas for violin, flute, and basso continuo.

ENGLAND. Henry Purcell wrote four-part fantasies in the old polyphonic style. He also wrote baroque trio sonatas, the most famous of which is the *Golden Sonata*. Handel wrote solo sonatas for flute, oboe, and violin without much idiomatic distinction between the specific instruments.

FRANCE. François Couperin wrote some chamber music. The principal name in the French school, however, is Jean Marie Leclair (1697–1764), who is considered the founder of the French school of violin playing.

Orchestral Music

In distinction from chamber music, orchestral music is for a larger body of instruments, and it involves the use of several instruments to a part.

Media. There was less standardization of instrumentation in large ensembles than in chamber music. A typical feature of baroque orchestration is that there was little or no attempt to bring out instrumental colors as such. As in the Renaissance, various instruments double on parts of a polyphonic composition with no regard

to blending, just so long as the part is within the range of the instrument. The strings invariably predominate in orchestras of the
Baroque. The bass part, particularly prominent in baroque orchestras, is invariably basso continuo. Orchestras were generally con-
ducted from the harpsichord, the harpsichordist having the dual
function of playing the continuo part and leading the ensemble.
Timpani (kettle drums) were not used, and brass instruments were
used only sparingly.

Forms. The baroque orchestra was used considerably in connection
with large vocal forms: operas, cantatas, oratorios, and choruses.
But it also developed special forms of its own.

OVERTURE. The Italian sinfonia (see page 76) and the French
overture (see page 77) became important orchestral forms in the
late Baroque. They were employed as overtures not only to operas
but to oratorios and cantatas, and even as opening movements to
orchestral suites.

ORCHESTRAL SUITE. The form of the dance suite was also employed
as an orchestral form. It used the same form and the same types
of dance movements as those found in keyboard suites and in the
chamber sonatas of the Baroque. It is often introduced by an elaborate prelude, overture, or sinfonia.

CONCERTO GROSSO. The most important orchestral form of the
Baroque period is the *concerto grosso*. It has a characteristic instrumentation. In addition to the main body of the orchestra, called
tutti or *ripieno,* from two to four solo instruments, called *concertino,*
are employed. The most characteristic feature of style of the concerto
grosso is the dynamic contrast of alternating sections of tutti and
concertino. Concerti grossi usually follow the plan of the four-
movement sonata: slow, fast, slow, fast. However, this plan is variable. Sometimes numerous shorter movements are used (Corelli),
and later a three-movement plan (fast, slow, fast) is to be found
(Vivaldi, Bach). The last movement, as in the church and chamber
sonatas, is often gigue-like in character, and it is apt to be more
fugal than the other movements.

SOLO CONCERTO. Music for orchestra with one or two solo instruments, usually violins, is called a *solo concerto*. It differs from the

concerto grosso in that the solo instrument is more prominently featured, plays more continuously, and does not provide the contrast between tutti and concertino that is so characteristic of the concerto grosso.

TURMSONATE. A less significant form of instrumental ensemble, called *Turmsonate* or *tower sonata,* was developed in Germany. It arose from the current practice of sounding the hours of the day from church or municipal towers. Chorales were often used for this purpose. Tower music was played mostly by brass instruments. The tower sonata consists of several movements of varying character, some dance-like, some chordal, others contrapuntal. Johann Pezel (or Petzold) (1639–1694) is the principal composer of Turmsonaten.

Schools and Composers. Orchestral music of one sort or another was written in all countries where dramatic forms flourished. Special orchestral forms such as the orchestral suite and concerto grosso were developed principally in Italy and Germany.

ITALY. The principal composers of orchestral music, chiefly the concerto and concerto grosso, are Stradella (c. 1645–1682), Corelli, Torelli, Geminiani (1674–1762), and Vivaldi.

GERMANY. The principal German composers of orchestral music are Abaco, Fux, Telemann, and J. S. Bach, whose six *Brandenburg Concertos* are among the finest orchestral music of the period.

ENGLAND. Little orchestral music was written in England. Handel wrote concerti grossi patterned after the Corelli plan. He also wrote two extended works for wind instruments intended for outdoor festival performance, *Fireworks Music* and *Water Music.* These consist of a large number of movements in varying forms and styles.

FRANCE. Separate orchestral music was not extensively employed in France. The greater portion of French orchestral music is that written for French opera and ballet, including instrumental dances of all kinds.

RECORDS

Organ Music

Frescobaldi, "Toccata for the elevation." AS 4.

Daquin, "Noël sur les flutes." VM 616.

German organ music (Pachelbel, Scheidt). AS 10.

Bach, Collection of toccatas, fantasias, preludes, and fugues. CM 270.

Bach, Collections of chorale preludes. CM 310. VM 652, 697, 711.

Bach, Organ trio sonata No. 1. Technichord 1388.

Harpsichord Music

French harpsichord music. AS 7.

Couperin, Miscellaneous harpsichord works. Couperin Society Album. His Master's Voice.

Rameau, Suite. VM 593.

Purcell, Suite. C DB501.

Handel, Suite. CHM, vol. 2.

Kuhnau, *Biblical sonata:* "Combat between David and Goliath." AS 3.

Bach, Prelude and fugue. Numbers 1 and 21. CHM, vol. 2.

Bach, Partita (suite). V 14146/7.

Chamber Music

Corelli, Trio sonata. PM 106.

Leclair, Trio sonata. AS 48.

Blavet, Sonata (flute and harpsichord). AS 9.

Rameau, "Pièce de clavecin en concert." AS 30.

Trio sonata (anonymous). AS 19.

Dall' Abaco, Trio sonata. AS 46.

Purcell, Golden sonata. AS 22.

Purcell, String fantasias. English Music Society Album, vol. 1.

Handel, Sonata (oboe and harpsichord). AS 11.

Handel, Sonata (viola da gamba and harpsichord). AS 49.

Telemann, Tafelmusik. AS 26.

Bach, Trio sonata. G DB5125/6.

Bach, Unaccompanied cello sonata. VM 611.

Bach, Sonata (violin and harpsichord). VM 887.

Orchestral Music

Pezel, Turmmusik. AS 2.

Orchestral suites of the late 17th century. AS 52.

Corelli, Concerto grosso. VM 600.

Vivaldi, Violin concerto. AS 37.

Handel, Concerto grosso. D 25659/60.

Handel, *Water Music.* C CMX13.

Bach, Concerto for 2 harpsichords. AS 41/2.

Bach, *Brandenburg concertos* (1–6). CM 249, 250.

Bach, Violin concerto. VM 221.

Bach, Orchestral suite. V 11996/8.

SCORES
Lute Music
SB 181b, 215, 216. HAM 211, 233.

Harpsichord Music
SB 205, 207, 218, 244, 253, 264, 279, 282, 296. HAM 192, 196, 199, 212, 216, 229, 232, 247, 250, 262, 264, 265, 274, 284, 285, 288, 289, 292, 296, 297, 302, 309.

Organ Music
SB 158, 185, 196, 243, 249, 263, 265, 283, 291, 292, 302. HAM 190, 191, 215, 217, 231, 234, 236, 237, 240, 249, 251.

Chamber Music
SB 155–157, 182–184, 219, 228, 229, 237–241, 245, 251, 294, 295, 307. HAM 197, 198, 199, 210, 219, 220, 230, 238, 245, 246, 252, 253, 256, 261, 269, 271, 275, 278, 287, 305.

Orchestral Music
SB 213, 214, 220, 221, 224, 232, 233, 252, 257, 276, 277, 278. HAM 208, 223, 224, 246, 259, 260, 270, 294, 295, 310.

CHAPTER XV

Bach and Handel

THE culmination of the Baroque period is represented in the works of two great German masters: Johann Sebastian Bach (1685–1750) and George Frederick Handel (1685–1759). Unlike the masters of the early 17th century, Bach and Handel perfected rather than invented forms and styles. Although both were German by birth, their music, taken as a whole, reflects an amazing amalgamation of all national schools and styles—an important factor in their universal greatness.

Bach and Handel Compared

Lives. A comparison of the biographies of Bach and Handel shows many striking differences and a few similarities. (1) Bach was provincial in the sense that he spent his entire life within a geographical area of about a forty-mile radius; whereas Handel was cosmopolitan, spending large parts of his life in Germany, Italy, and England. (2) Bach was very much of a family man, who by two successive wives had twenty children. Handel never married and never seemed to need domestic life. (3) Bach's life was largely concerned with small ventures and commonplace problems, whereas Handel's life centered around big ventures. (4) Whereas Bach had a long line of musical ancestors (to such an extent that in Germany any musician was apt to be referred to as "a Bach"), Handel had virtually no musical ancestry. (5) It is a curious coincidence of fate that both these great masters ended their last years in blindness.

Character, Personality. Bach and Handel were both devoutly religious, but Handel was more mundane. Handel was pompous and lordly, whereas Bach, although on occasions willful, was generally more humble and even obsequious.

Kinds of Music. (1) Bach's musical output was chiefly in church music (church cantatas and sacred organ music); Handel dealt in large dramatic forms (opera and oratorio). (2) Bach's music is utilitarian for the most part, written for specific occasions or functions, whereas Handel wrote music on a grand scale and often for no particular occasion or function. (3) Whereas Bach used the chorale extensively in his music, Handel made virtually no use of it. (4) Bach's output and greatness in organ music are well known, a contrast to the fact that Handel, although a great organist, wrote very little organ music. (5) Both composers were great masters of choral music. (6) Whereas Bach's music is of an impersonal nature, it may be said that Handel is the first composer to reveal his personality through his music.

Differences of Musical Style. (1) Bach's music is predominantly polyphonic; Handel's music is predominantly homophonic, although both were great masters of baroque polyphony. (2) Bach's vocal music shows a strong tendency toward instrumental idiom, whereas Handel displays a more idiomatic vocal writing. (3) Although both composers were fond of regular rhythms, Bach often has a stronger, more driving rhythm. (4) Bach's harmony, on the whole, is richer and more ingenious than that of Handel.

Bach

Style. (1) Bach's contrapuntal ingenuity has never been surpassed, rarely equalled. The beauty of contrapuntal lines and the mastery with which they are combined in polyphonic textures are evident in such works as the fugues for organ and for harpsichord, the *Art of Fugue* (*Die Kunst der Fuge*), and the *Musical Offering* (*Das musikalische Opfer*). (2) The driving rhythm of many of the organ toccatas, some of the fugues, and most of the orchestral works is a characteristic of Bach's style. (3) Bach's harmonic ingenuity is on a par with his great contrapuntal skill. Richness, variety of progression, and considerable chromaticism are generally evident in his music. (4) Bach's instrumentation, characteristic of baroque instrumental music in general, is unidiomatic and rather uncolorful. (5) Bach had an extraordinary architectural sense of form, and subtlety and continuity of phraseology are everywhere manifest.

PICTORIAL EXPRESSION. According to Albert Schweitzer, an important aspect of Bach's music is his use of pictorial and symbolic expression. This is evident in his vocal music where the general meaning or mood of the text is brought out by various devices. For example, grief is often expressed by a descending chromatic line, as in the "Crucifixus" of the *B Minor Mass*. Joy, on the other hand, is often expressed in long, continuous lines of eighth or sixteenth notes as in the well-known choral setting "Jesu, Joy of Man's Desiring." Expressive words, such as "eternity," "still," "quiet," "pain," "fall," "ascend," etc., are pictorially treated. Such expression is to be found in the chorale preludes as well as in the vocal music. It was not an original idea with Bach, but he probably employed it more extensively than any of his contemporaries or predecessors.

Origins of Bach's Style. Bach's style, an assimilation of baroque practices in general, can be traced to various sources.

ORGAN MUSIC. The principal features of Bach's organ music are derived from the great and numerous German masters before him. He seems to have derived his fugal style from Pachelbel. The trio sonata and the trio chorale preludes come from Hofhaimer, Buchner, Kotter, and Kleber of the 16th century. His style of coloration comes from the 15th-century style of Paumann, through Finck, Isaac, and Schlick in the 16th century. Variation technique comes from the English virginal school, through Sweelinck and Scheidt. The toccata style is traced from Frescobaldi in Italy, through Froberger, and more immediately from Buxtehude.

HARPSICHORD MUSIC. The style of Bach's partitas and suites for harpsichord comes directly from the French clavecin school. This is noticeable in the contrapuntal treatment and in the use of embellishment.

ORCHESTRAL AND CHAMBER MUSIC. A direct Italian influence on Bach's instrumental ensemble music is to be seen in the use of string figuration, sequence, and clear phraseology. The driving rhythm of his orchestral music comes from Corelli and more from Vivaldi.

CHORAL MUSIC. Bach's choral technique comes from the Venetian school of Giovanni Gabrieli through Schütz (a pupil of Gabrieli's) to Buxtehude and Telemann.

HARMONY. Bach's harmony is solidly German.

Summary of Works. Bach's great versatility can be seen from the following classified summary of his music.

VOCAL CHURCH MUSIC. Bach wrote some 300 church cantatas of which only about 200 have been preserved, and several secular cantatas. In addition to the famous *St. Matthew Passion* he wrote Passion music to the St. John gospel, 4 short Masses, the great *B Minor Mass,* a setting of the Magnificat, and several choral compositions called "motets." He harmonized nearly 400 chorales in four-part harmony.

HARPSICHORD MUSIC. Bach's harpsichord music includes 15 two-part inventions (short, imitative contrapuntal pieces), 15 "symphonies" (three-part inventions), 6 partitas (suites), 6 English suites, 6 French suites, 48 preludes and fugues (*The Well-Tempered Clavichord*), miscellaneous suites, toccatas, preludes, fugues, etc., and the *Goldberg Variations.*

ORGAN MUSIC. Bach's organ music includes 6 trio sonatas, numerous preludes and fugues, toccatas, fantasias, a passacaglia and fugue in C minor, the *Orgelbüchlein* (a set of short chorale preludes for the liturgical year), various sets of 6, 18, 25, and 28 chorale preludes, and chorale variations (called "partitas").

CHAMBER MUSIC. Bach's chamber music includes 3 sonatas for harpsichord and flute, 6 sonatas for harpsichord and violin (3 church sonatas and 3 chamber sonatas), 3 sonatas for harpsichord and viola, one trio sonata for flute, violin, and basso continuo, 1 sonata for 2 violins and basso continuo, 6 sonatas for violin alone, and 6 sonatas for cello alone.

ORCHESTRAL MUSIC. His orchestral music includes 1 concerto grosso for harpsichord, flute, and violin, 6 *Brandenburg Concertos* (concerti grossi), 3 concertos for violin and orchestra, 1 concerto for 2 violins, 4 orchestral suites, 2 concertos for harpsichord, 3 concertos for 2 harpsichords, 2 concertos for 3 harpsichords, and 1 concerto for 4 harpsichords.

COLLECTIONS. Bach wrote several collections that are of great historical as well as musical interest. The *Musical Offering* is a collection of contrapuntal pieces (various canons, ricercares, fugues, and a trio sonata) all based on a theme by Frederick the Great and presented to him by Bach. *Anna Magdalena Bach's Music Notebook* is a collection of rather simple pieces presumably for the musical edification of his second wife. It consists of two volumes of diverse pieces for harpsichord and some songs. *The Art of Fugue* was Bach's last great work. It is a collection of fugues and canons all based on one thematic idea. The final piece is an incomplete quadruple fugue one of the themes of which spells out Bach's name, *B A C H* (the letter *H* in German stands for B natural, while *B* stands for B flat).

Handel

Style. (1) Handel's style is a mixture of national elements: Italian, German, and English. (2) His style includes most of the traits generally characteristic of the late Baroque: formal, strict structures, ornamentation, artificiality of stereotyped cadences and harmonic progressions, and certain melodic formulae. (3) Handel's music is predominantly homophonic. (4) Handel's harmony is conventional, more diatonic than Bach's. Specifically, Handel makes extensive use of tonic and dominant progressions and of first inversion chords. (5) Handel's rhythm is generally strong, and he favors dotted rhythm patterns. (6) Handel is fond of contrasts of tempo, material, polyphonic and homophonic sections, range, and timbre. (7) Handel's phrases are more clearly definite on the whole than those of Bach; they are also inclined to be long. (8) Cantabile melody, often beginning with a long sustained note, is characteristic of his melodic style. (9) In his choral music he often gains a special effect by writing tenor and bass parts high and soprano and alto parts low. (10) Handel frequently makes use of a special final cadence: a pause or complete rest in all parts following a climax, and then a few solid cadential chords.

Summary of Works. Handel's principal contributions are in opera, of which he wrote forty-three, mostly in Italian style, and in oratorio, of which he wrote twenty-seven, mostly in his later life after his operatic ventures had failed.

OTHER VOCAL WORKS. Handel's other vocal works consist of 22 Italian duets, numerous anthems, a masque (*Acis and Galatea*), Italian cantatas with basso continuo and other instruments, and Italian, German, and English songs.

INSTRUMENTAL MUSIC. Handel's instrumental music includes 17 harpsichord suites, 12 harpsichord pieces of varying nature, 6 fugues for harpsichord, 15 solo sonatas for violin, oboe, and viola da gamba, all with figured bass accompaniment, 6 trio sonatas for 2 oboes and basso continuo, 15 sonatas for 2 violins, 6 oboe concertos, 12 organ concertos, 22 orchestral concertos (concerti grossi), *Water Music, Fireworks Music,* and both French and Italian types of overture to his 43 operas and 27 oratorios.

PART FOUR

The Classical Period (1750–1820)

Structure of music was very formal
music was simple.
homophonic -- simple harmony,
counterpoint...

CHAPTER XVI

General Considerations

THE second half of the 18th century and the first quarter of the 19th century is a period marked by momentous events in general history, and by significant changes in musical form and style.

THE MEANING OF CLASSICISM. The term "classical" in music conforms to the ideals of the Apollonian cult of Ancient Greece: objectivity, emotional restraint, clarity of form, and adherence to certain structural principles. Classical ideals in music are not confined to the late 18th century. They appear in the ars antiqua; they are manifest in certain aspects of the 20th century. Classicism is also characteristic of the late baroque music of Bach and Handel, for example. To distinguish the classicism of the early 18th century from that of the late 18th century, the latter is often referred to as the *Viennese Classical* period, because Vienna was the musical capital of Europe at that time.

General Historical Background. The period between 1750 and 1820 is generally marked by the rise of the lower and middle classes in a democratic spirit which asserted itself in the French Revolution. The French Revolution and the Napoleonic Wars dominate the period. Before the French Revolution, a widespread conflict, known as the Seven Years' War (1756-1763), in which Prussia, allied with England, fought against Austria and France, spread through Europe, India, and America (the French and Indian Wars). The American Declaration of Independence (1776) and the American Revolution belong to this period. The predominant philosophy was rationalist; it is manifest in the works of the German Kant and of the French

Diderot and the Encyclopedists. Voltaire and Rousseau are important names in literature and philosophy. In sociology Adam Smith's
The Wealth of Nations (1776) is a milestone. Important artists of
the period are Goya, David, Reynolds, Gainsborough, and Copley.
Rococo is the term applied to the general spirit and style of the
art and music of this period.

THE MEANING OF ROCOCO. *Rococo* is defined in Webster as "a
florid style of ornamentation characterized by curved lines and
decoration of pierced shellwork, popular in Europe in the 18th
century." The term has come to have a somewhat broader meaning
and application. It is used to connote a sort of preciosity, overrefine-
ment, and delicacy that pervades not only decoration but also
painting, architecture, literature, poetry, and music. At best the
rococo is a delicate, polished, restrained, and somewhat superficial
art; at worst it is a degeneration of the baroque spirit.

General Musical Characteristics of the Classical Period. In general,
classical music can be described as objective, showing emotional restraint, polish, refinement, and a certain amount of superficiality.
The classical spirit is more clearly manifest in instrumental music
than it is in opera and other dramatic forms.

FORM. Clarification of formal structure is generally evident.
Modern sonata form emerges in the Classical period.

MELODIC STYLE. A new type of melody is developed. It has an individual and compact character, and it is often folk-like in its clarity
and simplicity. It replaces the long lines and the figuration styles of
baroque polyphony.

HOMOPHONIC STYLE. A new importance of distinct thematic material gives homophonic style a decided precedence over polyphonic
style. A special aspect of this characteristic is the *Alberti bass,* a special type of broken-chord accompaniment.

COUNTERPOINT. Counterpoint is still employed, especially in thematic development, but it is of secondary importance. Contrapuntal
forms are generally abandoned.

HARMONY. Classical music generally shows a remarkable simplicity.
On the whole, there is less harmonic complexity and ingenuity than
in the works of J. S. Bach, for example. No significant harmonic

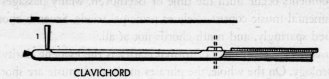

CLAVICHORD

1. Tangent which strikes string when key is depressed.

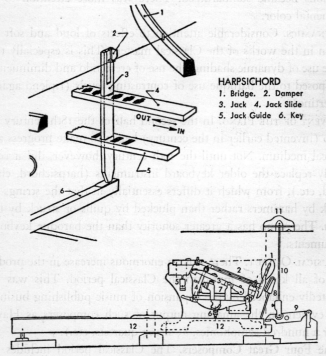

HARPSICHORD

1. Bridge. *2.* Damper
3. Jack *4.* Jack Slide
5. Jack Guide *6.* Key

MODERN PIANO

1. Hammer Head. *2.* Hammer Shank and Butt. *3.* Repetition Lever. *4.* Tack. *5.* Set-off
Button. *6.* Capstan Screws. *7.* Repetition Spring. *8.* Check Head and Wire. *9.* Damper
Body. *10.* Damper Wire. *11.* Damper Head. *12.* Key.

Harpsichord reprinted by permission of the publishers from Willi Apel, Harvard Dictionary of Music, Cambridge,
Mass.: Harvard University Press, 1945. Clavichord and Piano reprinted by permission of the publishers from
Grove's Dictionary of Music and Musicians. New York: The Macmillan Company.

Herzog & Gibbs, N. Y. C.

ACTION OF KEYBOARD INSTRUMENTS

developments occur until the time of Beethoven. Many passages in instrumental music consist solely of principal triads. Seventh chords are used sparingly, and ninth chords not at all.

PHRASEOLOGY. An aspect of formal clarity is the evident clarity of phraseology. On the whole, the phrases in classical music are shorter and more regular than those in the Baroque period.

the same — simplicity

ORCHESTRATION. The basis of modern orchestration and instrumentation was established in the Classical period. Instrumental combinations became standardized. There was more attention to instrumental color.

DYNAMICS. Considerable attention to effects of loud and soft are shown in the works of the Classical masters. This is especially true in the use of dynamic shading, the use of crescendo and diminuendo, as opposed to the baroque use of contrasting levels (ripieno against concertino).

ADVENT OF THE PIANO. In the second half of the 18th century the piano (invented earlier in the century) began to make progress as a musical medium. Not until the 19th century, however, did it completely replace the older keyboard instruments (harpsichord, clavichord, etc.), from which it differs essentially in that the strings are struck by hammers rather than plucked by quills or struck by tangents. The piano has a greater sonority than the baroque keyboard instruments.

MUSICAL OUTPUT. There was an enormous increase in the production of all kinds of music in the Classical period. This was undoubtedly enhanced by the expansion of music publishing business. It is evident in the amazing output of such composers as Haydn (over a hundred symphonies, 83 string quartets, etc.).

musical publishing started now.

The Four Great Composers. The Classical period includes the lives and works of four first-rank composers: (1) Christoph Willibald Gluck (1714-1787), noted for his operas and for opera reform, (2) Franz Joseph Haydn (1732-1809), who wrote symphonies, chamber music, and oratorios, and who is credited with having established the basis of modern orchestration and sonata form; (3) Wolfgang Amadeus Mozart (1756-1791), who was equally great in symphonic music, chamber music, and opera; and (4) Ludwig van

Gluck

Haydn

Mozart

Beethoven

*Mozart copied from Haydn in the beginning.
After Mozart died, Haydn copied from Mozart.*

Beethoven (1770–1827), who, in his great symphonies, chamber music, piano music, Mass, opera, and oratorio, represents the culmination of the classical styles and forms and the transition to 19th-century romanticism. Beethoven will be taken up separately in Part Five, Chapter XXI.

RECORDS

An interesting comparison of classical and baroque music can be made in the study of Haydn's *Surprise Symphony* (No. 94, in G major), and Handel's *Concerto Grosso*, No. 1, in G major. There are excellent recordings of both these works.

Haydn started symphanies with a slow movement.

Symphony had 4 movements.

Finaly is fast.

CHAPTER XVII

Instrumental Music of the Classical Period

I n the Classical period instrumental music became more important than vocal music. With certain reservations, it may be said that the most important developments in style and form took place in the field of instrumental music. Objectivity, clarity of form, and other aspects of classicism are generally more apparent in the instrumental music of the period than they are in dramatic music.

Classical Sonata Form

The most significant structural principle evolved and established in the Classical period is *sonata form*. Subject to certain modifications, it is the basis for nearly all instrumental music of the period: the symphony, the concerto, chamber music, and the keyboard sonata. It was eventually established as a group of three or four movements which follow certain structural plans.

First Movement. As opposed to the baroque sonata which usually begins with a slow movement, the classical sonata opens with an allegro movement. Occasionally, as with Haydn symphonies, a slow introduction is used. The first movement usually follows a basic structural plan known as *sonata-allegro form,* which consists of three principal sections: *exposition, development,* and *recapitulation.*

Exposition. The exposition consists of the presentation of two principal thematic materials in the following manner: (1) The first theme is presented in the key of the sonata (tonic key). (2) An *episode* or *bridge passage* modulates to a contrasting key (the dominant key if the sonata is in major, the relative major key if the sonata is in a minor key). (3) The second theme (sometimes called *subordinate theme*) is then presented in the contrasting key. It is usually more lyric and less dynamic and forceful than the first theme. (4) The exposition frequently has a closing section called *coda* or *closing theme*. The classical exposition invariably ends with a double bar and repeat sign, although in performance the exposition is no longer repeated.

DEVELOPMENT. The middle part of the sonata-allegro form is called the development section. It consists of free treatment or development of any or all of the thematic material presented in the exposition. There is no set plan of organization in the development section. It usually passes through several keys according to the fancy of the composer.

RECAPITULATION. The recapitulation consists of a restatement of thematic material similar to that of the exposition, except that normally all themes are in the tonic key. The development and recapitulation were repeated in classical sonata-allegro form.

Second Movement. The second movement of the classical sonata is in a slow tempo (andante, largo, etc.). It is usually in the subdominant key (four degrees above the tonic key), or it may be in the relative major key (three degrees above the tonic in minor keys), or in the dominant key. A variety of structural plans are employed for the second movement. The most common of these are: (1) *first rondo,* in which the form, according to contrast of thematic materials, is *A B A,* (2) *song form,* which includes the use of shorter themes in variously related plans (*A A B A, A A B A' B A',* etc.), (3) variations, (4) sonata-allegro form, and (5) sonatina form, which is sonata-allegro form abridged by omission of the development section in favor of a brief transition.

Third Movement: Minuet. In the Classical period this movement is optional. It is used in all four-movement symphonies, quartets, and in a relatively few keyboard sonatas. But it is omitted in the concerto and in all three-movement symphonies and sonatas. It is in a moderate or fast tempo, and in three-four time. The minuet movement uniformly follows a structural plan called *song form with trio,* or *minuet and trio*. Each of the three main sections is a song form, so that the whole plan may be represented in a formula as follows:

$$A:\|:BA':\|\quad C:\|:DC':\|\quad ABA'\|$$

minuet   trio   minuet

The middle section, called trio, is in a contrasting key.

Fourth Movement: Finale. The last movement of sonata form is in a lively tempo (allegro or presto). It is in the tonic key. It is often a rondo form, following the plan of thematic materials: *A B A C A* (second rondo form), or *A B A C A B A* (third rondo form). Not infrequently the finale is in sonata-allegro form, as in the first movement.

The Classical Symphony

Perhaps the most important single contribution of the Classical period is the symphony. It embodies not only a new formal principle, the classical sonata form, but also new concepts of orchestration.

Origin of the Symphony. The term "sinfonia," from which the word symphony is derived, was used almost indiscriminately in the 17th century to apply to various kinds of instrumental music. It is similar in its broad application to the term "sonata." It was also applied to interludes and ritornelli in opera. Late in the 17th century its meaning came to be narrowed to the Italian overture. From the latter form the basic plan of movements of the symphony was derived (fast, slow, fast). By the middle of the 18th century the Italian sinfonia was developed as an independent instrumental form, not connected with opera. Haydn added the minuet between the second and last movements of the symphony. The four-movement symphony became standard by the end of the 18th century, although the minuet was sometimes omitted. The internal structure of the movements appears to have developed first in the first movement sonata-allegro plan. The bithematic scheme of sonata-allegro form emerged during the first half of the 18th century, largely in connection with keyboard sonatas and the sinfonia. Thus the classical symphony of the second half of the 18th century replaced the concerto grosso and the orchestral suite of the late Baroque period as the most important type of orchestral music.

Instrumentation and Orchestration. The Classical period established the basic plan of instrumental grouping for the symphony orchestra: strings, woodwinds, brass, and percussion.

STRINGS. The string instruments are divided into five parts: first violins, second violins, violas, cellos, and basses. The first and second violins often double in passages for emphasis. The cellos and basses usually double. Double and triple stopping is used for special chordal emphasis, particularly in final cadences. There is no subdivision of string parts in classical orchestration.

WOODWINDS. The instrumentation for the woodwind section is more variable in the Classical period. The most common plan is one flute, two oboes, and a bassoon. The clarinet is added or else it replaces the oboe in the later classical symphony (e.g., Haydn's *London Symphony* and Mozart's *Jupiter Symphony*).

BRASS. Two French horns (without valves) are generally used in the classical orchestra. Trumpets are occasionally used; trombones and tubas are not employed at all.

TIMPANI. Timpani or kettle drums are used in pairs, tuned to the tonic and the dominant tones of the key.

Schools and Composers. The development of the classical symphony took place at many different places and by many different composers exploring the new form and style. The principal activities were in Italy and Austria.

MILAN. A large school of talented musicians was centered in Milan. The principal figure among the preclassical symphonic composers is G. B. Sammartini (1701–1775), the teacher of Gluck, J. C. Bach, Wagenseil, and Mozart. Sammartini was chiefly responsible for the cultivation of the bithematic plan of sonata-allegro form.

VIENNA. Milan was under Austrian rule and so Austrians became conversant with the new style. The principal composers of the Viennese school are Georg Matthias Monn (1717–1750) and Georg Christoph Wagenseil (1715–1777). Among these composers the prototypes of Haydn's classical symphonies are to be found.

MANNHEIM. In Mannheim further developments leading to the classical symphony took place. The school centered around a famous court orchestra of that city. The principal contribution of the

Mannheim composers seems to have been new dynamic effects (forte, piano, sforzando, crescendo, diminuendo, etc.). The leading composers of this school are Johann Stamitz (1717–1757), his two sons, Karl and Anton, Ignaz Holzbauer (1711–1783), F. X. Richter (1709–1789), and Christian Cannabich (1731–1798).

OTHER COMPOSERS. Bach's sons, Carl Philipp Emanuel Bach (1714–1788) and Johann Christian Bach (1735–1782), contributed chiefly to the development of the sonata. Other composers of preclassical and classical symphonies are Michael Haydn (1737–1806, brother of Franz Josef), François Gossec (1734–1829), Karl Ditters von Dittersdorf (1739–1799), and Luigi Boccherini (1743–1805). The great masters of the classical symphony are Franz Josef Haydn, Mozart and Beethoven.

Style. The classical symphony is homophonic in style. Counterpoint is employed, but it is usually incidental to the style as a whole. Each theme is brought into prominence, and the themes are the nucleus of the music. The basso continuo and the use of the harpsichord disappear in the Classical period. Clear and regular phraseology is characteristic of the thematic material, which is compact rather than continuous and extended as with Bach and Handel. The harmony is in general simple, conventional. Effective use of dynamics is evident in a greater dynamic range, and there is more gradation and contrast between loud and soft. Form becomes conventionalized with standard relationship of thematic material and keys.

HAYDN AND MOZART. Although in similar fashion Haydn and Mozart represent the full realization of classical ideals in their symphonies, sonatas, chamber music, and concertos, and although each composer influenced the style of the other to some extent, still, there are some individual traits that should be pointed out. Haydn makes extensive use of slow introductions to the first movements of his symphonies, which Mozart seldom does. Haydn's themes are, on the whole, characteristically lively, folk-like in style, cheerful, and robust. Mozart's themes are more subtle, less folk-like. A cantabile style of melody is particularly characteristic of Mozart. Whereas Haydn has clear phraseology, Mozart's phraseology is more irregular, subtle, and extended. Haydn's melody and harmony are usually simple and diatonic, whereas Mozart is more inclined toward chromaticism. Ornamentation is more prominent with Mozart, and there is a greater delicacy of style, a sort of "laciness" characteristic of his music.

The Classical Concerto

The classical concerto developed directly from the baroque solo concerto. In a general sense it resembles the baroque concerto in that it is based upon the exchange of material between a solo instrument and the entire orchestral ensemble (tutti).

Form. The classical concerto is a three-movement form as is the baroque solo concerto. The minuet movement of the classical symphony is not used in the concerto. The formal structure of the movements differs considerably from that of the baroque concerto, making use as it does of a modified classical sonata form.

FIRST MOVEMENT. The first movement of the classical concerto is a modified sonata-allegro form. The exposition usually consists of three main parts: (1) The opening tutti, in which principal themes are introduced, ends in the tonic key. (2) The solo instrument then enters either with a brilliant introduction or immediately with the principal subject. There follows an exchange of material (first and second subject) between the solo instrument and the orchestra. (3) The exposition closes with a short tutti section. The solo instrument and the orchestra then take part in a short development section, which leads through various keys back to the tonic. The recapitulation begins with a tutti section corresponding to the first tutti section, but shorter. Then, there is a solo section corresponding to the first solo section of the exposition. A short tutti section, corresponding to the second tutti section in the exposition, ends on a six-four chord (tonic chord with the fifth in the bass). The solo instrument alone then plays a *cadenza*. This is a brilliant, virtuosic display of thematic material, freely and elaborately developed. Cadenzas are either written by the composer of the concerto, composed separately by the performer or someone else, or, most often in the classical period, improvised by the performer. The cadenza is followed by a brief tutti section, either with or without the solo instrument, concluding the movement.

SECOND MOVEMENT. The second movement is less virtuosic and more ornamental than the first movement. It is usually in some sort of enlarged song form, a first rondo, or a variation form. The cadenza is rarely employed in the andante movement.

FINALE. The third and last movement of the concerto is again in fast tempo. It is usually some form of rondo, resembling the last movement of the classical symphony. Occasionally a short cadenza is used.

Composers. The transition from the baroque solo concerto to the classical concerto is attributed mainly to Bach's sons, Carl Philipp Emanuel Bach and Johann Christian Bach. The Italians, Locatelli and Tartini, also show a departure from baroque methods.

HAYDN AND MOZART. Haydn wrote 20 piano concertos, 9 violin concertos, 6 cello concertos, and numerous other concertos for various instruments (flute, baryton, horn, clarino, etc.). Mozart wrote 25 piano concertos, 8 violin concertos, and concertos for other instruments: violin and viola, bassoon, flute, flute and harp, horn, and clarinet.

Small Orchestral Forms

In the second half of the 18th century large quantities of music were written for small orchestral ensembles. Such music was variously called *serenade* (*Nachtmusik*), *cassation,* and *divertimento*. These terms apparently were used interchangeably. They are the counterpart of the baroque orchestral suite in that they consist of from four to ten movements, many of which are dances such as minuets, gavottes, etc. They were written for small orchestras of highly diverse instrumentation, and they usually employed only a few instruments on a part. Haydn wrote about 65 of these, Mozart wrote about 30.

Chamber Music

Media. Music written for a small group of solo instruments continued to be important in the classical period. The chief difference between classical and baroque chamber music is that the former abandoned the use of the figured bass or continuo part. It is also more homophonic than the baroque chamber music. The instrumental combinations differ somewhat from those employed in earlier periods.

STRING QUARTET. By far the most important medium in classical chamber music is the string quartet, consisting of two violins, a viola, and a cello. It replaced the string fantasy ensemble of the Renaissance and the trio sonata of the Baroque. The music written for this ensemble, as well as the medium itself, is called *string quartet*. The form of the string quartet (as with the symphony) is the classical sonata form. The principal composers of string quartets in the Classical period are Luigi Boccherini (91 quartets), Haydn (83 quartets), Mozart (26 quartets), and Beethoven (16 quartets).

OTHER CHAMBER MEDIA. Combinations less extensively employed in the Classical period are the mixed quartet (three strings and one other instrument, usually piano, flute, or oboe), string trio, mixed trio, string quintet, and mixed quintet (string quartet plus piano, flute, or oboe).

THE VIOLIN SONATA. The violin sonata is the least important of classical chamber music media. Haydn wrote 12 violin sonatas, and Mozart wrote some 35 sonatas for violin and piano.

THE KEYBOARD SONATA. The keyboard sonatas of Haydn and Mozart are usually three-movement works; some are in two movements. Not until Beethoven is the four-movement sonata form usually employed. The structure of movements in the classical sonata is somewhat variable. Many of Haydn's earlier sonatas are in the older binary plan of movement rather than in sonata-allegro form. The same is true with many of the contemporary classical composers of keyboard music. A preclassical sonata form, showing transition from the older baroque binary plan of movement to the classical developed ternary (sonata-allegro) is exhibited in 12 keyboard sonatas by Domenico Paradisi (1710–1792). The sonatas of Carl Philipp Emanuel Bach, Wilhelm Friedemann Bach (1710–1784), and Johann Christian Bach, constitute an important literature in the development of the classical keyboard sonata. The sonatas of Muzio Clementi (1752–1832) lead up to the more advanced sonata style of Beethoven, whose 32 piano sonatas are the culmination of that form.

CHAPTER XVIII
Opera in the Classical Period

THE distinction between the baroque and the classical style in dramatic music is less clearly marked than in the field of instrumental music. The field of opera music expands enormously in the 18th century, and yet relatively few operas of this period are included in standard operatic repertory today.

Prevailing Types of Opera in the 18th Century. Italian opera seria dominated the 18th century. Opera buffa rivaled opera seria in the second half of the 18th century. In the same period opéra-comique predominated in France. In Germany Singspiel became increasingly important, although it never rivaled opéra-comique or opera buffa.

Italian Opera Seria. The Neapolitan school of opera, which began in the late 17th century, flourished and spread over all Continental Europe during the first half of the 18th century. As it became the model, or at least the point of departure, for all opera, it also became decadent, so that reform was inevitable as was the rise and growth of other operatic styles, particularly in the field of comic opera.

CHARACTERISTICS. 18th-century Italian opera was marked by characteristics most of which were the object of attack and reform in the second half of the 18th century: (1) Opera plots were overcomplex and artificial; they centered around intricate love intrigues and impossible situations. (2) There were usually six characters, representing three of each sex. (3) Dramatic truth was generally neglected. (4) From the dramatic standpoint, the overemphasis on arias was objectionable. Most of the operas consisted of chains of arias. Nevertheless, arias selected from 18th-century opera constitute an important repertory of vocal music; many of them are exceedingly fine and beautiful. Arias were artificially classified into various types and there were strictly observed rules concerning where, when, and by whom they could be sung. (5) There was little use of chorus. (6) There was an almost exclusive use of *castrati* (male sopranos and altos); women were generally barred from leading roles. (7) There was prominence of *parlando style* of recitative (i.e., rapid dialogue, half spoken, half sung). This was even more extensively employed in buffa opera.

COMPOSERS. The principal composers of Italian opera in the Classical period are: Niccolò Jommelli (1714–1774), Tommaso Traetta (1727–1779), Baldassare Galuppi (1706–1785), Antonio Sacchini (1730–1786), Christoph Willibald Gluck (1714–1787), Giuseppe Sarti (1729–1802), Nicola Piccini (1728–1800), Domenico Cimarosa (1749–1801), Giovanni Paisiello (1740–1816), who represents a transition from 18th- to 19th-century opera, and Antonio Salieri (1750–1825).

Gluck and Opera Reform. Because of his attempts to simplify and purify opera, Christoph Willibald Gluck (1714–1787) represents the classical spirit in opera as no other contemporary did. With Mozart, he is one of the two greatest opera composers in the Classical period.

RECOGNITION OF DEFICIENCIES IN NEAPOLITAN OPERA. Gluck was not the first to recognize the decadent aspects of Neapolitan opera. In 1720 Benedetto Marcello wrote a satire on opera, entitled *Il Teatro alla moda.* Another treatise by Count Algarotti, entitled *Saggio sopra l'opera in musica* (1755) sets forth principles similar to those later advanced by Gluck. Opera reform was further recognized in a work by Arteaga, entitled *Rivoluzioni del teatro musicale italiano* (1783–1788). These treatises, reflecting to some extent a growing antipathy to operatic trends, would have been of little avail were it not for the intrinsic greatness of Gluck, who put theories into actual practice.

GLUCK'S CONTRIBUTIONS AND STYLE. Gluck's importance to opera can be seen from the following list of his contributions: (1) Entirely apart from its historical significance, Gluck's music is great. (2) In general, his music represents the classical spirit by a return to simplicity of style. (3) Gluck improved the libretto by eliminating complex love intrigue and by returning to classical Greek mythology for the basis of his librettos. (4) He strove for dramatic truth by eliminating superfluous virtuosity and by creating music that follows the emotional and dramatic situations. (5) He placed more emphasis upon recitative and made less stylistic difference between recitative and aria. (6) He made dramatic use of the chorus. (7) Character delineation is an important attribute of Gluck's operas. (8) Effective instrumentation adds to successful characterization. (9) Gluck's overtures present the general mood of the work and are closely related to the opera.

GLUCK'S MOST IMPORTANT WORKS. Gluck began his career by writing some 20 typical Italian operas. The first important opera in the reformed style was *Orfeo ed Euridice* ("Orpheus and Eurydice"), produced in Vienna in 1762. It was not a success there, being generally misunderstood, but it was translated into French and successfully produced in Paris. Despite certain concessions to Italian operatic practices (the title role is for an alto castrato, and the story is altered to have a happy ending), it reveals most of the points in Gluck's reform. *Iphigénie en Aulide* (1774), *Armide* (1777), and *Iphigénie en Tauride* (1779) were all produced in Paris. The latter was the crowning work of Gluck's career. It was also the victorious work in a controversy between Gluckists and Piccinists, which was an outgrowth of the "war" between Italian buffonists in France and the French anti-buffonists.

GLUCK'S INFLUENCE AND SUCCESSORS. Gluck's influence was probably not of very considerable extent outside of Paris. At least for the time being, Italian tradition continued as before. Gluck's influence can be shown in Mozart's *Idomeneo*. Gluck's followers were Sacchini, Cherubini, Méhul, and Spontini.

Mozart Opera. Mozart was not a reformer. He wrote in the prevailing forms and styles of the day. His operas are considered great because they are musical masterpieces in themselves. In fact, Mozart's operas are the only 18th-century operas remaining in the standard repertory today.

STYLE. Mozart's operas show predominating Italian influence. He uses the parlando style extensively and highly complex plots (*Figaro* and *Don Giovanni*). Mozart's operas are greater than contemporary Italian operas (1) because of the greatness of Mozart's music and its importance to the dramatic work, (2) because of Mozart's great melodic genius, and (3) because of his ability in character delineation.

TYPES AND EXAMPLES OF MOZART OPERA. Mozart opera falls into three categories: Singspiel, opera seria, and opera buffa.

a. *German Operas, Singspiel Type.* The two principal German operas by Mozart are: *Die Entführung aus dem Serail* ("The Seraglio," 1782) and *Die Zauberflöte* ("The Magic Flute," 1791).

b. *Opera Seria.* Two Mozart operas which may be classed as Italian operas of the seria type are *Idomeneo* (1781) and *La Clemenza di Tito* (1791).

c. *Opera Buffa.* Most of Mozart's important operas belong to the opera buffa class. They are *La Finta giardiniera* (1775), *Le Nozze di Figaro* ("The Marriage of Figaro," 1786), which is probably Mozart's best-known opera, *Don Giovanni* ("Don Juan," 1787), called *dramma giocosa,* a mixture of opera seria and opera buffa elements, and *Così fan tutte* (1790).

CHAPTER XIX

Religious Music of the Classical Period

THE least significant developments in music in the Classical period are in the field of religious music, including oratorio and church music. They are decidedly overshadowed by opera and instrumental music.

Oratorio

Principal Composers and Works. A transition from the cantata style of J. S. Bach to the late 18th-century oratorio style of Haydn is shown in the works of Carl Philipp Emanuel Bach (*The Resurrection* and *The Israelites in the Wilderness*). By far the most important classical composer of oratorios is Haydn, whose oratorios fall in the late 18th century. His most important oratorio is *The Creation* (1798), which is based upon Genesis and upon an early adaptation of Milton's *Paradise Lost. Il Ritorno di Tobia,* an early work written in 1774, is the best example of 18th-century Italian oratorio. Haydn's last oratorio, *The Seasons* (1801), is a secular oratorio with very little religious content. Mozart's work in oratorio is negligible.

Church Music

In general, the church music of the Classical period is inferior. It is mostly of a dramatic nature and it appears to have been conceived for concert purposes rather than liturgical usage.

Forms of Church Music. The principal forms of 18th-century church music are: (1) The Mass, concert-like settings of the Ordinary of the Mass, with orchestra, soloists, and chorus, (2) Requiem

Mass, (3) motets, for chorus, solo voices, and instrumental accompaniment, (4) litanies, short choral pieces including responses, and (5) vespers, music for the penultimate Catholic canonic hour, and the only one permitting music other than plainsong. It includes antiphons, psalms, hymns, and settings of the Magnificat.

Composers. As in other fields of music of the 18th century, Haydn and Mozart are the greatest composers of church music.

HAYDN. Haydn wrote 14 Masses, 13 offertories, and miscellaneous religious choral music: motets, Salve Reginas, Ave Reginas, etc.

MOZART. Mozart wrote 15 Masses, 4 litanies, 2 vespers, a *Requiem Mass,* which is probably his most famous work in this field, and miscellaneous smaller works including motets, offertories, etc.

OTHER COMPOSERS. In Italy there is a long list of church composers who turned out enormous quantities of church music, mostly mediocre. The most notable of these are Galuppi, Paisiello (some 103 church compositions), Zingarelli (over 500 church compositions), Sarti, and Cherubini. To this list should be added the names of early 19th-century composers: Spohr, Schubert, and Beethoven, whose *Missa Solemnis* is a great festival Mass.

The Romantic Period (1820–1900)

PART FIVE

The Romantic Period (1820–1900)

CHAPTER XX

General Considerations

General Aspects of Romanticism. The 19th-century romantic point of view, expressed in philosophy, literature, arts, and music, may be summed up according to the following points: (1) individualism, (2) emotionalism, (3) subjectivity, largely replacing classical objectivity, (4) favorite subjects: the ancient (particularly medieval), the supernatural (magic, witches, fairies, ghosts, etc.), the weird, and the mystic, and (5) nationalism.

Historical Background. The cultural, economic, political, and social order was greatly affected by momentous progress in science and mechanics (electromagnetic induction, photography, food canning, the railway and steamboat, steel production, electric light, telephone, telegraph, etc.). The Industrial Revolution brought on new social and economic problems, and the rise of capitalism and socialism. Important wars of the 19th century are: the Crimean War (1854–1856), the Civil War in the United States (1861–1865), and the Franco-Prussian War (1870). The most important development in art is French impressionism by the painters Manet, Degas, Renoir, and the sculptor Rodin. Whistler is considered one of the great 19th-century painters. The outstanding philosophies of the period belong to the Germans: Schopenhauer, Nietzsche, and Hegel. In literature and poetry there is a long list of illustrious names. In England, Byron, Wordsworth, Scott, Thackeray, Dickens, Hardy, Carlyle (Scottish essayist and historian), Coleridge, and Keats are the most outstanding. In Germany, Goethe, Richter, Heine, and E. T. A. Hoffmann (author, musician, and painter) are the principal writers in addition to the philosophers named above. In France, Hugo, Flaubert, Lamartine, and Musset are the leaders. The United States produced some great writers, chief among whom are Emerson, Longfellow, Poe, Hawthorne, and Mark Twain.

General Musical Aspects of the 19th Century. All of the five general aspects of romanticism apply to the music of the 19th century. Individualism is manifest in the great diversity of styles of individual composers. Emotional expression, personal feeling, and sentimentality are everywhere present in 19th-century music. Romantic subjects are evident in the songs and operas of the period. Nationalism in music becomes one of its marked characteristics in the second half of the century, when countries consciously fostered their own styles centered around folk music. And, in general, subjectivity replaced objectivity in music. There was great expansion of instrumental music, particularly for the orchestra and for the piano. The choral music of the period is comparatively unimportant. In the 19th century, program music is more important than at any other period in the history of music. Virtuosity became a marked characteristic; the virtuoso composer-performer in piano and violin became a phenomenon typical of the century. Germany and Austria were the leading countries in the Romantic period.

Specific Musical Characteristics. The 19th century reveals marked changes in musical style and in formal concepts, both of which are highly diverse in comparison to style and form in the Classical period.

MELODY. Romantic melody is characterized by warmth of personal feeling. It is less regular in phraseology than classical melody.

HARMONY. The 19th century sees an important expansion of harmonic idiom: new chords and new chord progressions are to be found. There is a greater use of chromaticism than in the 18th century. More altered chords and seventh and ninth chords are employed. A freer use of nonharmonic or non-chordal tones is manifest. Modulation becomes more of an end than a means, used more for its own effect than as a function to get from one key to another.

TONALITY. The basic concept of key feeling is still intact in the 19th century, but there is more tonal obscurity, fluid modulations obscuring the key feeling of whole passages. More remote keys and more varied key schemes are employed. In the late 19th century there are definite signs of departure from conventional tonal concepts.

COUNTERPOINT. Contrapuntal forms as such hold virtually no place at all in 19th-century music. Counterpoint is seldom used other than in a very secondary role, and it is even more rarely strict.

FORM. There is a great expansion of formal concepts and of formal freedom in the 19th century. Extremes of formal dimensions are characteristic of the period: great popularity of small forms in piano and song literature, and the growth to enormous lengths in symphony and opera. The essentially new forms of the period are numerous. (1) New stylized dances are the waltz (the slow Ländler and the fast Viennese waltzes), mazurka, polonaise, etc. (2) The *étude,* a technical study for piano or violin, glorified for concert usage, becomes an important form. (3) In piano music the classical sonata form is largely replaced by various free forms called romanza, fantasy, arabesque, nocturne, ballad, etc., and also by descriptive pieces. (4) Symphonic music shows an expansion of classical symphonic form, and there are new symphonic forms: the symphonic poem, the symphonic suite, the program symphony, and the concert overture. (5) The most important formal development in opera of the 19th century is the Wagnerian music drama.

PREDOMINATING MEDIA. The 19th century is dominated by four principal media: (1) piano, (2) orchestra, (3) solo song with piano accompaniment, and (4) opera. Chamber music and religious and secular choral music are of less importance.

INSTRUMENTATION AND ORCHESTRATION. The 19th century sees an expansion of the art of orchestration. Three important names in this connection are Berlioz, Wagner, and Rimsky-Korsakov. Instrumental color is developed. Symphony orchestras are large and greater sonority is created by more extensive employment of brass, woodwinds, and percussion. Mechanical improvements and innovations had a great deal to do with the growth of the orchestra. The English horn added a new color to the orchestral palette. The invention and widespread use of valves for brass instruments greatly increased the usefulness of those instruments. The Böhm key systems applied to woodwind instruments greatly increased their effectiveness.

CHAPTER XXI

Beethoven

Ludwig van Beethoven (1770–1827) represents the end of the Classical period and the beginning of the Romantic period. Along with Palestrina, Bach, Haydn, and Mozart, he is one of the greatest masters of all time.

Beethoven's Place in Music History. Beethoven's music is of consummate greatness. Beethoven was a great individualist. More than any other master he freed music and musicians from servile status. He broke the confines and the artificial restraint of the Classical period by giving his own profound spirit free expression. Beethoven's early music is definitely classical, based upon the style of Haydn. His music of the middle and late periods reveals the subjectivity, emotionalism, and freedom of romanticism.

Beethoven's Style. Because he was the first great individualist in music history, Beethoven's music, though a product of his times, shows many remarkable features of style that reflect his character and at the same time set his music apart from that which went before and that which followed.

General Features. There are four general features of Beethoven's music. (1) The most important of these is the profoundness of emotional content. This has been aptly called the "appassionata spirit," in reference to the great piano sonata, Opus 57, which so definitely reveals this quality. (2) Beethoven had a great sense of humor; but unlike Haydn's cheerful, light-hearted humor, his is gruff, rustic, and profound. The scherzo of the Fifth Symphony and the peasant dance of the Sixth Symphony are good examples of this characteristic. (3) Beethoven's impulsiveness and sudden changes of emotion are well known to readers of biography. These traits are clearly manifest in his music. (4) Closely associated with Beethovenian humor and impulsiveness is the element of surprise in his music. This is created by prolonged passages of suspense, then sudden changes of rhythm, key, dynamics, and by tremendous climaxes followed by abrupt introduction of a simple, naïve tune.

SPECIFIC FEATURES. The more specific aspects of Beethoven's style may be considered under five headings: thematic material, counterpoint, form, choral music, piano music.

a. *Types of Thematic Material.* Beethoven is a great master of thematic material. He employs two broad types of melody: (1) short motival first themes in sonatas, symphonies, etc. (e.g., the "fate motive" of the Fifth Symphony), and (2) beautiful cantabile melody (e.g., the adagio cantabile movement of the piano sonata, Opus 13).

b. *Counterpoint.* In his early- and middle-period works counterpoint is masterful but it is definitely subordinate. In his late works, however, at a time when elsewhere counterpoint was generally abandoned, Beethoven returned to the old contrapuntal practices and revealed a great mastery of this art (e.g., the fugue for string quartet, Opus 133).

c. *Form.* Beethoven is one of the greatest masters of form. He is a master of thematic development. He expanded sonata-allegro form to include more than two principal thematic materials and he even occasionally introduced new material in the development section or in the recapitulation. He greatly varied the plan of movement in the sonata: (1) He used variation form as an opening movement (Opus 26), or (2) a free fantasy as in the opening movement of the *Moonlight Sonata.* (3) He replaced the third movement minuet with a scherzo, a change of style rather than of formal structure. (4) He varied the number and type of movements in late works (e.g., the string quartet in C sharp minor, Opus 131, and the Ninth Symphony with a choral finale).

d. *Choral Music.* Beethoven's choral music is great because of the greatness of Beethoven's musical ideas and the profoundness of his expression, but he exceeds the limits of choral idiom, and treats his chorus as additional instrumental color.

e. *Piano Style*. In addition to the general features of style which apply to his piano music, there are several minor traits peculiar to his style in that medium. He creates a special effect of texture by the use of widely separated hands. Heavy thick chords in the low register of the piano are frequently noticeable. Occasional long, sweeping chromatic scales, usually ascending, often lead to an emphatic objective in the music. He uses thirds moving in opposite directions.

Principal Contributions to Music Literature. In addition to three large vocal works, Beethoven worked principally in the fields of piano, orchestra, and chamber music.

PIANO LITERATURE. Beethoven's contributions to piano literature are chiefly 32 sonatas and 21 sets of variations.

ORCHESTRAL WORKS. Beethoven wrote 9 symphonies, the last notable for its choral finale, a setting of Schiller's *Ode to Joy*. Besides these, the *Leonore Overture* (revised overture to his opera *Fidelio*), the *Coriolanus Overture,* and the *Prometheus* ballet music are his principal orchestral works. The violin concerto and the 5 piano concertos should be added to the list of Beethoven's great orchestral music.

CHAMBER MUSIC. Beethoven's chamber music, with that of Brahms, is the greatest of the 19th century. He wrote 16 string quartets, 6 piano trios, and 10 violin sonatas. These are his most important contributions in the field of chamber music.

VOCAL WORKS. Three great vocal works by Beethoven are the opera *Fidelio,* the oratorio *Christus am Ölberg* ("Christ on the Mount of Olives"), and the *Missa solemnis in D.* In addition, Beethoven wrote some songs which are less important than the contemporary song literature of Schubert, although his song cycle, *An die ferne Geliebte,* should be mentioned.

CHAPTER XXII

19th-Century Opera

NINETEENTH-CENTURY opera was developed chiefly in Italy, France, and Germany. The 19th century also saw the rise of nationalism, which is particularly manifest in operatic production. Opera reached a peak of development in the second half of the century.

Italian Opera

Italy, which had led the field since the beginning of opera in the early 17th century, still held a front rank in opera in the 19th century, although its prominence was shared almost equally by the developments in France and in Germany.

General Characteristics of Italian Opera. In the 19th century, virtuosity for its own sake is less prominent. Dramatic profundity is hardly to be found until Verdi late in the century. The bel canto style of song prevails, as does also the rapid parlando style of recitative. The chorus is more often and more prominently used, but the orchestra still plays a secondary role. Realism becomes an important aspect of opera in the late 19th century.

Composers, Styles, Works. Italian opera in the 19th century is dominated by four composers: Rossini, Bellini, Donizetti, and Verdi.

ROSSINI. Gioacchino Rossini (1792–1868) was more successful in the comic opera style than in opera seria. He had great facility. His sparkling wit, the vivacity of his music, and the rapid parlando style are characteristic. His principal works are *L'Italiana in Algeri* (1813), *Il Barbiere di Siviglia* ("The Barber of Seville," 1816), *La*

Gazza ladra ("The Thieving Magpie," 1817), *Mosè in Egitto* (1818), *Semiramide* (1813), and *Guillaume Tell* ("William Tell," 1829). The latter, produced in Paris, is typical French grand opera.

BELLINI. Vincenzo Bellini (1801–1835) reveals a generally high quality of emotional content. He employs appropriate libretti (by Romani). Sentimentality of his melodies, warm and flowing, is characteristic of his style, and they influenced Chopin's melody. His principal operas are *La Sonnambula* (1813), *Norma* (1832), and *I Puritani* (1834).

DONIZETTI. Gaetano Donizetti (1797–1848) is the third and last important Italian opera composer of the first half of the 19th century. He was less gifted and less original than Bellini but his superior training and technique are shown in his operas. His principal operas, among some 65 that he wrote, are *Lucrezia Borgia* (1833), *Lucia di Lammermoor* (1835), *La Favorita* (1840), *La Fille du régiment* ("The Daughter of the Regiment," Paris, 1840, opéra-comique), and *Don Pasquale* (Paris, 1843, opera buffa).

VERDI. Giuseppe Verdi (1813–1901) is the greatest Italian composer of opera in the entire century. He developed great power of characterization and dramatization. His late works show a greater profundity of spirit than those in the first half of the 19th century. The orchestra is more important than it is with his predecessors. He is truly Italian in spirit, not an imitator of his German contemporary, Wagner. His principal operas are *Rigoletto* (1851), *Il Trovatore* (1855), *La Traviata* (1855), *Aida* (1871–1872), which is characterized by its colorful pageantry, and *Otello* ("Othello," 1887), on a libretto by Boito, faithful to the Shakespearian drama. *Falstaff* (1893), his last great opera, is a return to buffa style but with greater profundity.

OTHER COMPOSERS. Realism, or *verismo,* is typical of other late 19th-century works by Pietro Mascagni (1863–1945) (*Cavalleria rusticana,* 1890), Ruggiero Leoncavallo (1858–1919) (*I Pagliacci,* 1892), and Giacomo Puccini (1858–1924) (*La Bohème, Madama Butterfly,* and *Tosca,* 1900).

French Opera

Whereas in the 18th century there was a clear demarcation between the comic opera and serious opera types, this distinction gradually became less evident during the 19th century, until in the second
half of the century they merge. In France, in the first half of the
19th century, opéra-comique and grand opera exist side by side.

Opéra-Comique. The comic opera tradition which was paramount
in the 18th century continues to flourish during the first half of the
19th century. It gradually began to develop in two directions. On
the one hand it became more purely entertainment of the operetta
type. On the other hand, it approached the style, form, and subject
matter of serious opera, so that in the second half of the 19th century
it grows into lyric opera.

COMPOSERS AND WORKS. The principal composers and opéras-
comiques are François Boïeldieu (1775–1834) (*La Dame Blanche,*
1825); Daniel Auber (1782–1871) (*La Muette de Portici,* 1828, and
Fra Diavolo, 1830); Louis Hérold (1791–1833) (*Le Pré aux clercs,*
1832); Victor Massé (1822–1884) (*Les Noces de Jeannette,* 1853);
and Charles Gounod (1818–1893) (*Le Médecin malgré lui,* 1857).

Grand Opera. New developments took place in French grand
opera in the first half of the 19th century which made it a rival of
opéra-comique. This is often referred to as the "grand spectacle
opera," which describes its general character, featuring grandiose
schemes, heroic or historical subjects, extravagant characters and
situations, demons and men in conflict, plainsong or chorale juxta-
posed with ballet tunes, and great choral masses. The chief exponent
of this style of opera was Giacomo Meyerbeer (1791–1864), whose
principal works are *Robert le Diable* (1831), *Les Huguenots* (1836),
Le Prophète (1849), and *L'Africaine* (1860). In the second half of
the 19th century the French leaned toward a lyric style of opera as
well as retaining some aspects of the grand spectacle opera. Charles
Gounod's *Faust* (1859) and *Roméo et Juliette* (1867), Thomas'
Mignon (1866), and Massenet's *Manon* (1884) reveal a tender sentiment and no great heights of passion, characteristically French refinement of style, good declamation, and good stage orchestration.

COMPOSERS AND WORKS. In addition to the composers and works already mentioned, there is a long list of operatic works belonging to the second half of the 19th century: Jacques Halévy (1799–1862), an imitator of Meyerbeer, wrote *La Juive* (1835); Hector Berlioz (1803–1869), *Les Troyens* (1858); Georges Bizet (1838–1875), *Carmen* (1875); Edouard Lalo (1823–1892), *Le Roi d'Ys* (1876–1888); Léo Delibes (1836–1891), *Le Roi l'a dit* and *Lakmé* (1883); Jacques Offenbach (1819–1880), *Les Contes d'Hoffmann* (1881); Camille Saint-Saëns (1835–1921), *Samson et Dalila* (1877); Gustave Charpentier (1860–   ), *Louise* (1900); Jules Massenet (1842–1912), *Manon* (1884); Alexis Chabrier (1841–1894), *Gwendoline* (1886), resembling Wagner's *Tristan;* Vincent d'Indy (1851–1931), *Fervaal* (1895); and, finally, Debussy, the impressionistic opera *Pelléas et Mélisande* (1902).

German Opera

In Germany two significant developments in opera took place in the 19th century. The first is the rise of German romantic opera in the first half of the century. The second is the *music drama* of Richard Wagner.

German Romantic Opera. German romantic opera springs from the German Singspiel of the late 18th century and the early 19th century. It has even been said that all German opera from Mozart's *Entführung* and *Zauberflöte* to Wagner's music dramas are merely enlarged Singspiele in style. New elements come into German opera in the first half of the century.

CHARACTERISTICS. The fundamental characteristics of German romantic opera are: (1) The subjects are derived from German folklore and legend. (2) There is a romantic treatment of nature and natural phenomena. (3) There is an important use of supernatural agencies to heighten dramatic interest. (4) German folk song, or folk song style, is used along with more conventional operatic styles of aria.

COMPOSERS. The most important representative of German romantic opera is Carl Maria von Weber (1786–1826). In addition to the general characteristics of romantic opera, Weber's operas point toward Wagner in the attempt to fuse the arts, and to gain dramatic realism by avoiding repetition of lines or verses in arias. His principal operas are *Der Freischütz* (1821), *Euryanthe* (1823), and *Oberon* (1826). Other composers are Beethoven, *Fidelio* (1805); Ludwig Spohr, *Faust* (1818) and *Jessonda* (1823); E. T. A. Hoffmann, whose *Undine* (1816) forms a connecting link between literature and music; Heinrich Marschner (1795–1861), *Der Vampyr* (1828) and *Hans Heiling* (1833); Robert Schumann, *Genoveva* (1850); Konradin Kreutzer, *Nachtlager von Granada* (1834); Reissinger, *Felsenmühle* (1833); Friedrich von Flotow, *Martha* (1847); Albert Lortzing (1801–1851), *Czar und Zimmermann* (1837) and *Der Wildschütz* (1842); Otto Nicolai (1810–1849), *Die lustigen Weiber von Windsor* ("The Merry Wives of Windsor," 1849); and Richard Wagner's *Der fliegende Holländer* ("The Flying Dutchman," 1841).

Wagner and the Music Drama. The most important figure in 19th-century opera is Richard Wagner (1813–1883), who achieved a fusion of the arts in his music dramas. He is one of the greatest geniuses of all time.

CHARACTERISTICS. The fully developed music drama shows marked departure in general concept, style, and form from all other operatic production.

a. *Fusion of Arts.* Wagner conceived the music drama as a work in which music, poetry, and stagecraft are fused to form a new dramatic whole. He believed that no one art should at any time dominate the drama. This resulted in dramatic unity and dramatic truth surpassing anything in the operatic field.

b. *Libretto.* Wagner wrote his own libretti. They are perfectly conceived literary works for his music dramas. Three fundamental bases of his libretti are (1) German folklore, mythology, and legend, (2) romantic mysticism, the supernatural, and the medieval, and (3) the idea of redemption, often associated with some religious implications.

c. *Continuity.* One of the most notable features of Wagnerian music drama is continuity. This is achieved in part by the important innovation of abandoning the distinction between recitative and aria. The continuous melodic line, the nonperiodic rhythm, and the constant use of the orchestra all contribute to the over-all aspect of continuity.

d. *Leitmotif.* Another significant aspect of Wagnerian music drama is the use of themes, called *leitmotifs,* throughout the opera. These thematic ideas are connected with a particular person, idea, situation, or mood, and they are variable according to the dramatic requirement of the moment. They are developed symphonically throughout the opera. By their use Wagner attained musical unity and dramatic coherence.

e. *The Wagnerian Orchestra.* The orchestra is highly important to Wagnerian music drama, carrying as it does its share of dramatic content in a continuous flow of music. Aside from operatic consider-ations, important developments in instrumentation and orchestra-tion are found in the music drama. Wagner generally increased the size of the orchestra. He used complete choirs of instruments (e.g., three clarinets and bass clarinet). Brass choirs are used more extensively than heretofore. The strings are often divided, and spe-cial ethereal effects are obtained by using them in high registers and with tremolo. The significance of Wagner's orchestral music is re-flected in the fact that considerable portions of it are used in con-cert form.

f. *Other Aspects of Style.* Wagner's harmony is characteristically chromatic. Chromaticism also plays an important part in the melodic style. Wagner makes a significant use of counterpoint, an element heretofore neglected in opera. On the whole, he makes little use of the chorus (*Die Meistersinger* is a notable exception).

WORKS. Wagner set forth his ideas in several treatises on the sub-ject of music and drama. The principal ones are *The Artwork of the Future* (1850), and *Opera and Drama* (1851). These were writ-ten during a period of political exile (1849–1864). His operas are: *Die Feen* (1833); *Das Liebesverbot* (1836); *Rienzi* (1840), which is a spectacle opera reminiscent of Meyerbeer; *Der fliegende Holländer* (1841); *Tannhäuser* (1845); *Lohengrin* (1845), which is the last work Wagner called romantic opera; *Das Rheingold* (1854), which is Part I of the great operatic tetralogy entitled *Der Ring des Nibe-lungen; Die Walküre* (1856), which is Part II of the *Ring; Tristan und Isolde* (1859); *Die Meistersinger* (1867); *Siegfried* (1871), which is Part III of the *Ring; Götterdämmerung* (1874), which is Part IV of the *Ring;* and *Parsifal* (1882), Wagner's last opera.

Other 19th-Century Opera

The major developments in opera in the 19th century have been outlined under the three nationalities, Italian, French, and German. In addition there are a few outstanding works in other countries to be mentioned.

Russian National Opera. Nationalism in Russian music is said to begin with the opera by Michail Glinka (1804–1857), *A Life for the Tsar* (1836), which nevertheless shows strong Italian influence. *Russlan et Ludmilla* (1842) is a second important opera by Glinka. Other Russian composers and operas are: Alexander Dargomijski (1813–1869), *Roussalka* (1856) and *The Stone Guest* (1872); Modest Moussorgsky (1839–1881), *Boris Godunov* (1874), a highly important Russian work; Alexander Borodin (1833–1887), *Prince Igor* (completed and produced posthumously, 1890); Tschaikovsky (1840–1893), *Eugen Onegin* (1877), romantic but not nationalist; and Nicolai Rimsky-Korsakov (1844–1908), who produced a great number of Russian operas: *May Night* (1878), *Snow Maiden* (1881), *Mlada* (1895), *Sadko* (1896), *Tsar's Bride* (1898), *Tsar Saltan* (1900), *Pan Voyevoda,* and *Le Coq d'or* (before 1908).

Bohemian National Opera. National opera in Bohemia is chiefly represented by *Prodana nevesta* ("The Bartered Bride"), a comic opera by Friedrich Smetana (1824–1884). Anton Dvořák's *King and Collier* (1874) is also an example of Bohemian national opera.

Opera in England. Operatic production in England in the 19th century is of little consequence, with the exception of the famous Gilbert and Sullivan operettas in the last quarter of the century. The wit, humor, rollicking tunes, and clever satire of these creations are peculiarly English. The principal Gilbert and Sullivan operettas are: *Trial by Jury* (1875), *H. M. S. Pinafore* (1878), which ran for over 700 consecutive nights, *The Pirates of Penzance* (1880), *Patience* (1881), *Iolanthe* (1882), *Princess Ida* (1884), *The Mikado* (1885), *The Yeomen of the Guard* (1888), *The Gondoliers* (1889), and *Utopia Limited* (1893).

CHAPTER XXIII

19th–Century Oratorio and Choral Music

D ESPITE the fact that oratorio in the 19th century was overshadowed by opera, and that choral music was less popular than other media, there were some notable contributions to both fields.

Oratorio

Little oratorio of consequence was written from the time of Handel, who overshadowed all consequent attempts in the field of oratorio, until Mendelssohn's *St. Paul* and *Elijah,* which represent the peak of artistic creation in that form in the 19th century.

Mendelssohn Oratorio. The greatest 19th-century composer of oratorio is Felix Mendelssohn (1809–1847).

STYLE. The greatness of Mendelssohn's oratorios rests primarily upon his outstanding choral technique. His style in general is reminiscent of Handelian technique plus the addition of romantic elements. He wrote melody of high quality. He was skilled in instrumentation, and he had a great sense of form. All these factors combined to make his oratorios the principal masterworks of the century in that field.

PRINCIPAL WORKS. Mendelssohn wrote a symphony-cantata called *Lobgesang* ("Song of Praise"). His oratorio, *St. Paul,* makes use of chorales. *Elijah* (1846) is Mendelssohn's greatest oratorio. *Die Walpurgisnacht* (1842) is a secular cantata on a text by Goethe.

Other 19th-Century Oratorio. The first important oratorio of the 19th century is Beethoven's *Christus am Ölberg* ("Christ on the Mount of Olives," 1800). A work which enjoyed popularity until the appearance of Mendelssohn's oratorios is Spohr's *Das letzte*

Gericht ("The Last Judgment"). Other oratorios of the 19th century are: Schumann's *Das Paradies und die Peri* (1844), Berlioz' *Damnation de Faust* (1846), a secular oratorio, and *L'Enfance du Christ* (1854), which is a cantata trilogy, Liszt's *St. Elizabeth,* a concerto-oratorio with Wagnerian leitmotifs, and *Christus* (1873). Some important English oratorios of the late 19th century are: Stainer's *The Crucifixion* (1887), Hubert Parry's *Judith* (1888), *Job* (1892), and *King Saul* (1900), Elgar's *The Dream of Gerontius* (1900) and *The Kingdom* (1906).

Sacred Choral Music

Much of the sacred choral literature in the 19th century assumes the romantic operatic spirit, making it difficult to distinguish between cantata and oratorio on the one hand and liturgical church music on the other.

Principal Forms of Church Music. Settings of the Catholic Ordinary of the Mass and the Requiem continued to be made in the 19th century. Most of these were for concert rather than liturgical purposes. In addition there were numerous settings of the Psalms.

Composers of Religious Choral Music. Mendelssohn and Brahms are the two greatest choral composers of the 19th century. Mendelssohn's *Psalms* for chorus and orchestra, his *Lauda Sion* for chorus and orchestra, and his Opus 39, motets for female voices and organ, are his chief contributions to sacred choral literature. Brahms's *Deutsches Requiem* ("German Requiem") is his greatest work in sacred choral literature. It is based upon Biblical selections rather than upon the Catholic Requiem text. In addition, he wrote *Ave Maria* for female voices, orchestra, and organ, and settings of the Psalms. Other composers and works in this field are: Schumann, *Mass in C Minor;* Berlioz, *Requiem* and *Te Deum;* Liszt, *Graner Mass* and *Ungarische Krönungs-Messe* ("Hungarian Coronation Mass"); Cherubini, *Mass in D Minor;* Beethoven, *Missa solemnis;* Schubert, 6 Latin Masses, 1 German Mass, 5 Salve Reginas, 2 Stabat Maters, etc.; Verdi, *Requiem;* Gabriel Fauré, *Requiem,* César Franck, *Les Béatitudes* (an oratorio) and *Psalms;* and Bruckner, *Te Deum, Mass in F Minor,* and other Masses.

Secular Choral Music

The 19th century produced a dearth of high quality choral music. With a few exceptions, the secular choral music was of a decidedly cheap and popular nature. Notable exceptions are the fine part songs of Mendelssohn and numerous larger works by Brahms: the *Alto Rhapsody,* for alto solo, male chorus, and orchestra, *The Song of Destiny* for chorus and orchestra, *The Song of Triumph* for eight-part chorus, and *Nänie* for chorus and orchestra. Anton Bruckner also wrote some solid works for male chorus. The choral finales of Beethoven's Ninth Symphony and Liszt's *Faust Symphony* are notable examples of 19th-century symphonic works using chorus.

CHAPTER XXIV

The Solo Song

THE accompanied art song, as opposed to folk song, popular song, and operatic aria, is one of the most significant developments of the 19th century. The chief contributions to this form of music come from Germany, where the lied (German art song) was developed. Song composition in France and Russia in the second half of the century is also important. In Italy, where opera always eclipsed every other kind of musical activity, and in England, the solo song literature is negligible.

General Considerations. The rise of great German romantic poetry is an important factor in the development of the lied. Another factor is the rise of the piano in the early 19th century. Its increased sonority over earlier keyboard instruments provided an adequate support for the solo voice. Greater attention was given to appropriate musical setting of the text than ever before.

SONG CYCLE. Songs of a related character and subject, usually composed to the verses of one poet, were written. Such groups are called *song cycles* or *Liederkreise*. Important examples of song cycles are Beethoven's *An die ferne Geliebte* (1816), Schubert's *Die schöne Müllerin* (1823) and *Winterreise* (1827), Schumann's *Frauenliebe und Leben* (1840) and *Dichterliebe* (1840), Brahms's *Magelone* (1861–1868), Fauré's *La Bonne chanson* (1892), and Debussy's *Chansons de Bilitis* (1897).

FORM. Two structural plans are used in the accompanied solo song. One is the *strophic song* in which the same music is used for each stanza. The other plan is called *through-composed* (or *durchkom-*

poniert) in which the music changes with each stanza according to the nature of the text. The latter plan came to be used more extensively in song literature.

German Lied Composers. Early romantic song composers in Germany are Beethoven, Reichardt, Zelter, and Zumsteeg.

FRANZ SCHUBERT. Franz Schubert (1797–1828) is the greatest master of the lied. He is one of the greatest melodic geniuses of all time. His melodies and accompaniments show sensitivity to the text. He was one of the first to employ the through-composed plan of text setting. He wrote over 600 songs and two famous song cycles.

FELIX MENDELSSOHN. The song literature of Felix Mendelssohn (1809–1847) is characterized by its excellence of melody but a lack of variety, and a rather loose connection between music and text. He usually employed the strophic plan.

ROBERT SCHUMANN. The songs of Schumann (1810–1856) are typically romantic. The importance of the piano is to be seen in that the accompaniment is often more important than the melody. His songs are also sometimes declamatory in style. He is best in settings of Heine poems.

KARL LOEWE. Karl Loewe (1796–1869) was a master of 19th-century ballad form.

HUGO WOLF. Absorption in the text and great power in bringing out the mood of the text are characteristics of Wolf (1860–1903). Richness of harmony is also typical. Wolf was almost exclusively a song composer.

JOHANNES BRAHMS. The songs of Johannes Brahms (1833–1897) show characteristic attention to formal considerations. They are mostly strophic, and often strongly flavored with German folk song style. Richness and moodiness are generally typical of Brahms harmonies.

ROBERT FRANZ. Robert Franz (1815–1892) was exclusively a song composer. He limited his songs to subjects of extreme emotion and wrote only for the mezzo-soprano voice.

French Song Composers. All French opera composers contributed to some extent to song literature. The poets Verlaine and Baudelaire had a great deal to do with the excellence of French song literature in the second half of the 19th century. Refinement and taste are characteristic of the French song literature of this period. The principal composers of French songs are: Gounod, Duparc, Fauré, Chausson, and Debussy.

Russian Song Composers. The principal contributors to song literature in Russia in the 19th century are: Glinka, Tschaikovsky, Rachmaninoff, Gretchaninov, Glière, and Moussorgsky.

CHAPTER XXV

19th-Century Piano Music

PIANO music is one of the most important developments of the 19th
century. Interest in piano music from the middle of the century
eclipsed even interest in the orchestra.

General Characteristics. The piano came into general use early in
the 19th century. Its sonority, greater than that of earlier keyboard instruments, opened the way for new developments in idiom,
and its warmth of tone and its power were an inspiration for the
expression of romantic ideas. Keyboard technique reached new
heights and this resulted in the prominence, excesses, and even
extremes of virtuosity. The pianist-composer was a phenomenon of
the Romantic period.

FORM. The new medium of the piano plus the currents of romanticism combined to produce entirely new styles. Short pieces for
piano were generally characteristic of the period. Pieces with descriptive titles were also popular. Stylized dances of the 19th century
were the waltz, the mazurka, and the polonaise. Eighteenth-century
dances, such as the minuet, gavotte, bourée, etc., disappeared early
in the 19th century. Numerous free forms came into being, works
with no predetermined structural principles: romanza, fantasy, nocturne, ballade, novelette, etc. The variation form was employed
throughout the century, but it often revealed shallow virtuosity
rather than artistic skill. The étude is a piece based upon one or
more aspects of technique, it is often openly virtuosic, and it is glorified for concert performance. Sonata form was generally neglected
after Beethoven and Schubert. The suite and contrapuntal forms are
virtually absent from 19th-century piano literature.

Principal Composers. Nearly all the important piano music of the 19th century belongs to Germany.

BEETHOVEN. The first quarter of the 19th century is characterized by the expansion of classical forms in the hands of Beethoven. His 32 piano sonatas and his 21 sets of variations are the greatest achievements in these forms. Details of his style are discussed on page 140.

SCHUBERT. Schubert's piano music is a mixture of classical and romantic elements. He wrote sonatas based on classical patterns. He also wrote fantasies, impromptus, and numerous pieces of a decidedly romantic nature. Schubert was a genius of melodic invention but not of thematic development. His music is poetic and lyric rather than clever or profound.

SCHUMANN. Schumann is the arch-romanticist in all his music. In his piano music he wrote exclusively in romantic forms and in a completely romantic style. His piano works consist of the romantic free forms and, most extensive of all, pieces with descriptive titles. He wrote collections of short, descriptive pieces: *Davidsbündlertänze, Papillons,* and *Carnival.* Schumann's music for piano is seldom brilliant, seldom excessively virtuosic. His longer piano compositions seem to be constructed by joining together several smaller forms.

MENDELSSOHN. Mendelssohn's piano music is less significant than that of his principal contemporaries and less significant than his own music in other media. He wrote capriccios, scherzos, and concert variations in a style more virtuosic than that of Schumann. He also wrote short pieces of a poetic, lyric nature, such as the *Songs without Words.*

CHOPIN. Frédéric Chopin (1810–1849) was almost exclusively a composer for the piano. More than any other 19th-century composer he developed piano idiom through his astute awareness of the possibilities of the instrument. Chopin's music depends to a great extent upon the use of the sustaining pedal, or, more properly, the damper pedal. This mechanism enables the production of greater sonorities than can be sustained by the two hands alone, and it also paves the way to more modern effects of mixed harmonies. Chopin's melodic style is a lyric, cantabile style with melismatic variation, used principally in the nocturne type of composition. Virtuosity is

characteristic of the études and preludes particularly. Chromaticism
and fluctuating tonality are marked characteristics of Chopin's style.
His music represents Polish nationalism in the use of polonaises
and mazurkas. His style in general is a mixture of French and German romanticism. He wrote polonaises, ballades, mazurkas, waltzes,
nocturnes, preludes, études, impromptus, and freely romantic sonatas. He was essentially a piano composer, and his attempts in
other media (e.g., 2 piano concertos) are less successful, less
idiomatic.

LISZT. Franz Liszt (1811–1886) is the great virtuoso pianist-composer of the 19th century. Virtuosity is prominent in nearly all of
his piano compositions. He is fond of frequently introducing ca-
denza-like material. Chromaticism and unusual progressions characterize his harmonic style. His melodies are often romantic, sentimental. His music has a certain formal looseness. In addition to much
piano music, Liszt is noted for his numerous difficult and sometimes unidiomatic transcriptions for piano of works by Paganini,
Bach, Verdi, Wagner, etc.

BRAHMS. Johannes Brahms wrote a considerable amount of piano
music, less idiomatic than that of Chopin, but he shows great
attention to structural form. Rich, dark harmony, and special textures are characteristic of his music. His variations especially show
a more important use of counterpoint than is typical of the 19th
century in general. Brahms wrote intermezzi, variations, capriccios,
sonatas, rhapsodies, fantasies, ballades, and romances. His sonatas
are more reminiscent of the nobility and greatness of Beethoven
than are any other sonatas of the 19th century.

OTHER COMPOSERS. Other composers of 19th-century piano music
are Grieg, MacDowell, Albéniz, Granados, Reger, Busoni, and
Fauré.

CHAPTER XXVI

Instrumental Ensemble Music

THE instrumental ensemble music of the 19th century may be considered under two main categories: symphonic music which expanded enormously in the century, and chamber music which was one of the least popular fields.

Symphonic Music

General Considerations. During the 19th century the symphony orchestra and symphonic form show tremendous expansion. The technique of orchestration grew accordingly. The greatest names in this field of development are Beethoven, Berlioz, Wagner, and Rimsky-Korsakov.

Symphonic Forms and Styles. Whereas sonata form was largely abandoned in piano music after Beethoven, it was retained as the basic form of the symphony throughout the 19th century. Other forms were added.

SYMPHONY. Beethoven expanded the classical symphony with new freedom of expression. Romantic composers following Beethoven replaced classical style with romantic style and romantic treatment of thematic material. Although retaining the broad outlines of the classical symphonic structure, the romantic symphony handles the thematic material much more freely. Programmatic aspects of symphonic music were soon adopted by many romantic composers, Berlioz being the chief exponent of this idea.

CONCERTO. All the features of the romantic symphony except the programmatic aspects apply to the romantic concerto. Concertos were written principally for piano and for violin. Here is a notable extension of virtuosity, with characteristically elaborate and brilliant cadenzas.

SYMPHONIC POEM. The symphonic poem, developed in the second half of the 19th century, was an outgrowth of the earlier program symphony. It was originated by Liszt. It is a large, free form in one movement. It is usually programmatic: (1) either on a narrative basis (e.g., Strauss's *Till Eulenspiegel*) or (2) pictorial or descriptive but not narrative (e.g., Debussy's *L'Après-midi d'un faune* and Liszt's *Les Préludes*).

SYMPHONIC SUITE. The symphonic suite of the 19th century has no affinity with the baroque orchestral suite. The symphonic suite consists of several movements of a related programmatic nature but descriptive rather than narrative (e.g., Debussy's *La Mer* and Rimsky-Korsakov's *Scheherazade*). The symphonic suite also includes incidental music for drama (Grieg's *Peer Gynt Suite*) and ballet music (Tschaikovsky's *Nutcracker Suite*).

CONCERT OVERTURE. The overture not connected with opera was a form employed moderately often by 19th-century composers. It is usually in a modified sonata-allegro form, with more structural definitude than the symphonic poem. Several diverse examples of concert overture may be cited: (1) Beethoven's *Coriolanus Overture* and *Egmont Overture* are incidental or entr'acte music to plays. (2) Mendelssohn's *Overture to "A Midsummer Night's Dream"* belongs to the category of entr'acte music. The whole work, including the overture, is an orchestral suite because of its several movements and its descriptive nature. (3) Mendelssohn's *Hebrides Overture* is descriptive and programmatic. (4) Brahms's *Academic Festival Overture* is occasional music, i.e., written for a particular event or occasion.

SYMPHONIC VARIATIONS. Though not completely abandoned in the 19th century, variation form was not one of the most extensively employed for the symphony orchestra. Notable examples of symphonic variations are: Brahms's *Variations on a Theme by Haydn*, César Franck's *Symphonic Variations* for piano and orchestra, D'Indy's *Istar Variations*, and Elgar's *Enigma Variations*.

POPULAR TYPES OF ORCHESTRAL MUSIC. Considerable quantities of a more popular type of orchestral music were written in the 19th century. The most important of these are the Viennese waltzes of Johann Strauss (1825–1899). Other types of orchestral entertainment music, replacing the classical serenades of the 18th century, were the ballet suites and opera suites, and potpourri overtures from stage works.

Principal Composers, Works, Styles. The principal contributions to symphonic literature in the Romantic period came from Germany. In the second half of the century, however, France, Russia, and other countries began to contribute to the enormous literature of that period.

BEETHOVEN. 19th-century symphonic literature begins with Beethoven. (See Chapter XXI.)

SCHUBERT. Schubert wrote 8 symphonies and 8 overtures. He employs a conventional orchestration of the late Classical period, and classical symphonic form. His melodies are great, showing the typical lyric, songlike quality so characteristic of Schubert. But there is a deficiency of technical resources in his music and a decided lack of thematic development, his themes usually being merely repeated or transposed. His music is full of ingenious harmony and modulations.

SCHUMANN. Schumann wrote 4 symphonies, 4 concert overtures, and a piano concerto. His orchestration is romantic but rather uninspired in its thick, drab texture with almost constant mixing of strings, woodwinds, and brass. His melodic style is definitely romantic as is also his freedom with the symphonic form. Strong rhythmic traits are noticeable, especially his use of syncopation and dotted rhythms.

MENDELSSOHN. Mendelssohn wrote 5 symphonies, concert overtures, 1 violin concerto, and 2 piano concertos. His symphonic music leans rather heavily upon programmatic ideas. His orchestration is clear and bright, particularly in the very characteristic scherzo style he developed by the use of woodwinds and light strings in high registers playing rapid figures.

BERLIOZ. Berlioz, the most famous French symphonist of the first half of the 19th century, wrote 4 program symphonies and 5 dramatic concert overtures. His chief contribution to symphonic music is in the field of instrumentation and orchestration. In addition to advancing a more colorful orchestration in his music, he wrote a treatise on orchestration that in many respects is still standard today. He is one of the chief exponents of symphonic program music, an example of which is his *Fantastic Symphony*. In this and other works he uses the *idée fixe,* a sort of leitmotif recurrent throughout the work.

BRAHMS. Brahms is generally considered the greatest symphonic composer in the second half of the 19th century. He wrote 4 symphonies, 2 symphonic overtures, symphonic variations, 2 serenades, 1 violin concerto, 1 double concerto for violin and cello, and 2 piano concertos. Rich, full, and varied color characterizes his orchestration. His harmony is likewise rich and full, and often somber. Brahms is a great formalist and his symphonies show mastery of architectural proportions. Other prominent features of his style are the use of wide-range thematic material, important contrapuntal qualities, use of cross-rhythms and rhythmic modification of thematic material, and the use of root and third without the fifth in chords and themes.

LISZT. The principal contribution of Liszt to symphonic literature is the symphonic poem, in which form he wrote 13 works. In addition he wrote a *Faust Symphony* for orchestra, tenor solo and male chorus. Virtuosity plays an important part in Liszt's orchestral style. This is, of course, also evident in his concertos for piano in E♭ and A. His melodies are often romantic, sentimental. His rhythmic style is often influenced by Hungarian patterns. His harmony is characteristically chromatic. His formal structures are rather loose, rhapsodic, and improvisatory.

BRUCKNER. The symphonic works of Anton Bruckner (1824–1896) consist of an early overture and 11 symphonies, 2 of which are incomplete. Austrian romanticism and Schubertian style of melody are characteristic of his symphonic music. He uses Wagnerian orchestration and harmonic style. The great length of his formal structures is notable.

MAHLER. Gustav Mahler (1860–1911) wrote 10 symphonies (the last incomplete), of which No. 8 (the *Symphony of a Thousand*) is the most famous, as well as *Das Lied von der Erde,* a song cycle for symphony orchestra, tenor, and alto. Romantic sentimentality is present in most of his music. Like Bruckner, he employs a Wagnerian style of orchestration and harmony. He makes considerable use of solo instruments and solo voices (in Symphonies 2, 3, 4, and 8). His symphonies, like those of Bruckner, are of extraordinary length.

STRAUSS. Richard Strauss (1864–   ) is a transitional figure whose music represents a continuation of Wagnerian orchestral traditions and the symphonic poem into the realm of modern neoromanticism. (See page 172.) His principal orchestral works are: *Till Eulenspiegel, Don Juan, Also sprach Zarathustra* ("Thus Spake Zarathustra"), *Don Quixote* (fantastic variations for violoncello and orchestra), *Ein Heldenleben* ("A Hero's Life"), and *Symphonia Domestica.*

French Symphonic Literature. Relatively few French composers of the 19th century are included in standard symphonic repertory, and they are all from the second half of the 19th century. To summarize the principal symphonic contributions of this school: Saint-Saëns wrote 5 symphonies, symphonic poems, and 2 orchestral suites. Lalo is noted primarily for his *Symphonie espagnole* for violin solo and orchestra. César Franck's *Symphony in D Minor* continues to be popular. His pupil, Chausson, wrote 1 symphony. D'Indy wrote program symphonies, symphonic poems, and 3 symphonic overtures. Bizet's *L'Arlésienne Suite* is his most popular orchestral work.

Russian Symphonic Literature. Russian symphonic literature begins in the last quarter of the 19th century. Its expansion parallels the development of Russian nationalism.

TSCHAIKOVSKY. The highly romantic works of Peter Ilich Tschaikovsky (1840–1893) have enjoyed a popularity out of proportion to their artistic merits. Tschaikovsky wrote 7 symphonies (including the *Manfred Symphony*), 6 orchestral suites, 11 symphonic poems and overtures, 3 piano concertos, the best known of which is that in B-flat minor, and the violin concerto in D. His melody is romantic, and only partly Russian in quality. His harmony and orchestration are basically German. His symphonic works all reveal structural weaknesses, particularly in long passages of aimless padding and repetition. In all his works there is to be found brooding melancholy and noisy ebullience.

RIMSKY-KORSAKOV. Of all symphonic works by Rimsky-Korsakov (1844–1908), the orchestral suite *Scheherazade* is the best known. He wrote 3 symphonies, of which *Antar* is the most famous, as well as symphonic poems, and overtures. His most significant contribution is his masterful and brilliant orchestration. His treatise on orchestration is standard. His music is characterized by Orientalism, and exotic harmony and subjects. He is also one of the most prominent exponents of Russian nationalism.

MOUSSORGSKY. The symphonic music of Modest Moussorgsky (1839–1881) is not extensive, but it is important in that it shows signs of departure from romantic styles toward a more modern Russian idiom. His principal orchestral work is the symphonic poem *Night on Bald Mountain.*

OTHER RUSSIAN COMPOSERS. Alexander Borodin (1833–1887) wrote 3 symphonies, a few symphonic poems, the best known being *The Steppes of Central Asia.* Balakirev (1837–1910) wrote 2 symphonies, 3 symphonic poems, 3 overtures, and 1 orchestral suite. These are rarely performed on symphony programs.

Other Symphonic Works of the 19th Century. A few additional composers and works should be mentioned: Dvořák's *Symphony from the New World,* Grieg's *Peer Gynt Suite,* Smetana's symphonic cycle, *My Fatherland,* Albéniz's *Iberian Suite,* originally written for piano, and Elgar's *Enigma Variations.*

Chamber Music

Chamber music, on the whole, was one of the least popular media during the 19th century. The limitations of chamber music media point toward the absolute rather than the emotional or programmatic, toward the objective rather than the subjective, toward the classical rather than the romantic spirit. Nevertheless, some great chamber music was composed in the 19th century.

Summary of Principal 19th-Century Chamber Music Composers.
Beethoven and Brahms are the two greatest masters of 19th-century
chamber music. The following summary of the works of the principal composers of chamber music shows a variety of instrumental
combinations.

BEETHOVEN. Beethoven wrote 10 violin sonatas, 5 cello sonatas,
6 piano trios, 4 string trios, 1 horn sonata, 1 string quintet, and 16
string quartets.

SCHUBERT. Schubert wrote 14 string quartets, 2 piano trios, a quintet, a string quintet, and an octet.

SCHUMANN. Schumann wrote 3 string quartets, a piano quartet,
a piano quintet, 3 piano trios, 2 violin sonatas, and numerous ro-
manzas, fantasies, etc., for various instruments with piano.

MENDELSSOHN. Mendelssohn's output in chamber music was 7
string quartets, 3 piano quartets, 2 string quintets, 2 string trios,
a violin sonata, 2 cello sonatas, an octet, and concert variations for
cello and piano.

BRAHMS. Brahms wrote 3 string quartets, 2 string quintets, 3 piano
quartets, a piano quintet, 3 piano trios, a clarinet quintet, a *Horn
Trio* (for French horn, piano, and violin), a clarinet trio, 2 clarinet
sonatas, 3 violin sonatas, 2 cello sonatas, and 2 sextets. In addition
to the extensive literature for chamber ensembles, Brahms also wrote
some significant organ music: fugues and chorale preludes.

FRANCK. César Franck wrote 1 string quartet, 4 piano trios, and
a piano quintet. His organ music is of substantial value.

FAURÉ. Gabriel Fauré wrote 2 piano quintets, 2 piano quartets,
and a piano trio.

CHAPTER XXVII

Summary of Principal Composers

THE principal composers of the 19th century have been mentioned in the foregoing chapters of Part Five in connection with each of the principal fields of musical development. The following summary lists the great masters of the period according to country and the fields of musical activity and chief contributions to musical development.

Germany. Germany is the leading country of the 19th century, and is represented in all fields of music.

BEETHOVEN: transition from classical to romantic; symphony, sonata, and chamber music.

WEBER: romantic opera and symphonic works; some piano music.

SCHUBERT: song, piano music, and symphony.

SCHUMANN: song, piano music, and symphony. Schumann is also the most noted 19th-century critic. As editor of the *Neue Zeitschrift für Musik* ("New Musical Journal") he wrote many essays and valuable criticisms championing the cause of good music and musicians through the fictitious "Davidsbündler" (i.e., the society of David against the musical Philistines).

MENDELSSOHN: choral music, oratorio, symphony, piano music, and organ music. Mendelssohn was also one of the leading conductors of the first half of the 19th century. In this connection his greatest contribution was the revival of Bach's *St. Matthew Passion* in 1829, marking the beginning of a great revival of interest in Bach's music which had been forgotten for nearly a century.

BRAHMS: symphonic music, chamber music, choral works, song, piano and organ music.

LISZT: piano virtuosity in composition and performance, symphonic poem, numerous transcriptions. Although Hungarian by birth, Liszt really belongs to the school of German romantic composers.

WAGNER: music drama, opera.

STRAUSS: symphonic poem, opera, songs.

Italy. The sole contribution of Italy in the 19th century is opera, instrumental fields being almost totally neglected.

ROSSINI: opera; especially excelled in buffa opera.

BELLINI: romantic Italian opera.

DONIZETTI: romantic Italian opera.

VERDI: the greatest master of 19th-century Italian opera.

France. The chief contribution of France in the 19th century is opera. In the second half of the century instrumental music and the solo song were developed.

MEYERBEER: romantic French opera.

BERLIOZ: orchestration, program symphony.

CHOPIN: exclusively a composer of piano music. Although Chopin was Polish by birth and exhibits Polish nationalist traits in some of his music, he may be considered as belonging to the French school because of his residence and associations in Paris.

SAINT-SAËNS: symphony, opera, oratorio.

GOUNOD: opera, romantic church music.

FRANCK: symphonic works, chorus, organ. Although Franck was Belgian by birth, he, like Chopin, spent almost his entire life in Paris.

FAURÉ: song, piano music, *Requiem*.

England. English music, which had been eclipsed by Continental activities since the time of Purcell, did not again rise to a position of eminence until the 20th century. In the 19th century it was largely under the influence of German romanticism and later of French impressionism, despite certain nationalistic and individual traits that appear here and there.

SAMUEL WESLEY (1766–1837): organ music, church music.

SAMUEL SEBASTIAN WESLEY (1810–1876): English church music.

JOHN FIELD (1782–1837): piano music (nocturnes predating Chopin style).

WILLIAM STERNDALE BENNETT (1816–1875): piano and orchestral music.

JOHN STAINER (1840–1901): *Crucifixion,* cantatas, anthems.

ARTHUR SULLIVAN (1842–1900): operettas.

CHARLES H. PARRY (1848–1918): oratorios, anthems, cantatas.

CHARLES STANFORD (1852–1924): Irish nationalism, church music, oratorios, operas, and chamber music.

EDWARD ELGAR (1857–1934): oratorios, cantatas, orchestral works.

Russia. Russia came into the group of prominent musical nations in the second half of the 19th century when the strong current of Russian nationalism began.

GLINKA: Russian nationalist opera.

"THE FIVE": a group of Russians who consciously fostered the spirit of Russian nationalism in music: Moussorgsky, Borodin, Balakirev, César Cui, and Rimsky-Korsakov.

MOUSSORGSKY: symphony, opera, song.

BORODIN: symphony, opera.

BALAKIREV: symphony, songs, piano.

RIMSKY-KORSAKOV: brilliant orchestration, symphonic poem, opera, orientalism, and Russian nationalism.

TSCHAIKOVSKY: romantic symphonic works, opera, song.

RACHMANINOFF: romantic symphonic works, piano concertos, songs. He was perhaps the last of the great pianist-composers of the romantic tradition.

Norway. Norway boasts of one famous composer: Grieg, who was a champion of Norwegian nationalism in his piano music, piano concerto, and numerous songs.

Bohemia. The two Bohemian nationalists of the 19th century are Smetana in the fields of opera and symphonic works, and Dvořák in symphony and chamber music.

Spain. Working principally in the fields of orchestral and piano music, the Spanish nationalists are Albéniz, Granados, and De Falla, the last named representing 20th-century Spanish nationalism.

Music in the United States. Music in America before 1700 was largely confined to Psalm singing, partly because of the rigors of pioneer life and partly because of the severe attitudes of the Puritans.

THE 18TH CENTURY. Concert life began in the second quarter of the 18th century in Boston, Charleston, New York, and Philadelphia. Francis Hopkinson (1737–1791) may be considered the first native American composer. He wrote songs in the current English style. Musical activities were virtually halted by the period of the American Revolution, and the development of native American talent was arrested by the influx of European musicians and composers who had the advantages of tradition and better training.

THE 19TH CENTURY. In the 19th century the influx of European musicians continued to increase. This was particularly true of Germans, musicians and teachers, whose romantic German culture colored the American musical point of view. The result was that not until the 20th century was there any considerable development of indigenous American art music. A native American style did develop, however, in the field of entertainment: the minstrel show with its strongly flavored Negro style. The folk-like songs of Stephen Foster (1826–1864) are also truly American, although somewhat limited to Southern melodic style and subject matter. In the second half of the 19th century there was a beginning of a real school of American composition which was to flower in the 20th century. The principal names connected with the development of American composition in the late 19th century are: John Knowles Paine (1839–1906), whose symphonies are basically German and solid in workmanship; his pupils, Arthur Foote, Frederick Converse, John Alden Carpenter, and Daniel Gregory Mason; others of the New England group, Chadwick, Parker, Whiting, Kelley. Because of his individuality of style Edward MacDowell (1861–1908) is considered one of the most important American composers of the 19th century. He is noted primarily for his piano music and his second piano concerto.

PART SIX

Modern Music (1880-1947)

CHAPTER XXVIII

General Considerations

THE first half of the 20th century is a revolutionary period in the history of music, comparable with the ars nova of the 14th century and the nuove musiche at the beginning of the 17th century.

General Historical Background. The first half of the 20th century is dominated by two great wars: World War I (1914–1918) and World War II (1939–1945). Tremendous scientific and mechanical progress has affected the entire civilization, beginning with the advances of electrical science, radio, the airplane, and achieving jet propulsion, radar, and atomic energy. In the arts and literature the modern spirit is represented by a return to objectivity, realistic expressionism, and functionalism. This spirit is expressed in the works of such artists as Picasso in painting, Frank Lloyd Wright in architecture, and by many diverse points of view in poetry and literature.

The Development of Modernism

Modernism in music may be broadly defined as that in which there is manifest some aspect of musical style or form that departs in some significant respect from common practices of the preceding period. Three periods in the development of modernism in music can be seen.

The Late 19th Century (1880–1900). It is impossible to say at just what time modernism was first manifest. The last two decades of the 19th century show definite signs of departure from general 19th-century styles, although the latter continued to dominate music well into the 20th century. Reaction against the dominant German romantic traditions was manifest in two channels: (1) nationalism, in which other European countries championed their own nationalistic styles, particularly in Russia, and (2) the developments of the French school of impressionism, the central musical figure of which is Claude Debussy.

The Early 20th Century (1900–1914). The period, roughly defined as beginning with the turn of the century and continuing to the opening of World War I, is one of open revolt against German romanticism, and is marked by radical experimentation. Here the new styles were predominant although much conservative romantic music was still being written and played. The most important pioneer composers of this period are Scriabin, Stravinsky, and Schönberg.

The Present (1918–1947). Although we are too close to get an adequate perspective of it, the period from the close of World War I (during which musical activity was retarded) until the close of World War II seems to be one of assimilation of new principles. This is confused by the fact that much experimentation still goes on, and romanticism is not completely abandoned. But there is clear evidence of a prevailing objectivity in music of the present period. This is manifest in the general restraint of emotional content, in the simplification of materials and structures, and in the greater attention to musical craftsmanship. In other words, a classical spirit prevails; and this is called "neoclassicism."

Broad Tendencies of Modernism

Neoromanticism. The term *neoromanticism* is applied to the continuance, if not the decadence, of German romantic traditions. Post-Wagnerian style continued well into the 20th century. It is characterized by a somewhat overripe emotionalism, enormous orchestras, great symphonic lengths, but also by advances in harmonic idiom and orchestration. The principal composers whose music belongs largely to this category are Mahler, Bruckner, Richard Strauss, and in some respects Sibelius.

Impressionism. A widespread movement in the arts took place in France in the second half of the 19th century. In poetry (Verlaine,

Baudelaire, etc.) and in painting (Manet, Monet, Degas, Renoir, etc.) new techniques were developed that produced veiled, "atmospheric" impressions rather than clear, dynamic expression. This movement carried over into music at the hands of Debussy as a direct reaction against Wagnerian romanticism. *Impressionism* is not devoid of romantic elements, however. Impressionistic music may be described as having refinement, delicacy, vagueness, and an over-all "luminous fog" atmosphere. The technical aspects of impressionism will be discussed in connection with Debussy in Chapter XXX (see page 184). The principal composers who used impressionistic styles are Debussy, Roussel, and Ravel in France, Delius in England, Palmgren in Finland, Scriabin in Russia, and Charles Griffes in the United States.

Expressionism. The term *expressionism,* like "impressionism," was borrowed from art. In general it was intended to mean the expression of the inner self (i.e., the subconscious) as opposed to impressionism as an impression of external things. Expressionism in art, which gave rise to abstraction (e.g., Piet Mondrian, Brancusi's *Bird in Space,* etc.) and surrealism (Dali), found a parallel in music around 1910 in the radical and highly experimental works of such composers as Schönberg and his followers, Webern, Berg, Křenek, and others. Polytonality and atonality are special techniques of this broad tendency. Expressionism lasted until about 1925 when it was generally replaced by neoclassicism.

Neoclassicism. The last of the broad tendencies to develop in the first half of the 20th century is that of *neoclassicism.* More than neoromanticism, which is a continuation or a deterioration of the Romantic period, neoclassicism is a definite return to a classical point of view. Romantic subjectivity, thrown aside, is replaced by a modern objectivity. It consists in general of a simplification of material, form, and medium, sometimes to the point of severity. More specifically, it is represented by a recognition of 18th-century ideals in the use of counterpoint and formal clarity but clothed in 20th-century harmonic idiom, key schemes, orchestration, and melodic style. The principal leaders in the neoclassical trends are Paul Hindemith (counterpoint and forms), Stravinsky (simplification of style from about 1920), and the modern Russian Prokofiev (simplicity and clarity of texture and form).

American Jazz. Although distinctly a popular art, American dance-band style, generally referred to as jazz, has had such a widespread influence upon serious or nonpopular music that it may be counted among the broad tendencies of modernism. Further, in view of its self-contained importance as a phenomenon of the 20th-century United States, it will be well to consider its development, aside from its implications with serious art music.

THE DEVELOPMENT OF JAZZ. Popular music in the United States has passed through several stages of evolution in its comparatively brief history. These broad currents of style often overlap and influence one another so that the chronology is not always clear.

a. *Ragtime.* Popular music known as *ragtime,* probably derived from minstrel shows, makes its appearance somewhere in the late 19th century. It is essentially a pianistic art characterized by prominence of syncopation in various patterns, conventional harmony (I, IV, and V), and regular phraseology. Ragtime bands originated in New Orleans a little before the turn of the century. They consisted mainly of small groups of Negro musicians who improvised upon ragtime tunes.

b. *Blues.* A style type of popular music known as *blues* influenced both ragtime and later jazz. W. C. Handy's "Memphis Blues" (1909) and his famous "St. Louis Blues" (1914) are early examples of this style. Blues style is unquestionably of Negro origin. The subject matter deals with an atmosphere of self-pity, a lost or absent lover, etc. Blues style consists of the following features: (1) predominant use of twelve-measure periods instead of the more conventional eight and sixteen, (2) preponderant use of major keys, (3) emphasis upon plagal or subdominant harmonies, (4) use of the lowered third and seventh degrees in the melody and harmony, (5) wavering above or below true pitch, and (6) progressions of dominant seventh chords, known as "barbershop harmony," a style now considered obsolete.

c. *Jazz.* The elements of the style known as jazz began to make their appearance around 1910, derived from ragtime and blues.

Jazz became a distinct style in the 1920's with the beginning of "name" bands (Whiteman, Ted Lewis, Guy Lombardo, etc.). In general, jazz is essentially an orchestral art in terms of arrangement (commercial arrangements called "sweet" or "straight" jazz) or improvisation (called "hot jazz"). The arranger or the performer then becomes more important than the composer, the original melody and harmony becoming secondary in importance to its treatment. Other characteristics of jazz in general are: (1) a more suave, more melodic, and more vocal melody than that of ragtime, (2) a sustained melody over a throbbing accompaniment, (3) superimposition of complex rhythmic patterns, (4) more major than minor tonalities, (5) use of added tones in harmony (particularly the added sixth and/or second degrees in the final tonic), (6) parallelism or seventh and ninth chords, (7) instrumentation: little use of strings, prominence of percussion, woodwinds (particularly saxophone and clarinet), and brass (trumpets and trombones with or without mutes), and special instruments such as the banjo (used in the 1920's, later replaced by the guitar), vibra-harp, etc. Special mention should be made of a pianistic development which began in the middle 1930's, called *boogie-woogie*. This consists of a strongly rhythmic ostinato figure carried in the bass over which the right hand carries variations in diverse figures. The term *swing* usually implies a later style (Benny Goodman, c. 1935) of jazz of a more improvisatory nature.

INFLUENCE OF JAZZ. The indigenous popular styles outlined above have had a widespread influence upon serious music. This influence is to be seen largely in (1) instrumentation, (2) certain harmonic devices, (3) rhythmic styles, and (4) use of blues. Concert jazz in larger forms began with George Gershwin's *Rhapsody in Blue* (1924). Other examples of rather ambitious employment of jazz idiom are his *Concerto in F* and Morton Gould's *Chorale and Fugue in Jazz* (1936). Evidence of employment of jazz or popular styles in serious works is to be found in Stravinsky's *Sacre du printemps* ("Rite of Spring") and *Histoire du soldat* (1918, movement entitled "Ragtime"), Carpenter's *Skyscrapers* and *Krazy Kat* (ballets), Ravel's *Sonata for Violin and Piano* and *Concerto for Piano*, Milhaud's ballets *Le Boeuf sur le toit* and *La Création du monde*, Krenck's jazz opera *Jonny spielt auf*, Aaron Copland's *Concerto for Piano and Orchestra* and *Music for the Theatre*, Constant Lambert's *Rio Grande* (1928) for voices and orchestra, Gruenberg's *Daniel Jazz* for small ensemble and solo voice, and Shostakovitch's *Suite for Jazz Orchestra* (1934).

Fields of Musical Activity

The 20th century has seen some important changes in the relative importance of various musical media. It has also seen the rise of new musical outlets: the cinema, the radio, and the phonograph. A widespread interest in music is also significant.

20th-Century Media. In general, instrumental music still dominates the field.

SYMPHONIC MUSIC. The symphonic forms that were developed in the 19th century continue to be used in the 20th century: the symphony, the symphonic poem, the symphonic suite, and various other less important forms.

CHAMBER MUSIC. There has been a significant revival of interest in chamber music, particularly from about 1920, in connection with neoclassical trends. New instrumental combinations have been exploited.

PIANO MUSIC. Piano music in general does not hold as prominent a place as it did in the 19th century. Nevertheless, much significant modern piano music has been written.

CHORAL MUSIC. A renewed interest in choral music is to be seen in the 20th century. There has been a revival of interest in renaissance *a cappella* choral music and a considerable new literature in this medium has been written. Large choral forms with symphony orchestra (e.g., Stravinsky's *Symphony of Psalms*) are being written.

SOLO SONG. Neither the output nor the popularity of solo song is as great as in the Romantic period. The solo voice with chamber music combinations has had a considerable vogue (e.g., Vaughan Williams' *On Wenlock Edge*).

BALLET. The ballet as a separate form not connected with opera has had a tremendous growth of popularity in the 20th century. The

Russian choreographer Diaghilev is the most important leader in this modern renaissance of the ballet. A long list of important ballet music (presented in symphonic concert form as well as in complete ballet form) began in the 20th century with Stravinsky's *Firebird* (1910), *Petroushka* (1912), and *Rite of Spring* (1913). There is an almost continuous production of ballets and ballet music up to the present.

OPERA. Although there have been some notable productions in the field of modern opera (e.g., Debussy's *Pelléas et Mélisande,* Strauss's *Der Rosenkavalier,* Berg's *Wozzek,* Hindemith's *Cardillac,* and Shostakovitch's *Lady Macbeth*), there has been a sharp falling off of interest in this medium in general. For the most part, 19th-century opera still dominates the repertory.

Musical Outlets. In addition to various musical media there are new musical outlets that have affected 20th-century music in one way or another.

RADIO. Radio broadcasting has had a tremendous influence upon creative and interpretive music. Probably more than any other factor it has created an interest in music unknown to such extent in any previous period in music history. Radio music, in addition to concert broadcasts, includes specially commissioned works for radio performance (e.g., Roy Harris' *Four Minutes and Twenty Seconds*), incidental music, commercial "theme songs," background music for radio plays, advertisements, etc.

CINEMA. Although music has come to be used extensively in film productions it is of little importance to the development of serious art music. It is an agent for popular music of the revue type. The efforts of serious composers have turned to some extent to the writing of background music for motion pictures, but this has rarely become a factor in concert music.

PHONOGRAPH RECORDING. Another important musical agent of the 20th century is the phonograph. Tremendous expansion of the recording industry has further increased public interest in music, in both the popular and serious fields.

Gebrauchsmusik. The German term *Gebrauchsmusik,* or "functional music" as it may be translated, expresses another important aspect of 20th-century music. It represents a conscious effort on the part of composers to lessen the breach between modern music and the musical public. More specifically it means music in a simplified style for performance by musical amateurs. It also implies music written for special purposes or particular occasions. The leader of the Gebrauchsmusik movement is Paul Hindemith, although the idea has had a widespread acceptance by many modern composers.

CHAPTER XXIX

Specific Aspects of Style

IT is important to keep in mind that no one of the revolutionary aspects of the 20th century—either the broad tendencies considered in the preceding chapter, or the specific features of style to be considered in the present chapter—represents all modern music, which is a complex stream of crosscurrents and eddies.

Tonality. One of the most significant aspects of modern music concerns new concepts of tonality.

EXPANSION AND MODIFICATION OF CONVENTIONAL CONCEPTS. Departure from conventional tonality began in the 19th century with the use of more and more remotely related keys within a composition, and with the practice of obscuring tonality by means of prolonged modulations and chromaticism (Chopin, Reger, Franck, Wagner, etc.).

MULTITONALITY. A typical feature of 20th-century tonality is the use of numerous remotely related keys introduced one after another with daring modulations or even without any modulation. This common practice may be referred to as *multitonality,* as opposed to the more commonly employed term "polytonality," to be explained later.

NEOMODALITY. A departure from the conventional major and minor diatonic scales led to the use of the old church modes. These are employed not in the strict sense but freely in modern settings and for certain archaic effects (Debussy, Ravel, Vaughan Williams, *et al.*).

NEW SCALE SYSTEMS. Composers further departed from conventional scale systems by experimenting with new scale patterns. One of these is the *whole-tone scale* (a scale of six tones within an octave, each separated by a whole step) which, however, is never employed exclusively throughout a composition, but more for special effects. Debussy was the principal composer to feature this device. Adaptations of various Oriental modes have been employed (Rimsky-Korsakov, Roussel, *et al.*). New scales have been invented (R. Strauss, Busoni, *et al.*).

POLYTONALITY. A more extreme innovation of the 20th century is the use of two or more keys simultaneously, called *bitonality* (in the case of only two keys) or *polytonality* (for several keys). This idea may have had its origin in prolonged pedal point and then in multiple pedal point (i.e., two or more tones held through a passage of changing harmony). Polytonality is seldom employed throughout one composition. The result of polytonality is great dissonance and the obscuring of any tonal feeling.

ATONALITY. The most extreme innovation of the 20th century in regard to tonal practices is *atonality*, which implies a complete negation of any tonal feeling at any time in a composition. The outstanding technique employed toward this end is the *twelve-tone system* devised by Arnold Schönberg and taken up by a school of atonalists (Webern, Wellesz, Berg, Křenek, *et al.*). Atonal music is consistently and extremely dissonant, consonance being studiously avoided because of its dangerous implication of key feeling.

NEW DIVISIONS OF THE SCALE. Fantastic rather than practical experiments have been carried on in the direction of dividing the octave into more than twelve equal parts. *Quarter tones* (24 different pitches to the octave), *eighth tones* (48 different pitches to the octave), and even *sixteenth tones* have been used. Because such division is impractical from the standpoint of instrumentation and notation, and because it is too remote from auditory tradition it has remained within the realm of experiment. The principal exponents of quarter-tone music are Alois Hába and Hans Barth. The Mexican Carrillo has produced some fantastic music in sixth tones, eighth tones, and sixteenth tones.

Harmony. Modern harmony in general makes more extensive use of sharp dissonance.

SPECIFIC ASPECTS OF STYLE 181

CHORD CONSTRUCTION. From the earliest dawn of harmonic concepts chords have been built in thirds. The 20th-century experiments have produced chords built on other intervals: fourths (Scriabin), fifths (resulting from inversion of chords built on fourths), sevenths, and seconds. A group of adjacent tones (chords built on seconds) sounding simultaneously is called a *tone cluster* (Henry Cowell, Leo Ornstein, Charles Ives, *et al.*). Chords without thirds (open fifths and octaves) have been used primarily for archaic effects. Chords are also built on altered degrees of the diatonic scale (e.g., in C major such a chord as D♯–F–A–C♯).

CHORD PROGRESSION. Evolution of practices in regard to chord progression has been almost continuous from the beginning of part music. Perhaps the most radical changes have taken place in the 20th century. Elision of chords in an otherwise conventional progression is fairly common. A more radical device is the use of *parallelism* which violates the "rules" of conventional harmony. This consists of open fifths, triads, seventh chords, or ninth chords moving in parallel motion. This is referred to as *chord streams*. Still another aspect of 20th-century chord progression is the use of unusual root progressions: root progression by half step, or by augmented fourth, etc.

MIXED CHORDS. The use of two different chords sounding simultaneously is found as far back as the 18th century or earlier as a result of double or triple suspensions. For example, a cadential measure might consist of the tones C–E–G combined with the tones B–D–F in which the latter resolve to the former. More extensive application of this principle led to *mixed chords* or *mixed harmony*. It is also an attribute of bitonality.

NEW TREATMENT OF DISSONANCE. Departure from conventional treatment of dissonance begins with a freer use of nonchordal or nonharmonic tones (passing tones, appoggiatura, suspensions, etc.) in their preparation and resolution. This led to freely introduced and unresolved nonchordal tones, and finally to what is now called *added tones* (e.g., the chord C–E–G plus the tone D♭). In general, modern harmony is characterized by sharper dissonances and prolongation of dissonant material. This may be brought about by any of the above-mentioned harmonic practices, by bitonality, atonality, and as a result of clashes of independent contrapuntal lines in 20th-century counterpoint.

Modern Counterpoint. One of the most significant developments of the 20th century is the revival of interest in polyphonic writing, an attribute of the neoclassical tendencies of the present. Baroque contrapuntal forms are again employed (fugue, canon, cantus firmus), but with the linear freedom allowed by modern harmonic concepts. Greater attention is given to the melodic contour of lines, the linear aspect, than to harmonic effects. Perhaps the two most important names in this field of development are Schönberg and Hindemith. A recent example of Hindemith's counterpoint is to be seen in his *Ludus Tonalis* for piano.

Meter and Rhythm. The 20th-century composers have exploited the field of rhythm and meter. In general, the characteristics of modern rhythm are: (1) greater complexity of rhythmic structure, (2) greater variety of rhythmic patterns, and (3) greater elasticity of rhythm.

NEW METRIC SCHEMES. There is a prominence of new metric schemes in 20th-century music. Time signatures such as five-eight, seven-eight, and ten-eight are to be found. Also, by use of accents an eight-eight measure may consist of irregular accents: 3 3 2 (rumba), 3 2 3, 2 3 3, etc. Various metric schemes are sometimes combined to produce *polyrhythmic* music or, more correctly, *polymetric* music (e.g., the three-four in one part against four-four in another part at the same time).

NONMETRIC MUSIC. A revolt against the monotony of incessantly recurrent measures of equal length is definitely manifest in the 20th century, sometimes expressed aptly by the phrase "breaking down the tyranny of the bar line." A return to the free nonmetric rhythms of plainsong was sought through several means: (1) abolishing the bar line altogether (not practical for ensemble music), (2) frequent change of time signatures, and (3) use of accent marks and ties across the bar line.

Melody. On the whole, melodic style has undergone less radical change than that occurring in other elements. Importance of melody ranges from its paramount function in polyphonic music to a relatively few instances where it is insignificant or even absent (Honegger's *Pacific 231* and Mossolov's *Iron Foundry*). Perhaps the most notable feature of modern melodic style is a tendency toward more extreme *angularity* (use of wide interval skips in the melodic line). A melodic style that might be termed dissonant is not uncommon (i.e., a melody in which there are numerous skips of dissonant intervals—major sevenths, minor ninths, diminished and augmented octaves, etc.). Still another characteristic of much 20th-century melodic material is the use of brief motives, or fragmentary melody, rather than a continuous melodic line. Of course, melodic style is also affected by such trends as neomodality, whole-tone scale, twelve-tone technique, etc.

Form. No essentially new forms as such have developed in the first half of the 20th century. Treatment of formal structures is even freer than in the 19th century. On the other hand, formal structures generally show a definite trend toward simplicity and clarity. This is another attribute of the neoclassical trends of the present. Formal clarity is achieved by a general shortening of length of compositions, by elimination of nonessentials, and by a more economic use of materials.

CHAPTER XXX

20th-Century Composers

France

General Considerations. The 20th-century revolution in music begins in France. Impressionism is the point of departure from German romanticism. French innovations were largely in the field of harmony and orchestration. Instrumental music became more important to French music than it was in the 19th century.

Debussy and Impressionism. Claude Debussy (1862–1918) identified himself with the impressionist movement in French art and produced a highly original style. His innovations became the tools of impressionist technique.

STYLE. Impressionism in music is characterized by the following devices and elements: (1) the use of neomodality, (2) the use of triads without thirds (i.e., open fifths), (3) the use of parallelism, (4) new chord progressions, (5) the whole-tone scale, (6) extensive use of ninth chords, (7) general vagueness of form, (8) free rhythm and less prominence of bar-line regularity, (9) long, flowing melodic lines, (10) the use of pseudo-Oriental and Spanish color effects, and (11) in piano music a special effect by simultaneously using the extreme registers of the instrument.

MEDIA. Debussy's principal fields are piano music (mostly free preludes and descriptive pieces), orchestral works (tone poems and impressionistic suites), songs, an impressionistic opera *Pelléas et Mélisande,* and an impressionistic choral work, *La Damoiselle élue.*

Ravel. Maurice Ravel (1875–1937) combined impressionistic technique with his own individual traits. He is considered by many authorities to be the most important French composer of the first half of the 20th century.

STYLE. His style consists of (1) all impressionistic devices, but less whole-tone scale, and more use of the eleventh chord than Debussy, (2) greater clarity and simplicity of form, (3) important development of orchestral color, Ravel being one of the greatest orchestrators the 20th century has yet produced, (4) prevalent use of Spanish rhythms, harmony, and color, (5) a sparing use of dissonance, (6) fondness for baroque forms and styles (derived from Couperin, Rameau, etc.), and (7) a sparing use of polytonality.

MEDIA. Ravel wrote orchestral music of all sorts, piano music and piano concertos, chamber music, and the ballet *Daphnis et Chloé*.

Roussel. Albert Roussel (1869–1937) was, on the whole, more progressive from a 20th-century point of view than Ravel.

STYLE. Roussel's style is eclectic, consisting of impressionistic and contrapuntal elements, and an apparent influence of Stravinsky. Strong Oriental flavor is apparent, probably acquired from his visits to the East when he served in the French navy. After 1910 harmonic dissonance and contrapuntal elements became more prominent in his music.

MEDIA. Roussel wrote an Oriental opera-ballet *Padmavati,* three symphonic poems entitled *Évocations,* considerable chamber music, and songs.

Eric Satie. Eric Satie (1866–1925) is noted primarily for his humorous satire against musicians and people taking music too seriously. He used grotesque titles (*Pieces in the Form of a Pear, Unpleasant Glances,* etc.) He made early uses of polytonality and atonality, although these are not consistent factors in his style. Satie was a strong influence upon the group of French composers known as "Les Six." His works are mostly piano pieces. He also wrote some orchestral music, ballet music, and songs.

"Les Six." A group of six French musicians came into prominence in the 1920's as champions of modern French composition. They are Milhaud, Honegger, Poulenc, Auric, Durey, and Tailleferre. Eric Satie was the leader (although not a member) and Jean Cocteau, a critic, was the literary spokesman of the group. Harmonic modernism, polytonality, and jazz influences are the chief attributes of their style.

Darius Milhaud. Darius Milhaud (1892–   ) is perhaps the most prominent of "Les Six." He now resides in the United States (Mills College, California).

STYLE. Milhaud's style is characterized by (1) influence of American jazz and South American rhythms, (2) polytonality, (3) polyharmonic style, (4) influence of Stravinsky primitivism (*La Création du monde*), and (5) certain aspects of neoclassicism.

WORKS. Milhaud has written much theater music (incidental music, ballet, opera, etc.), orchestral pieces, symphonies, a comic ballet *Le Boeuf sur le toit* which makes use of South American and United States dance rhythms, and a ballet *La Création du monde* in which American blues style is in evidence (1923—before the Gershwin *Rhapsody in Blue*).

Arthur Honegger. Although Swiss by birth, Arthur Honegger (1892–   ) belongs to "Les Six" and is the only other prominent composer of the group.

STYLE. The linear influence of Schönberg is evident, although Honegger does not employ the twelve-tone system. His music is often polytonal with the resulting dissonant harmonies.

WORKS. Honegger wrote theater music, ballets, incidental music, and orchestral works. He is principally noted for his symphonic work *Pacific 231* (1923) and a modern oratorio *Le roi David* (1923).

Other Composers of Modern French School. There is a long list of contemporary French composers whose work is less prominent or less known because of its recency. The principal ones are: Paul Dukas, who is known principally for his amazingly modern orchestral work written in 1897 *L'Apprenti sorcier* ("The Sorcerer's Apprentice"), Henri Rabaud, Florent Schmitt, Charles Koechlin, Jean Roger-Ducasse, Jacques Ibert, Jean Françaix, and Edgar Varèse. The latter, now in the United States, is listed again under American composers (see page 207).

Russia

General Considerations. Russia claims an important share of the credit for breaking away from 19th-century romanticism. The growing momentum of Russian nationalism was largely responsible for this. The general importance of music in Russia has grown in approximately the same proportions as it has in the United States in the 20th century. Russian style is strongly colored by folk music, and Russian composers have made important innovations in orchestration and in harmony. Under the regime of the U.S.S.R. there is a notable increase in the interest in music for the public, the proletariat, which lessens the breach between the composer and his musical public. The Russians have also been the leaders in the important 20th-century field of ballet.

Moussorgsky and Rimsky-Korsakov. The threshold of modernism in Russia is reached by Moussorgsky (1835–1881) and Rimsky-Korsakov (1844–1908), who are the most important of "The Five" in breaking away from 19th-century romanticism. Although much of their music is basically romantic, strong individuality and strong nationalistic tendencies are important factors in their styles. Rimsky-Korsakov's brilliant and colorful orchestration is his chief contribution to modernism. He wrote operas, symphonic works of which *Scheherazade* is the most famous, and a textbook on orchestration. Moussorgsky employed bold, individualistic harmony. His principal work is the opera *Boris Godunov*. He also made important contributions to song literature.

Alexander Scriabin. Alexander Scriabin (1872–1915) may be considered as one of the pioneers in the radical advances in modernism.

STYLE. Scriabin's principal innovation was the use of chords built on fourths and especially the "mystic chord" (e.g., C–F♯–B♭–E–A–D) which he used in *Poem of Ecstasy* (1908) and from then on. His music shows a transition from romantic styles (influence of Chopin, Liszt, and Wagner in early works), through impressionism, which influences most of his middle and later works, to a more individualistic and more radical style. His music in general is highly colored with rich harmonic and orchestral complexities, although in his later works the limitation to chords built in fourths creates a monotony of style. Mysticism played a prominent part in most of his music.

WORKS. Scriabin is noted primarily for his two orchestral poems, *Poem of Ecstasy* and *Prometheus, Poem of Fire,* and a large quantity of piano music.

Igor Stravinsky. To many a layman the name of Igor Stravinsky (1882–   ) is synonymous with modern music. There is perhaps a good deal of justification for this in view of the tremendous impact his music had on the musical world from about 1910. His music of that time represents most of the characteristics of revolt against romanticism.

STYLE. Two rather sharply defined periods in his music may be noted: (1) a style best described as *dynamism* until about 1920, and (2) neoclassicism from 1920 to the present.

a. *Dynamistic Style.* Prior to about 1920 Stravinsky's music shows a strongly progressive trend consisting of (1) brilliant, modern orchestration, including a new percussive use of the piano, (2) highly dissonant harmony, (3) polytonality, (4) strongly percussive rhythms, (5) frequent change of time signature or accentuation on odd parts of a measure, and (6) little emphasis upon melodic creation.

b. *Neoclassical Style.* From about 1920 Stravinsky's style is characterized by (1) simplification of texture, (2) economy of orchestration, (3) development of a more contrapuntal style, (4) less extreme harmonies and more conventional tonality, and (5) a greater clarity of form.

WORKS. Stravinsky is most widely known for his famous ballet music, but he has written highly successful music in various other media.

a. *Dynamistic Period.* His principal works in the first period are *Fireworks* (1908), written for the wedding of Rimsky-Korsakov's daughter; *L'Oiseau de feu* ("Firebird," 1910), a ballet showing the influence of his teacher, Rimsky-Korsakov; *Petroushka* (1911); *Sacre du printemps* ("Rite of Spring," 1913); and *Les Noces* (1918), which shows the beginning of a departure from the dynamistic style.

b. *Neoclassical Works.* Stravinsky's principal works since 1918 are *Histoire du soldat* (1918); *Pulcinella* (1919), based on themes and styles from Pergolesi; *Octet* for wind instruments (1923); *Symphonie des psaumes* ("Symphony of Psalms," 1930) for chorus and orchestra; *Oedipus-Rex* (1927), an opera-oratorio; *Apollon Musagètes* (1927); *Le Baiser de la fée* (1928), a ballet based upon themes of Tschaikovsky; and *Jeu de cartes* ("Card Party," 1936), called a "Ballet in Three Deals." Most of Stravinsky's ballet music has been rearranged in suite form for concert performance.

Serge Prokofiev. No other modern Russian composer has had the immediate popular appeal accorded to the music of Serge Prokofiev (1891–   ).

STYLE. Prokofiev's very individualistic and colorful style may be summed up as follows: (1) In general it is objective. (2) It is neoclassical in clarity of form and texture. (3) Counterpoint is used effectively but sparingly. (4) He is fond of abrupt and remote key changes (multitonality), and he uses some bitonality. (5) His melodic style is either angular or else diatonic, flowing, and cantabile. (6) He uses mostly a regular four-four meter, and regular periodic rhythms. (7) His harmonic style is acid, dissonant, but not excessively so. (8) His music is characteristically witty and humorous.

WORKS. Prokofiev has written (and played in concert) much piano music, orchestral works—perhaps the best known of which is the *Classical Symphony*—, a symphonic fairy tale entitled *Peter and the Wolf* (1936), violin and piano concertos, ballet music (*Chout*), an opera (*Love for Three Oranges*), and considerable quantities of chamber music.

Dmitri Shostakovitch. The Russian composer who claims first place in world popularity today is Dmitri Shostakovitch (1906–   ). Perhaps more than any other Russian he represents the point of view of Soviet Russia.

STYLE. Although his music is popular and represents the Soviet point of view, it is at the same time highly individualistic. It is characterized by the following: (1) objectivity, (2) a denial of the mystic and the somber romantic, (3) the use of 20th-century subjects, satirical treatment (e.g., the ballet *The Golden Age,* a satire on capitalism), (4) use of conventional symphonic form with the scherzo as the second movement, (5) reversing the order of themes in the recapitulation of sonata-allegro form, (6) the use of duple time (triple time is often in minor keys and a waltz caricature), (7) a favorite rhythmic figure: eighth note followed by two sixteenth notes (♪♫), (8) highly rhythmic first subjects that are essentially diatonic but with chromatic embellishment, (9) angularity of thematic material, (10) sudden modulations, (11) individualized instrumentation, (12) division of strings and special effects (e.g., use of glissando), (13) exploitation of high and low registers, (14) independent role of percussion (e.g., timpani solo), (15) use of piano in orchestral scores, (16) use of inverted pedal point: tremolo in high strings, (17) extensive use of scale runs, and (18) an individualistic piano style: percussive and characterized by extreme registers.

WORKS. Shostakovitch has written important works in nearly all media. His principal contributions are in the fields of symphony, opera, and ballet. His best known works are *The Nose* (1929), an opera after Gogol; *The Golden Age* (1930); an opera, *Lady Macbeth of the District of Mzensk* (1934); 8 symphonies, the most popular of which are the first, and the fifth through the eighth; a suite for jazz orchestra. He also reorchestrated Moussorgsky's *Boris Godunov*.

Choral and Religious Music. During the late 19th and first half of the 20th centuries much fine choral music has been written in Russia. Significant activity in the field of choral music has been given impetus by the famous Russian choral societies (Don Cossack choirs), and by the important emphasis on choral music in the Greek Orthodox Church. Russian church music has a profound religious atmosphere about it, reminiscent of the *a cappella* style of Renaissance church music. The principal composers are Alexander Archangelsky (1846-1924), Alexander Kastalsky (1856-1926), and Alexander Grechaninov (1864-   ).

Other 20th-Century Russian Composers. A large school of Russian composers has grown up in the first half of the 20th century. Their works are on the whole little known outside of Russia. The most important of these are Myaskovsky, Glazunov, Glière, Ippolitov-Ivanov, Vassilenko, Tcherpnin, Rebikov, and Mossolov.

Austria and Germany

General Considerations. There has been a notable decline of creative music in Germany in the first half of the 20th century, because Germany was preoccupied with military aggression and because cultural development was not an essential part of the Nazi regime. Important innovations have come from Austria in the development of atonality.

Schönberg and Atonality. Certainly one of the most influential figures of the 20th century is Arnold Schönberg (1874–   ). Although his music has had no general popularity, it has had, nevertheless, a considerable influence upon composition style and technique in general. Schönberg's early works are clearly in a post-Wagnerian style, showing influence of Mahler (*Verklärte Nacht*). In the first decade of the 20th century Schönberg shows definite tendencies toward atonal music (e.g., *Gurre-Lieder*).

THE TWELVE-TONE SYSTEM. The *twelve-tone system* devised by Schönberg is a technical means of arriving at atonality. Its basic assumption is that there is absolute tonal equality of all twelve tones within the octave. All suggestion of tonality must at all times be avoided. The thematic basis of a composition in the twelve-tone system is the *tone row*. It is a theme constructed of the twelve different tones into which an octave is divided. No tone may be repeated in a given voice until all twelve tones have been sounded. The tone row does not have to stay within the limits of one octave. The basic tone row is subject to infinite rhythmic changes. Subsequent statements of the theme may be melodically altered by inversion, complete retrograde statement (the entire theme played backwards), or retrograde by 2, 3, or 4 (e.g., retrograde by 2 would mean playing the original tone row in the order of tones 2 1 4 3 6 5, etc.). Further limitation of the tone row is that at no time must there be a suggestion of a triad or any tonal relationship.

SCHÖNBERG STYLE. Other elements of Schönberg's style, most of which result from the twelve-tone system, are: (1) extreme angularity of melodic line, (2) skips of dissonant intervals (melodic dissonance), (3) formal obscurity, (4) extreme use of dissonance (no consonance is permitted because it suggests tonality), (5) *Sprechstimme* employed in vocal music (half-sung, half-spoken texts), and (6) a fondness for morbid subjects (*Pierrot lunaire*).

CRITICISMS OF SCHÖNBERG SYSTEM. In its attempt to get away from all conventional practices in music, the twelve-tone system is aesthetically a negative rather than a positive art. It is a negation of tonality, of harmonic progression, of consonance, and of formal clarity, without sufficient positive elements to replace these factors. The system of tone rows does give a certain obscure unity to the music, but that unity is theoretical rather than practical since even the trained musician cannot grasp the construction on hearing the music (close, technical analysis of the score is necessary to determine what is going on). And because of the arbitrary and severe limitations of the system, twelve-tone music has an objectionable sameness about it.

PRINCIPAL SCHÖNBERG WORKS. The principal works by Schönberg are: *Verklärte Nacht* ("Transfigured Night," 1899), a neoromantic symphonic poem; *Gurre-Lieder* (completed 1911), for soloists, orchestra, and chorus; *Die hängenden Gärten,* a song cycle; *Pierrot lunaire* (1912), a work for Sprechstimme and five instruments the combinations of which vary with each setting of twenty-one verses by Albert Giraud; numerous piano works, orchestral works, concertos, and songs.

Other Composers of the Viennese School. Schönberg disciples of atonality and the twelve-tone technique are referred to as the Viennese School. They have created a considerable following by teaching, performing, and composing in various parts of the world. They are Anton von Webern (1883–1946), who has written songs, chamber music, and some orchestral works; Alban Berg (1885–1935), who is noted primarily for his atonal opera *Wozzek;* Ernst Křenek (1900–), now in the United States, noted chiefly for his jazz opera *Jonny spielt auf* (1927); and Egon Wellesz (1885–), now in England, who has written opera, ballet, orchestral works, and songs.

Richard Strauss. The music of Richard Strauss (1864–) belongs to the late 19th century and to the first two decades of the 20th century. Although he is still living, his musical productivity has been negligible during the past thirty years.

STYLE. His style may be broadly classified as neoromantic because of his use of enormous orchestras and massive though brilliant and colorful orchestration. His harmonic and melodic style is 20th century although not as extreme as that of Schönberg and Stravinsky.

WORKS. Strauss's orchestral works consist chiefly of symphonic poems (see page 161). In addition he has written operas (*Salome, Der Rosenkavalier, Elektra,* and *Die Frau ohne Schatten*). He has also contributed notably to late romantic song literature.

Paul Hindemith. The contributions of Paul Hindemith (1895–   ) to modernism are neoclassical modern counterpoint and Gebrauchs-musik. He is without doubt one of the foremost composers of the first half of the 20th century.

STYLE. The style of Hindemith is (1) essentially contrapuntal, (2) harmonically dissonant as a result of linear independence, (3) often melodically angular with dissonant skips, (4) essentially tonal in that it begins and ends in a key, but tonality is often ob-scured and remote from the starting point, (5) neoclassical in its economy of material and clarity of texture.

WORKS. The principal works by Hindemith are *Cardillac* (1926), an opera; *Neues vom Tage* (1929), an opera; *Das Marienleben* (1924), a song cycle; *Mathis der Maler* (1934), an opera, arranged as a symphonic suite; a considerable quantity of chamber music; *Plöner Musiktag,* a collection of festival concert pieces (Gebrauchs-musik); and a recent collection of preludes and contrapuntal pieces for piano entitled *Ludus Tonalis* (1944).

Ernest Bloch. Ernest Bloch (1880–   ) is a native Swiss, but his training and style are German. He is now a resident of the United States. He is the most important modern composer of Jewish music.

STYLE. His style is notable for free rhythmic elements and frequent changes of meter. His forms are free, rhapsodic, and do not adhere to conventional symphonic structures. There is a decided romantic quality to most of his music.

WORKS. His principal works are *Trois poèmes juifs* (1913), a sym-phonic poem; *Israel,* a symphony with voices; *Jézabel,* an opera; a *Concerto grosso* for string orchestra and piano (1925); and numerous other symphonic works and chamber music.

Ernst Toch. Another composer of modern Germany (now residing in the United States) is Ernst Toch (1887–   ). He has written principally in chamber music media and also motion-picture music (Hollywood).

England

General Considerations. England, which had not been among the leading musical nations since the Elizabethan era, has come to the fore in the 20th century. Although England has contributed no pioneers in 20th-century innovations, she has produced some top-rank composers. There has been a rise of interest in national music and an increased interest in the writing of symphonic music.

Cecil Sharp. Development of interest in English music is headed by the name of Cecil Sharp (1859–1924), who collected over 2800 folk songs.

Ralph Vaughan Williams. Probably the most important English composer of the first half of the 20th century is Vaughan Williams (1872–   ).

STYLE. The principal elements of his style are: (1) extensive use of neomodality (e.g., *Fantasy on a Theme of Thomas Tallis*), (2) extensive use of English folk song material and style, (3) some parallelism, (4) occasional cross-relations, and (5) some extensive and extreme dissonance.

WORKS. He has written a considerable amount of choral music; *A Sea Symphony* for soprano and baritone soloists, chorus, and orchestra; orchestral works; symphonies, including the *London Symphony;* concertos; chamber music (*On Wenlock Edge* for tenor solo, string quartet, and piano); and *Fantasy on a Theme of Thomas Tallis* for string orchestra.

Gustave Holst. The works of Gustave Holst (1874–1934) are not generally known outside England although he wrote much fine music in a 20th-century style.

STYLE. Holst adopted 20th-century idiom, but he is also an individualist. He has great melodic inventiveness. Between 1907 and 1912 he showed a fondness for Sanskrit texts. He has a penchant for quasi-ostinato treatment and reiterated motives. He also uses odd metric schemes (five-four, seven-four, etc.) and occasionally does away with the bar line. He seems to have a proclivity for mysticism in music.

WORKS. His most famous work is a symphonic suite entitled *The*

Planets. He made considerable contribution to military band music. He wrote some unconventional sacred and secular choral music, and made numerous folk song arrangements.

Frederick Delius. Frederick Delius (1863–1934) was not a progressive modernist, nor was he strongly nationalistic in his style.

STYLE. Delius' style is eclectic, consisting of various influences: (1) American Negro, from his residence in Florida as an orange planter, (2) French impressionism, (3) German romanticism from studies in Leipzig, and (4) Scandinavian from his travels in the north. Of all these influences impressionism seems to be the most prominent and the most general in his music.

WORKS. Delius wrote opera (*A Village Romeo and Juliet, Fennimore and Gerda*); numerous symphonic poems (*Brigg Fair, In a Summer Garden,* etc.); choral works such as *Sea-Drift* for baritone solo, chorus, and orchestra; and a few songs and some chamber music.

Other 20th-Century English Composers. Granville Bantok (1868–1946) writes in a pseudo-Oriental style for orchestra and for chorus. *Omar Khayyám* is a work for soloists, chorus, and orchestra. Cyril Scott (1879–   ) is impressionist and Oriental in his style. He has written music in various media, principally piano. John Ireland (1879–   ) is somewhat modern and dissonant in style. He has written chamber music and piano music and some orchestral works. Frank Bridge (1879–1941) has written chiefly chamber music. Arnold Bax (1883–   ) writes in a romantic-impressionistic style. He has written 6 symphonies, chamber music, and piano works. Arthur Bliss (1891–   ) shows influences of Ravel and of Stravinsky. He has written in various media. Constant Lambert (1905–   ) is a modern English composer, conductor, and critic. His principal works are a ballet (*Pomona,* 1927); a work for chorus, piano solo, and orchestra, making use of jazz idiom (*Rio Grande,* 1929); and *Music for Orchestra*. Later works have been written for piano, a piano concerto, and 8 Chinese songs. Benjamin Britten (1913–   ), another of the younger English composers, has written in all media, considerable music for films, stage, and radio.

Italy

General Considerations. Not since the 17th century has Italy played a significant role in the development of instrumental music. This is still true in the 20th century. A continued interest in romantic opera overshadows any serious development in instrumental music or modern idiom. Italy has had a revival of interest in its own musical history and has made some substantial musicological contributions.

Ferruccio Busoni. One of the first and most important champions of 18th-century ideals in the modern period is Ferruccio Busoni (1866–1924). As teacher, composer, pianist, critic, editor, and arranger he greatly influenced musical thought both at home and abroad. His own music shows originality of ideas though it is basically romantic.

Ottorino Respighi. One of Italy's foremost modernists is Ottorino Respighi (1879–1936), who adopted modern style with a certain amount of individuality.

STYLE. Respighi shows attention to structural design. He uses modern orchestral color. In general his style is slightly impressionistic and sensuous. He made some use of plainsong in his works (*Gregorian Concerto*).

WORKS. Respighi is known chiefly for his orchestral works: *The Fountains of Rome* (1916) and *The Pines of Rome* (1924). In addition he wrote a considerable number of operas, songs, and chamber works.

Francesco Malipiero. Although his music is heard little outside of Italy, Francesco Malipiero (1882–   ) is undoubtedly one of the strongest composers in that country. He has produced numerous orchestral works and operas in a modern idiom for which he has written his own libretti. He has also written some fine religious choral music. In general his is a neoclassicism derived from Italian baroque styles and forms. In addition to composition he has been one of the leaders in revival of interest in old Italian music. He edited the complete works of Monteverdi.

Alfredo Casella. The most progressive of modern Italian composers is Alfredo Casella (1883–   ). He has ventured into atonal music and extremities of dissonances not generally favored by Italians.

Nevertheless, his style is basically Italian. He has shown marked neoclassical tendencies in the use of concerto grosso technique and other Italian baroque elements (*Scarlattiana,* 1926). His fields of activity are opera, orchestra, chamber music, and piano works.

Ildebrando Pizzetti. The tradition of Italian opera has been carried on largely by the modern-styled works of Ildebrando Pizzetti (1880–   ). His operas include *Fedra* (1915), *Debora e Jael* (1922), *Fra Gherardo* (1931), *Lo Straniero* (1930), *Orseolo* (1933), and a scenic oratorio *La Rappresentazione di Abramo e Isacco* (1928).

Other 20th-Century Italian Composers. Less well-known composers in modern Italy are Alfano, Davico, Lualdi, Mule, Pick-Mangiagalli, Sinigaglia, Tommasini, Labroca, Massarani, Mortari, Pilati, and Rieti.

Hungary

General Considerations. Although Hungarian nationalism was reflected in the 19th century by the works of Franz Liszt (*Hungarian Rhapsodies*) and the little known nationalist operas of Ferenc Erkel (1810–1893), it was not until the 20th century that Hungarian music received widespread acclaim. Hungarian composers are among the most important modernists.

Béla Bartók. One of the top-ranking names in progressive modern music as well as one of the principal leaders of Hungarian nationalism is Béla Bartók (1881–1945). He collected more than 6000 folk songs of Magyar, Slovac, and Roumanian origin, and he made extensive studies of this music.

STYLE. Bartók's music is highly colored by Hungarian folk style, with some of his thematic material drawn directly from folk music. But his style is also strongly personal and original. His early works show influence of Brahms, then of impressionism. Influence of Schönberg and Stravinsky can also be traced in his later music. Neoclassicism affects his style to some degree (e.g., the contrapuntal treatment in the first piano concerto and in much of the piano music). The most arresting features of his style are rhythms which are percussive, dynamic, and often intricate as he draws from Hungarian dance patterns. He is also progressive in his use of polytonal harmony and bitter dissonance. His harmonic style also shows influence of Hungarian modality. Bartók has a good sense of formal structure.

WORKS. Bartók wrote in a variety of media: orchestral works, concertos, piano music, chamber music, and choral works. Special mention should be made of a collection of graded piano pieces called *Mikrokosmos,* which pieces reveal most aspects of Bartók's modern Hungarian style.

Ernst Dohnányi. The music of Ernst Dohnányi (1877–   ) is more conservative and less nationalistic than that of Bartók and Kodály. He is individual and charming in his style, which is more 19th-century than 20th-century. He has written works for orchestra, chamber music, and piano music.

Zoltán Kodály. Zoltán Kodály (1882–   ) is equally important with Bartók in the collection of Hungarian folk music, and of exploiting it in his music.

STYLE. Kodály's style is strongly Hungarian in flavor. He has an exceptional melodic gift, particularly in a lyric style. Conciseness of expression and a fondness for the picturesque are characteristic of his music.

WORKS. Kodály's chamber music is his most important contribution to modern literature. He has also written a humorous folk opera *Háry János,* and an important choral work *Psalmus Hungaricus.*

Paul Kadosa. Paul Kadosa (1903–   ), a younger Hungarian composer, has written numerous works for piano, concertos, and chamber music. He is a pupil of Kodály.

Spain

General Considerations. Twentieth-century Spanish music is highly colored by national style. There is little ultramodern music; most of it is basically romantic or impressionistic. As in Italy, there has been an awakening of interest in nationalism and in Spanish music of the past.

Manuel de Falla. The most important 20th-century composer in Spain is Manuel de Falla (1876–1946).

STYLE. De Falla does not use actual folk tunes in his music, but the Spanish folk element is very pronounced. He has assimilated the styles of various regions, Catalonia, Andalusia, etc. A characteristic melodic pattern of the Andalusian cadence is frequently used (e.g., A G F E or A G♯ F E). There is prominence of the Phrygian mode. Some tonal obscurity is to be found in his music which, as a rule, is tonal. De Falla frequently modulates to a key a minor third lower than the tonic in the final cadence. Rhythm is highly important in De Falla's music. In addition to Spanish rhythmic patterns he uses polyrhythm and considerable rhythmic complexity. His melodies usually have a narrow range. His orchestral style is derived from the modern French school.

WORKS. De Falla has written *La Vida breva,* a lyric drama; *El Sombrero de tres pecos* ("The Three-cornered Hat"), a ballet, arranged as orchestral suite; *Noches en los jardines de España* ("Nights in the Gardens of Spain"), a work for piano and orchestra; a *Harpsichord Concerto* (harpsichord, flute, oboe, clarinet, violin, and cello, 1926); and considerable amounts of chamber music, piano music, and songs.

Felipe Pedrell. The leading Spanish musicologist is Felipe Pedrell (1841–1922). Not only did he make important investigations of Spanish folk music, but he was responsible for editing and bringing out modern publications of the works of Victoria, Morales, Milan, and others.

Other Spanish Composers. Isaac Albéniz (1860–1909) wrote music in a 19-century romantic style which is also impressionistic. He made prominent use of Andalusian elements. His best-known work is the *Iberian Suite* for orchestra. He wrote much piano music. Enrique Granados (1867–1916) also belongs in style to the 19th century in addition to his music being typically Spanish. His best-known opera is *Goyescas* (1916), based upon an earlier set of piano pieces. He is noted chiefly for his piano music. Two famous Spanish musicians should be mentioned. One is Andreas Segovia (1894–   ), guitarist, who in addition to making world tours has arranged much music for guitar. Pablo Casals (1876–   ) is a world-famous cellist and a conductor.

Finland

Jean Sibelius. The works of Jean Sibelius (1865–   ) have had a tremendous popularity in the United States; they are less popular in Europe. Sibelius may be considered as one of the great composers of the 20th century.

STYLE. Although he makes no direct use of Finnish folk music, his style is strongly nationalistic. His music is basically romantic in its subjective nature and its programmatic proclivity. Sibelius is highly individualistic, and has not followed the course of 20th-century innovations in music. Details of his style are: (1) He makes use of short motives rather than extended melodic material, although examples of the latter are also to be found. (2) He is fond of ostinato treatment, an incessant reiteration of a short theme or motive. (3) His melodies seem to gravitate around the third degree of the scale. (4) His harmonies are characteristically stark, although not extremely dissonant. (5) A favorite device is the use of sudden crescendos, usually in brass, followed by abrupt rest. (6) He makes prominent use of the timpani. (7) His symphonies and tone poems show unusual formal sense, seldom conforming to strict symphonic structures. (8) Over all his music there is a brooding melancholy.

Other Finnish Composers. Selim Palmgren (1878–   ) is a pianist and impressionist composer who has written songs and much piano music. Armas Jaernfelt (1869–   ) is a Finnish conductor who has written symphonic overtures, suites, and symphonic poems.

Argentina

General Considerations. The 20th century has seen a notable increase of interest in the music of Latin American countries and the rise of national developments. This has resulted in a general development of music education and musical organizations and of large numbers of native composers. Latin American styles, as a rule, have a European basis with more or less strong infusion of indigenous traits.

Alberto Williams. The most important figure in present-day Argentine music is Alberto Williams (1862–   ). He is the director of the Conservatory of Buenos Aires which he founded in 1893. His style is generally a mixture of European and national traits. He is a prolific composer, having written 9 symphonies, symphonic poems, concerto overtures, piano pieces, songs to his own texts, choral works, chamber music, and treatises on music.

Other Argentine Composers. Other 20th-century Argentine composers are Juan Castro, José Castro, Siccardi, Gianneo, Jacobo Ficher, and Juan Paz (a radical exponent of the twelve-tone system). Composers of opera are: Boero (*El Matrero*), Rogatis, Espoile, Casella. Collections and arrangements of Argentine folk music have been made by Beltrame, Chazarreta, Forte, Vegi, and Wilkes.

Brazil

General Considerations. Brazilian music is composed of Portuguese, some Spanish, African, and native Indian elements. Of these the African element seems to be the strongest. Brazilian music was strongly influenced by early Jesuit organizations, which brought European culture to that country.

19th-Century Brazilian Music. Brazilian music had a considerable growth in the 19th century. The principal composers of this period are: José Garcia (1767–1830), a composer of religious music; Francisco Manoel (1795–1865), the composer of the Brazilian national anthem and the founder of the Conservatory of Rio de Janeiro (1841); Carlos Gomes (1836–1896), the most famous Brazilian opera composer (*Il Guarany*); Leopold Miguez (1850–1902), who wrote the first symphonies in Brazil.

Heitor Villa-Lobos. The most prominent of all Latin American composers today is Heitor Villa-Lobos (1881–   ). He is a prolific composer, having produced some 1400 works to date. His style is somewhat uneven but it is highly original and national. He is the most prominent promoter of public school music in Brazil. His works include all media. He has developed a new and original style of piano music. Well known are his *Chôros No. 8* for orchestra and *Chôros No. 10* for orchestra and chorus. His best-known symphonic works are *Amazonas* and *Dansas Africanas. Momo Precoce* is a work for piano and orchestra. A recent work is *Bachianas brasilieras,* which includes five suites for varied instrumental ensemble.

Other Contemporary Brazilian Composers. Prominent Brazilian nationalists are Itiberé (1846–1913) and Nazareth (1863–1934), particularly in popular music. Other contemporary moderns are: Braga (1868–   ), Fernândez (1897–   ), and Mignone.

Other Latin American Countries

Chile. José Zapiola (1804–1885) is the most important 19th-century Chilean composer. Chile has produced two outstanding composers of the 20th century. Humberto Allende (1885–   ) has written symphonic poems (*Escenas campesinas chilenas* and *La Voz de las calles; Tres tonadas* for soloists, chorus, and orchestra; *Tonadas de caracter popular chileno* for piano; and a violin concerto and chamber music. Domengo Santa Cruz Wilson (1899–   ) is active in various Chilean musical organizations. His style is distinctly modern with polytonal tendencies. He is also a teacher and a musicologist. His most important work is *Cinco poemas tragicos* for piano. He has written a considerable number of songs and chamber music.

Colombia. Guillermo Uribe-Holguín (1880–   ) is the leading Colombian composer. He has written numerous symphonic works, *300 Trozos en el sentimiento popular* for piano, a *Requiem* and other church music, and chamber music.

Peru. Daniel Alomias Robles (1871–1942) was one of the leading composers of Peru. He made numerous folk song collections and wrote symphonic poems, songs, piano pieces, and an opera *Illa-Cori.* Theodore Valcárcel (1902–1942) is known principally for a ballet-opera *Suray-Surita.* Younger Peruvian contemporaries are Málaga, Carpio, Verneuil, and De Silva.

Venezuela. Vicente Emilio Sojo (1887–   ) is the leading Venezuelan composer. He has written much church music, chamber music, choral works, songs, and collected and harmonized Venezuelan folk songs.

COMPOSERS 203

Mexico. Mexican music was at an early time influenced by Aztec culture and Spanish music, and later European training. Carlos Chávez (1899–   ) is the leading composer and conductor in modern Mexico. His work is directed strongly toward Mexican nationalist music and much of it has been performed in the United States. His principal works are: *Sinfonía India, Sinfonía de Antigona;* ballets *H.P.* ("Horsepower") and *Los Cuatro soles,* and *Energía* for small orchestra. Manuel Ponce (1886–   ) is noted for his piano work *Danzas mexicanas.* Julián Carrillo (1875–   ) is famous for his new system of composition called "Sonido 13" based upon further division of the octave (quarter tones, eighth tones, etc.). Silvestre Revueltas (1899–1940) wrote highly individual music touched by popular Mexican idiom. He wrote motion-picture music for the film *Redes* ("The Wave"), symphonic poems *Caminos, Cuanahuac, Esquinas,* and *Sensemaya* with chorus, several ballets, chamber music, and piano pieces. Younger Mexican composers are Sandi, Ayala, Moncayo, Contreras, and Galindo. Jiménez (1910–   ) has written much church music.

The United States

General Considerations. The United States has become in the 20th century one of the leading musical nations of the world. Although it has produced no top-ranking composers such as Stravinsky, Prokofiev, Hindemith, etc., it has nevertheless produced an amazing number of excellent composers. The notable growth of interest in the music of American composers is largely attributable to three things: (1) conductors including more and more American compositions on programs, (2) the establishing of composers' guilds and other organizations to foster native composition, and (3) the establishing of scholarships, prizes, and funds to encourage talent.

NATIONALISM IN THE UNITED STATES. There is no established nationalism as such in the United States; there is no indigenous American style. American music has no one style, but is rather a complexity of heterogeneous styles. There are several reasons for this.

a. *European Influence.* Strong traditions of European music have worked against an indigenous American style. The influx of European musicians, conductors, composers, and teachers in the 19th and early 20th centuries is in part responsible. Until comparatively recently there was a prevalent notion that musicians and composers had to be trained in Europe to acquire sound musicianship. The products of our excellent music schools and conservatories have now almost completely abolished this erroneous notion.

b. *Eclecticism*. Composers in the United States have been eclectic, following various musical innovations originating in Europe: impressionism, atonality, classicism, French school, etc.

c. *Individualism*. American individualism has also played an important part in the heterogeneous styles of this country; and it has worked against the development of a uniform national style.

d. *Scarcity of Native Folk Music*. Because the country is young and because it is a nation of heterogeneous peoples, the United States has no national folk music. Its place is in part supplied by: (1) composed songs such as the Stephen Foster melodies, (2) cowboy songs, (3) American Indian music (of little influence on American composition), and (4) Afro-American folk music, which has had the greatest influence upon American music in general.

JAZZ. The only truly American development has been that of jazz (see pages 174 ff.). This has greatly influenced the styles of composers both here and abroad. Although its influence has been widespread, however, jazz does not constitute an all-inclusive American style. It is only one of many factors.

American Symphony Orchestras. No small commentary upon the importance of music in the United States is the number and excellence of symphony orchestras in this country, in both respects far surpassing such organizations anywhere else in the world today.

American Composers. It is impossible to make a complete list here of all American composers of the first half of the 20th century. Furthermore, any attempt at a complete evaluation of styles and works is futile because they are constantly changing with the individual as well as in general trends, a fact equally true of other schools of the 20th century. Nevertheless, the following list, arranged chronologically according to year of birth, attempts to summarize the chief elements of style and the contributions of each composer in terms of the present point of view.

EDGAR STILLMAN KELLEY (1857–   ). Kelley, long associated with the department of composition at Cincinnati Conservatory, has written a variety of works for orchestra. The best known of these is *New England Symphony* (1913). He has also written incidental music, a comic operetta (*Puritania*), and some choral works of a romantic nature.

CHARLES LOEFFLER (1861–1935). Alsatian-born Charles Loeffler spent his creative life in the United States. His style is a combination of French and individualistic traits with little American influence to be seen. His style is on the whole quite conservative. He wrote orchestral works, choral music, chamber music, and songs.

FREDERICK CONVERSE (1871–1940). A pupil of John Knowles Paine at Harvard, Converse also taught and composed. He wrote operas, orchestral works, and is noted mostly for his symphonic poem *Flivver Ten Million* (1927).

HENRY HADLEY (1871–1937). Hadley was a prominent United States conductor (Seattle, San Francisco, New York Philharmonic), and a promoter of American music. His style is conservative. He wrote stage, orchestral, and choral works.

EDWARD BURLINGAME HILL (1872–   ). A pupil of John Knowles Paine, among others, Hill has taught music at Harvard since 1908 (now emeritus). In addition to being a composer of some esteem he is an authority on Russian and modern French music. He is not a progressive modernist, but his music has a pleasing individuality about it. His works, mostly for orchestra, have been performed by the Boston Symphony Orchestra. They include symphonies, symphonic poems (*Lilacs*), two sinfoniettas, and some chamber music.

CHARLES IVES (1874–   ). The music of Charles Ives has recently attracted considerable interest. He has a remarkable range of style. He is largely a self-taught amateur, writing music for his hobby. Early experiments before 1900 predate many of the innovations of Stravinsky, Schönberg, etc. He uses tone clusters, polyharmony, polyrhythm, strong dissonance, atonal passages, rapid metric changes, jazz rhythms, as well as some extremely conservative styles. He has written orchestral works, chamber music, some piano music (*Concord Sonata*), and numerous songs.

JOHN ALDEN CARPENTER (1876–   ). Carpenter has written numerous songs, orchestral works, and ballet music. He is best known for his ballet music *Skyscrapers* and *Adventures in a Perambulator*, both of which make use of ragtime and jazz idiom.

ERNEST SCHELLING (1876–1939). Schelling is noted primarily for his postwar orchestral work *Victory Ball* (1923) and for some piano music.

CARL RUGGLES (1876–   ). Numerous features make up the individualistic style of Carl Ruggles: (1) a sustained melodic line, (2) nonrepetition of theme until the tenth progression (tenth note), (3) avoidance of regular phrasing, (4) freedom of rhythm with practically no metric accent and with change of time signature, (5) extremely varied chordal material, (6) short, compact forms, and (7) a rhapsodic style not based upon development of thematic ideas. His principal works are an opera (*The Sunken Bell*) and several symphonic works (*Men and Angels, Men and Mountains, Portals*) and *Vox Clamans* for solo and chamber orchestra.

LOUIS GRUENBERG (1884–   ). Symphonic jazz is essayed in Gruenberg's *Jazz Suite* (1925) and *Daniel Jazz* (1923), a chamber work for tenor and 8 instruments. He has contributed to modern American opera with *Emperor Jones* (1932).

CHARLES T. GRIFFES (1884–1920). Griffes used a modified impressionistic style. He wrote songs, piano pieces, and a symphonic poem *The Pleasure Dome of Kubla Khan* (1920).

WALLINGFORD RIEGGER (1885–   ). The music of Riegger is eclectic in style. He shows a fondness for canonic and fugal forms. He uses atonality in his *Prelude and Fugue* for orchestra and organ. There is also an element of humor in much of his music. He has written orchestral works (*American Polonaise*), chamber orchestral works (*Dichotomy*), chamber music, and stage works.

DEEMS TAYLOR (1885–   ). Well known to the American public through his service as commentator on the New York Philharmonic broadcasts, as well as through his music, is Deems Taylor. His operas *The King's Henchman* and *Peter Ibbetson* have had numerous performances at the Metropolitan in New York. He is not an extreme modernist and his style shows certain marked Wagnerian tendencies.

EDGAR VARÈSE (1885–   ). French born, Edgar Varèse brought influence of the French school to American music. His style is acrid, has a certain hardness of line, is characterized by emphasis on percussion. He is apparently more interested in orchestral effects than in harmonic effects, although the latter are extremely modern in use of minor seconds, ninths, etc. He has made use of odd time signatures such as three-four and a half (i.e., adding half beats to a measure).

JOHN BECKER (1886–   ). Becker uses a neo-Palestrina technique with modern dissonances. He is an individual who does not follow fads of modernism, but also fights conservatism.

ADOLPH WEISS (1891–   ). Adolph Weiss is an avowed atonalist and one of the extreme modernists among American composers. In addition to playing bassoon with the New York Philharmonic and teaching, he has produced symphonic works (*American Life*), choral works, and chamber music.

DOUGLAS MOORE (1893–   ). As well as being a teacher (Columbia University) and author (*From Madrigal to Modern Music*), Douglas Moore has shown himself to be a composer of considerable talent. He has written principally orchestral and choral works (*Moby Dick* for orchestra and chorus), and an opera *The Devil and Daniel Webster* (1933).

BERNARD ROGERS (1893–   ). Rogers is one of the more progressive moderns teaching at Eastman. His symphonic works (*Adonais, To the Fallen, The Faithful,* and several symphonies) have been widely performed. He has also written works for chamber orchestra (*Rhapsody, Nocturne, Soliloquy,* etc.) and chamber and choral works.

WALTER PISTON (1894–   ). Walter Piston is professor of composition at Harvard University. He writes much near-atonal music. Vigorous rhythms are characteristic of his music. His thematic material makes notable use of augmented fourths and major sevenths. He studiously avoids tonic-dominant relations in his harmony. His music shows a high degree of craftsmanship and a facile technique. He has a directness of expression and a fondness for contrapuntal writing. He has written works for orchestra (symphonies and a violin concerto), for chorus (*Carnival Song* for male chorus and brass instruments), a varied quantity of fine chamber music, and a ballet *The Incredible Flutist.*

WILLIAM GRANT STILL (1895–   ). William Grant Still is the leading Negro composer in the United States. His chamber and orchestral works make extensive use of Negro themes and styles.

LEO SOWERBY. Leo Sowerby (1895–   ), who is not an extreme modernist, has written much church music and organ music, as well as orchestral and chamber music. He has made use of jazz idiom in a few works.

HOWARD HANSON (1896–   ). As head of the Eastman School of Music Howard Hanson is one of the foremost music educators of the country. Through his various important activities he has promoted American music perhaps more than any other one individual. He has written numerous highly successful works: several symphonic works, choral works (*Lament for Beowulf*), and opera (*Merry Mount*).

ROGER SESSIONS (1896–   ). Sessions teaches at Berkeley. In his attempt to be independent musically he has avoided any musical dogmas or "isms." He makes use of fractional repetition in his melodic lines, lending unity to long sustained melodies in slow tempo. He has employed polyrhythm (two-four against three-eight) for brief passages. His music is of considerable technical difficulty. Perhaps his best-known work is an orchestral suite *The Black Maskers.*

VIRGIL THOMSON (1896–   ). Virgil Thomson is music critic for the *New York Herald Tribune.* He has a gift for vocal declamation which makes English texts sound natural when sung. He strives for musical simplicity, against extreme modern complexities. He is noted mainly for his opera *Four Saints in Three Acts* on a text by Gertrude Stein, and his ballet *Filling Station.* He has written a large quantity of chamber music of all kinds, and some film music.

HENRY COWELL (1897–   ). Cowell might be called the No. 1 experimentalist in the United States. He is the author of a book called *New Musical Resources,* and until recently he was editor of *New Music.* He has experimented with numerous musical effects such as tone clusters, complex rhythms, pizzicato and glissando on piano strings, etc. He invented the "rhythmicon," an instrument to play any metric combination (e.g., 2's against 3's, 3's against 5's, etc., up to 16 notes in a group). His music shows a scientific combined with an artistic approach.

QUINCY PORTER (1897–   ). Porter's style is individual without being progressively modern. His principal orchestral work is the *Ukrainian Suite* for strings. His principal field of composition is chamber music. He was the director of the New England Conservatory; he now teaches at Yale University.

GEORGE GERSHWIN (1898–1937). George Gershwin represents the link between Tin Pan Alley and the concert stage. His Broadway successes are well known. He successfully applied jazz idiom to serious music in his famous *Rhapsody in Blue* and in his piano concertos. *Porgy and Bess* (1935) is an American jazz opera.

ROY HARRIS (1898–   ). Roy Harris has often been heralded as *the* American composer. This is highly erroneous because, even though he is certainly one of the leading American composers, his style no more than that of any other single composer can be labeled strictly American, or representative of American style. Harris' style reflects rugged individualism. He is not an extremist. His contrapuntal style is often forced. His thematic development is reminiscent of Beethoven. He makes use of unequal divisions of regular measure, and of odd meters (seven-eight, etc.). Upon occasion he introduces polytonality. He has written numerous orchestral works, choral works (*Symphony for Voices,* 1935), and chamber music.

RANDALL THOMPSON (1899–   ). Thompson has written a quantity of excellent choral music and some orchestral music. He writes in a modern polyphonic idiom.

GEORGE ANTHEIL (1900–   ). Antheil's music is sensational, shows some imitation of Stravinsky dynamism, exaggeration, and recently the use of Gebrauchsmusik and neoclassical trends.

AARON COPLAND (1900–   ). Copland is one of the leading protagonists of modern American music, which he has promoted through concert organization and numerous articles in the field of modern music. He has written music for radio, cinema, and theater, as well as large concert forms. He has made effective use of jazz idioms (*Music for the Theatre, Piano Concerto*), and has shown unusual ability in melodic creation.

OTTO LUENING (1900–   ). Luening is a composer, teacher, conductor, and flutist. He uses a dissonant modern style in his orchestral works and chamber music.

RUTH CRAWFORD (1901–   ). Ruth Crawford's music may best be described as a heterophonic style which features complete rhythmic, tonal, harmonic, and melodic independence of parts. She uses extreme polyrhythmic construction.

WILLIAM SCHUMAN (1910–   ). Although he is one of the younger American composers, William Schuman is today recognized as one of the leading composers. He employs a linear style with considerable contrapuntal imitation. He used parallelism of fourths and fifths in his music from 1937 to 1941. His harmonic style is important. It is based upon contrast between degrees of dissonance rather than between consonance and dissonance. He uses polytonality. His rhythms are extremely varied by shifting of metric bases and by accenting of off-beats. He uses instrumental choirs as separate blocks of color. He has assimilated jazz elements in his individualistic style. General traits are boldness, originality, and intensity of feeling. He has written much choral music, as well as string quartets and symphonies. He now heads the Julliard School of Music.

MORTON GOULD (1913–   ). Like Gershwin, Gould has made use of popular styles in serious music (*Chorale and Fugue in Jazz,* 1933). His harmonies are inclined to be sharply dissonant and his orchestration is brilliant and colorful.

HENRY BRANT (1914–   ). Brant is one of the younger composers of United States music. He has original ideas and original manner of saying them. He insists on the listener's using a score for better understanding of his music. He is the inventor of "oblique harmony," a scheme of harmonic relationships existing between the bass of one chord, the tenor of a second chord, the alto of a third chord, and the soprano of a fourth chord. He also originated a variation form of four parts with no specified instrumentation except that they be contrasting colors in which four themes are announced simultaneously and contrapuntally. Then all variations directly utilize one of the four themes.

YOUNGER AMERICAN COMPOSERS. Among the many promising American composers of a younger generation not already mentioned are: Samuel Barber (1910–   ), Leonard Bernstein (1918–   ), Paul Bowles (1911–   ), Paul Creston (1906–   ), David Diamond (1915–   ), Bernard Herrmann (1911–   ), Gail Kubik (1914–   ), Gian-Carlo Menotti (1911–   ), Paul Nordoff (1909–   ), Gardner Read (1913–   ).

Glossary

A CAPPELLA. Sung without accompaniment; i.e., chorus without instrumental support.

ACCENT. Emphasis or stress placed upon a tone.

AIR. A melody.

ANTIPHONAL. One choir answered by another choir.

ARIA. A song, usually employed in connection with a dramatic work such as opera or oratorio.

ARPEGGIO. An ascending or descending series of tones of a chord, played consecutively.

ATONALITY. Absence of key feeling.

AUTHENTIC CADENCE. The dominant chord followed by the tonic.

AUTHENTIC MODE. Any church mode in which the range of the melody lies between the final and the octave above.

BAR LINE. Vertical line through the staff to indicate metric divisions of a composition.

BASS. The low register of instrumental or vocal music.

BEAT. A measured pulse. E.g., in 4/4 time there are four beats to a measure.

BITONALITY. The use of two different keys simultaneously.

BRASS. Wind instruments in which the tone is produced by lip vibration.

BROKEN CHORD. The tones of a chord played consecutively.

CADENCE. The chord progression or melodic progression used to terminate a phrase or a section of a composition.

CANON. A contrapuntal form in which two or more parts in succession take up the same melody.

CANTABILE. In a singing style.

CANTUS FIRMUS. A borrowed melody used as the basis of a polyphonic composition.

CHAMBER MUSIC. Music for a small group of solo instruments, intended for performance in a small room rather than a large auditorium.

CHANSON, French word for "song."

CHANT. Liturgical melody, nonmetric, and monodic. E.g., plainsong.

CHOIR. A group of singers, usually associated with liturgical performance; or an instrumental group in the orchestra (e.g., brass choir, woodwind choir, etc.).

CHORALE. Protestant hymn tune.

CHORALE PRELUDE. A contrapuntal composition for organ based upon the chorale melody.

CHORD. A group of simultaneously sounding tones.

CHORUS. A body of singers; also a composition or part of a composition written for vocal ensemble.

CHROMATIC. Tones foreign to the key. A scale proceeding by semitones.

COLORATION. Melismatic ornamentation applied to melody such as plainsong.

COLORATURA. Rapid scales, figures, ornaments, usually applied to an operatic aria.

CONSONANCE. Combinations of tones in harmony that produce agreeable repose.

CONTRAPUNTAL. In the style of counterpoint; i.e., several individual melodies combined.

CONTRARY MOTION. Two melodies moving in opposite pitch directions; one melody ascends while the other descends.

COUNTERPOINT. The combination of two or more melodies; almost synonymous with polyphony.

CRESCENDO. Gradual increase of loudness.

DECLAMATION. Questions involving setting of music to text: proper accenting of syllables, pronunciation, stress on important words, etc.

DIATONIC. The use of the natural tones of the scale, excluding chromatic or altered tones.

DIMINUENDO. Gradual decrease of loudness.

DISSONANCE. Combinations of tones in harmony that produce unrest and require resolution; i.e., consonance following dissonance.

DOMINANT. The fifth tone of the scale, or the chord built on that tone.

DOTTED RHYTHM. Rhythm produced by recurrent use of a dot following a note which adds half its value to the note.

DOUBLE BAR. Two vertical lines drawn through the staff to indicate the end of a principal section in the composition or the final close.

DOUBLE STOPPING. Bowing on two strings of the violin simultaneously, producing a harmonic interval.

DUPLE METER. Two strong beats to the measure.

DYNAMICS. The aspect of music related to loudness and softness.

EIGHTH NOTE. One eighth the time value of a whole note.

ELEVENTH CHORD. A chord of six different tones.

EMBELLISHMENT. Melodic ornamentation consisting of trills, grace notes, mordents, etc.

ENSEMBLE. Any group of singers and/or instrumentalists.

FIGURATION. Recurrent melodic pattern.

FIGURED BASS. The use of numerals below a bass melody to indicate harmony.

FLAT. A symbol meaning to lower the tone in front of which it appears.

FLORID. Highly ornamented melodic line.

FORM. The structure of a musical composition.

FORTE. Loud.

FUGAL. In the style of a fugue; i.e., making use of contrapuntal imitation.

FUGHETTA. A short fugue or fugal section in a composition.

GLISSANDO. The execution of rapid scales by sliding the finger along the keyboard or violin string.

HALF NOTE. Half the time value of a whole note.

HARMONY. The practices of chord construction and chord progression.

HOMOPHONIC. A predominating melody with subordinate accompaniment.

HYMN. A religious song in verse and stanza form.

IMITATION. The use of a theme or melodic fragment consecutively in different parts of a polyphonic composition.

INSTRUMENTATION. The problems of instruments and instrumental combinations employed in ensemble music.

INTERVAL (HARMONIC). The pitch difference between two simultaneously sounding tones, referred to as 2nds, 3rds, 4ths, etc.

INTERVAL (MELODIC). The pitch difference between two consecutive tones, referred to as 2nds, 3rds, 4ths, etc.

INVERSION. Melodic inversion means the alternation of a given melody so that each melodic interval of the original melody is represented by the same interval moving in the opposite direction, up instead of down and vice versa.

KEY. The tone around which melodic and harmonic progressions gravitate.

KEYBOARD INSTRUMENT. Any instrument, such as the piano, organ, harpsichord, etc., which is manipulated by means of a series of black and white keys.

LIBRETTO. The text of an opera or oratorio.

LIED, LIEDER (*pl.*). German word for "song."

LIEDERBUCH. German song book.

LINE. The horizontal or melodic aspect of a composition.

LITURGICAL. Pertaining to the church service.

LYRE. A small, harplike instrument.

LYRIC. Songlike style, opposed to dramatic and coloristic styles.

MAJOR. Based upon a scale that has half steps between the 3rd and 4th degrees and between the 7th and 8th degrees.

MEDIUM, MEDIA (*pl.*). The instruments and/or voices required for the performance of a given composition.

MELISMA. An ornamental melodic passage, usually vocal, in which case it implies the use of numerous melodic tones to one syllable.

MELODY. A succession of tones of different pitch and usually different duration.

METER. The measuring of music according to a recurrent group of regular pulses.

METRIC. Measured: regular groups of regular pulses.

MINOR. Based upon scales that have a half step between the 2nd and 3rd degrees of the scale.

MODALITY. Use of the church modes.

MODE. The arrangement of half steps and whole steps in scales; hence major mode, minor mode, Dorian mode, etc.

MODULATION. The harmonic process of changing from one key to another.

MONODY, MONODIC. Music which is limited to a single melodic line without accompaniment.

MOTIVE. A group of tones in a melody that have a special rhythmic and/or melodic character.

MOVEMENT. The main sections of a large work (symphony, sonata, concerto, etc.) which are complete compositions in themselves.

MULTITONALITY. Numerous remotely related keys used consecutively in a composition.

MUSICOLOGY. The scientific study of music, as differentiated from the art of composition, performance, interpretation, etc.

NATURAL. A sign placed before a note indicating cancellation of a sharp or flat.

NINTH CHORD. A chord consisting of five tones.

NONCHORDAL TONES. Tones sounding with a chord that are not part of that chord.

NONHARMONIC TONES. The same as nonchordal tones.

GLOSSARY

GLOSSARY

NOTATION. The graphic representation of music by symbols that indicate pitch and duration of tone.

OCTAVE. An interval of eight degrees; the tones on the staff that have the same letter names are one or more octaves apart.

ORCHESTRATION. The study of effects produced by the combination of various instruments and instrumental resources.

OSTINATO. A short melody repeated over and over, usually in the bass.

OVERTURE. The instrumental form used to precede large dramatic works such as opera and oratorio.

PARALLEL MOTION. Two or more melodic lines moving in the same direction and the same intervals at the same time.

PART. The single melodic line of a polyphonic composition.

PEDAL POINT. A sustained or repeated tone, usually in the bass, which sounds through changing harmonies.

PENTATONIC. A five-tone scale.

PERCUSSION. Instruments, such as drums, gongs, triangles, etc., that are played by being struck.

PHRASE. A small section of a musical composition that is terminated by some form of cadence (harmonic close, melodic close, rhythmic pause).

PIANO. To play or sing quietly or softly.

PICKUP BEAT. The tone of a phrase beginning with an unaccented tone and preceeding an accented beat; anacrusis.

PITCH. The degree of highness or lowness of tone. Determined by rate of vibration.

PIZZICATO. A plucked string (as opposed to a bowed string).

PLAGAL CADENCE. The subdominant chord followed by the tonic chord.

PLAGAL MODE. The modes that range a fifth above and a fourth below the final.

PLAINSONG. Ecclesiastical melody, nonmetric, unaccompanied, modal.

POLYPHONY. Music employing two or more parts or melodies.

POLYTONALITY. The use of several different keys simultaneously.

PREPARATION. A dissonant note is prepared when it occurs immediately before as a consonant or chordal tone.

PROGRAM MUSIC. Music that has extramusical associations, is narrative or descriptive.

PSALM. Song based on the biblical Book of Psalms (which includes 150 religious poems).

QUADRUPLE FUGUE. A fugue with four distinct subjects or themes.

QUARTER NOTE. A note having one fourth the value of a whole note.

RANGE. The distance between the highest and the lowest note of a melody.

REGISTER. The range or a section thereof in a voice, instrument, or melody.

REGISTRATION. The combination of stops used in organ playing.

RELATIVE MAJOR. The major key, a third above the minor having the same key signature.

RESPONSORIAL. The chant of a priest answered by a choral chant, either in unison or polyphonically.

RHYTHM. The patterns of long and short durations of notes, also involving accented and unaccented tones.

ROOT. The tone on which a chord is built (e.g., the tonic is the root of the tonic triad).

SCALE. Any series of adjacent tones arranged in a plan of half steps and whole steps.

SCORE. The vertical alignment of two or more staves in a composition consisting of several parts.

SEQUENCE (PATTERN). The repetition of a melodic pattern at successively higher or lower intervals.

SEQUENCE (PLAINSONG). Prose text added to the melismatic alleluia of a plainsong.

SEVENTH CHORDS. A chord consisting of four tones.

SFORZANDO. Term meaning suddenly loud.

SHARP. Symbol meaning to raise the tone in front of which it appears.

SIXTEENTH NOTE. A note having one sixteenth the time value of a whole note.

SONORITY. Richness or fullness of sound.

STAFF. Parallel horizontal lines (normally 5) on which notes are placed to indicate exact pitch.

STRINGED INSTRUMENT. Any instrument (but usually referring to the bowed instruments) which produces musical tone by the vibration of a string from bowing or plucking.

STYLE. The character of music determined by musical elements such as harmony, rhythm, melody, tone color, etc.

SUBDOMINANT. The fourth degree of the scale or the chord built on that degree.

SUBJECT. The theme or melody of a fugue.

SUITE. A group of instrumental compositions; often, but not necessarily, implying a group of instrumental dances.

SYNCOPATION. Accenting weak or unimportant beats or parts of beats in a measure.

TEMPO. The speed at which a composition is performed, indicated by such terms as andante, moderato, largo, etc.

TETRACHORD. A section of a scale consisting of four adjacent tones.

THEME. A melody which is the basis of a composition or part of a composition.

TIE. A curved line connecting otherwise repeated notes.

TONALITY. The gravitation of music around a key or a tonal center.

TONIC. The first tone of a scale or the chord built on that tone.

TRANSCRIPTION. Rewriting a musical composition for another medium.

TREBLE. The high register.

TREMOLO. Rapid reiteration of a note on a string instrument by drawing the bow back and forth quickly in very short strokes across the string.

TRIAD. A chord consisting of three tones (root, third, fifth).

TRIPLE METER. Three beats to the measure.

TRIPLE STOPPING. Causing three tones to sound simultaneously on a bowed string instrument.

TUNE. A melody.

TUTTI. Played by the entire orchestral ensemble.

UNACCOMPANIED. Without instrumental support.

UNISON. Two or more parts singing or playing the same melody at the same time.

UNPREPARED DISSONANCE. *See* Preparation.

VIRTUOSITY. Brilliant display of technical facility.

VOICE. The individual part in a polyphonic composition. (It does not necessarily mean "to be sung.")

WHOLE NOTE. The basic unit of time in music.

WHOLE-TONE SCALE. A scale of six tones all a whole tone or whole step apart.

WIND INSTRUMENT. Any instrument which is played by blowing.

WOODWIND. Wind instruments that produce musical tone by vibration of a reed.

Bibliography

General Histories of Music

Dickinson, E., *The Study of the History of Music* (1908).

Einstein, A., *A Short History of Music* (1938).

Ferguson, D., *A History of Musical Thought* (1935).

Finney, T., *A History of Music* (1935).

Kinsky, G., *The History of Music in Pictures* (1929).

Láng, P., *Music in Western Civilization* (1941).

Leichtentritt, H., *Music, History, and Ideas* (1938).

Moore, D., *From Madrigal to Modern Music* (1942).

Nef, K., *An Outline of the History of Music* (1939).

Oxford History of Music, The (7 vols. 1929–34).

Pratt, W., *The History of Music* (1935).

Prunières, H., *A New History of Music* (1943).

Scholes, P., *The Listener's History of Music* (1925).

Stanford, C., and C. Forsyth, *History of Music* (1922).

Special Periods and Subjects

Abraham, G., *A Hundred Years of Music* (Beethoven to the present) (1938).

Allen, W., *Philosophies of Music History* (1939).

Apel, W., *Notation of Polyphonic Music* (1944).

Barrett, W., *English Glees and Part-Songs* (1886).

Beaumont, W., *Complete Book of Ballets* (1937, 1942).

Bekker, P., *The Changing Opera* (1935).

Bekker, P., *The Story of the Opera* (1936).

Brisay, A. de, *The Organ and Its Music* (1935).

Burney, C., *A General History of Music from the Earliest Ages to the Present Period* [1789] (1935).

Cabrol, A., *The Mass, Its Doctrine and History* (1931).

221

Cagey, E., *Ballad Opera* (1937).

Carse, A., *History of Orchestration* (1925).

Casella, A., *The Evolution of Music through the History of the Perfect Cadence* (1924).

Cobbett, W., *Cyclopedic Survey of Chamber Music* (2 vols., 1929).

Copland, A., *Our New Music* (1941).

Cowell, H., *New Musical Resources* (1930).

Dannreuther, E., *Musical Ornamentation* (2 vols., 1893).

Davison, A. T., *Protestant Church Music in America* (1933).

Dent, E., *History of Opera* (1942).

Dickinson, E., *Music in the History of the Western Church* (1902).

Dolmetsch, A., *Interpretation of the Music of the XVIIth and XVIIIth Centuries* (1915).

Douglas, W., *Church Music in History and Practice* (1937).

Dyson, G., *The New Music* (1924).

Ewen, D., *Twentieth Century Composers* (c. 1937).

Finck, C., *Songs and Song Writers* (1925).

Forsyth, C., *Music and Nationalism* (1911).

Foster, M., *Anthem and Anthem Composers* (1901).

Glyn, M., *About Elizabethan Virginal Music and Its Composers* (1924).

Harding, R., *Origins of Musical Time and Expression* (1938).

Haydon, G., *The Evolution of the Six-Four Chord* (1933).

Heyman, K., *The Relation of Ultramodern to Archaic Music* (1921).

Jeppesen, K., *The Style of Palestrina and the Dissonance* (1927).

Krenek, E., *Studies in Counterpoint* (1940).

Mackinley, M., *Light Opera* (1926).

Mason, D. G., *The Romantic Composers* (1930).

Merritt, A., *Sixteenth Century Polyphony* (1939).

Niecks, F., *Programme Music* (1907).

Patterson, A., *The Story of the Oratorio* (1909).

Reese, G., *Music in the Middle Ages* (1940).

Richardson, A., *The Medieval Modes* (1933).

Robeck, N. de, *Music of the Italian Renaissance* (1928).

Sachs, C., *The History of Musical Instruments* (1940).

Sachs, C., *A World History of the Dance* (1937).

Slonimsky, N., *Music since 1900*.

Streatfield, R., *The Opera* (1925).

Vaughan Williams, R., *National Music* (1934).

Veinus, A., *The Concerto* (1944).

Wagner, P., *Introduction to the Gregorian Melodies* (1907).

Wallaschek, R., *Primitive Music* (1893).

Westerby, H., *The History of Pianoforte Music* (1924).

Note. For related articles and further bibliography in periodicals and works in foreign languages, see Willi Apel, *Harvard Dictionary of Music* (1944).

Nationalities

Abraham, G., *Studies in Russian Music* (1935).

Calvocoressi, M., and G. Abraham, *Masters of Russian Music* (1936).

Chase, G., *The Music of Spain* (1941).

Dent, E., *Music of the Renaissance in Italy* (1934).

Fuller-Maitland, J., *Master of German Music* (1894).

Hill, E. B., *Modern French Music* (1924).

Howard, J. T., *Our American Music* (1931).

Howard, J. T., *Our Contemporary Composers* (1940).

Idelssohn, A., *Jewish Music in Its Historical Development* (1929).

Kaldy, G., *A History of Hungarian Music* (1903).

Lasserre, P., *The Spirit of French Music* (1917).

Luper, A., *The Music of Brazil* (1943).

Newmarch, R., *The Music of Czechoslovakia* (1942).

Rayson, E., *Polish Music and Chopin Its Laureate* (1916).

Reis, C., *Composers in America* (1938).

Sabanief, L., *Modern Russian Composers* (1927).

Slonimsky, N., *Music of Latin America* (1945).

Streatfield, R., *Masters of Italian Music* (1895).

Trend, J., *The Music of Spanish History to 1600* (1926).

Urban, L., *The Music of Bohemia* (1919).

Walker, E., *History of Music in England* (1924).

Biography

For details of biography, articles in one of the numerous music dictionaries are suggested (Groves, Baker, Oscar Thompson, *et al.*) and comprehensive bibliography under each article.

Record Anthologies

Anthologie Sonore (13 vols.).

Columbia History of Music (5 vols.).

Score Anthologies

Apel, W., and A. T. Davison, *Historical Anthology of Music* (2 vols., scheduled for publication, 1946).

Einstein, A., *Beispielsammlung zur Musikgeschichte*, 4th ed., Teubner, Leipzig (1930).

Riemann, H., *Musikgeschichte in Beispielen*, Breitkopf & Härtel, Leipzig (1930).

Schering, A., *Geschichte der Musik in Beispielen*, Breitkopf & Härtel, Leipzig (1931).

Steinitzer, Max, *Musikgeschichtlicher Atlas*, Fuckmich, Freiburg (1908).

Wolf, J., *Sing- und Spielmusik aus älterer Zeit*, Quelle & Mayer, Leipzig (1931).

Supplementary Bibliography

Apel, Willi, *Masters of the Keyboard* (1947).
Bukofzer, Manfred, *Music in the Baroque Era* (1947).
Einstein, Alfred, *Music in the Romantic Era* (1947).
Grout, Donald, *A Short History of Opera* (1948).

MUSIC HISTORY CHRONOLOGICAL CHART

	800	900	1000	1100	1200	1300	1400	1500	1600	1700	1800	1900

General Periods

P O L Y P H O N I C   P E R I O D   B A R O Q U E

ARS ANTIQUA   ARS NOVA   CLASSICAL   MODERN

← MIDDLE AGES →   RENAISSANCE   NUOVE MUSICHE   ROMANTIC

Instrumental Forms

ENGLISH VIRGINAL SCHOOL   Dance Suite   Classical Sonata . . . .
Variation   Sonata . . . .   String Quartet
Estampie . . .   Rota . . . .   Basse - danse . . . .   Toccata, Prelude and Fugue . . . .   Symphony . .
Danse - royale . . Saltarello . . . .   Tourdion . . | . . . .   Chorale Prelude . . . .   Serenade . . . .
Pavane · Galliard . . . .   Trio Sonata . . . .
Ricercare . . . .   Symphonic Poem .
Canzona . . . .   Concert Overture
Prelude . . . .   Concerto Grosso . . . . .   Ballet
Solo Concerto . . . .

Vocal Forms

Troubadour and Trouvère Monody   Polyphonic Settings of the Mass . . . .   Opera
Organum . . . .   Motet . . . .   Oratorio
Plainsong Tropes and Sequences . . . . . .   Clausula   Cathedral Anthem   Cantata   Large Works for Orchestra, Soloists, Chorus . . . .
Conductus   Solo Song
Verse Anthem
Motet . . . . . .   Isorhythmic Motet   French Chanson . . . .   Recitative
Ballade   Villota   Italian Madrigal
Madrigal   Canzonetta   English Madrigal
Caccia   Balletto
Ballata   Polyphonic Lied . . . .

Documents and Works

Musica En-chiriadis   Winchester Troper   Montpellier Codex   Old Hall MS.   *Fitzwilliam Virginal Bk.*   Beggar's Opera   *Lohengrin*   *Wozzek*

Trent Codices   *Odhecaton*   *Euridice*   Serva Padrona   *Elijah   Ring*   *Rite of Spring*

Nuove Musiche   *Freischütz*   *Rhapsody in Blue*

Ars Nova   Lochaimer Liederbuch   *Ballet Comique*   *Cento Concerti*   *Messiah   Seasons*   *L'Apres-midi*

1st polyphonic setting of Mass (Machaut)   Glogauer Liederbuch   Huguenot Psalter   *Brandenburg Concertos*   *Aida*   *Till Eulenspiegel*

Münchner Liederbuch   *L'Amfiparnasso*   *Orpheus*   *Barber of Seville   Carmen*   *Pierrot Lunoire*

COMPOSERS

French

Troubadours . . . .   BURGUNDIAN SCHOOL   Lully . . . .   Gounod . . . . Honegger
Trouvères . . . .   Dufay . . . FLEMISH SCHOOL . . . .   Chopin . . . . . Debussy
Leonin   Pérotin   De la Croix   Obrecht . . . | .   Couperin . . . . .   Ravel . . . .
De Vitri . . . .   Ockeghem . . . . Lasso . . . .   Berlioz . . . . . . Franck
Machaut . . . .   Desprez . . . . Lejeune . . . . .   Rameau . . . .   Bizet . . Faure . . . . . Milhaud . . . . . .
De la Rue . . .   Jannequin   Saint · Saëns . . . . . | . . .
Mouton . . . . .   Goudimel   Meyerbeer   Roussel . . . . . .

Italian

Cavalli . . . . A. Scarlatti . . . .   Rossini . . . .   Busoni . . . .
A. Gabrieli . . . . . Frescobaldi . . .   D. Scarlatti . . .   Bellini . .   Respighi . . . . . .
Landini . . . .   Willaert . . . . . G. Gabrieli . . . .   Corelli . . . | . .   Donizetti . . .   Malipiero . . . .
PALESTRINA . . . . .   Vivaldi . . . . . .   Verdi . . . . . . Puccini . . . .
Carissimi . . . . .   Casella . . . . . .
Monteverdi . . . . .   Bartok (*Hung.*) . . . . .
De Falla (*Sp.*) . . . . .

German

Minnesingers . . . .   Schütz . . . . . .   Telemann . . . .   BEETHOVEN . .   R. Strauss . . . . . .
Meistersingers . . . .   Gluck . . . . .   Weber . . Wagner . . . .
Gallus . . . . | Froberger . . .   BACH   Mendelssohn . . Mahler . . . .
Praetorius . . .   HANDEL . . . .   Schubert . . . .   Schönberg . . . .
Senfl . .   Schein . . . .   Pachelbel . . | . . . . MOZART . . . . .   Schumann .   Sibelius (*Fin.*) . . .
Isaac . . . . .   Hassler . . . .   Brahms . . . . . Hindemith . . . . .
Hofhaimer . . .   Scheidt . . . . .   HAYDN . . . .   Liszt . . . .

English and others

Dunstable . . . . . .   Purcell . . . . . .   R U S S I A   Glinka . . . . .   Scriabin
Victoria (*Sp.*) . . . . . .   Tschaikovsky . . . Stravinsky . . . .
Byrd . . . . . .   Rimski · Korsakov   Prokofieff . . . .
Morley . . . . .   Borodin . . . . .   Shostakovitch . . . . . .
Bull . . . . . . | .   Moussorgsky . Elgar (*Eng.*) . . . .
Vaughan Williams (*Eng.*)
Gibbons . . .   Rachmaninoff . . .

Index

A

A Cappella music, in the Renaissance, 38, 39; in baroque church music, 86; in French baroque church music, 87; in 20th century, 176; in modern Russian church music, 190
ABACO, FELICE DALL' (1675–1742), 101
Academic Festival Overture, Brahms, 158
Académie Royale de Musique, 77
Accompanied solo song, 69
Acis and Galatea, Handel, 79, 109
Act-tunes, 79
ADAM DE LA HALLE, 11
ADAM OF ST. VICTOR, 10
Adam und Eva, Theile, 78
Added tones, 181
Addison, 67
Adonais, Rogers, 207
Adventures in a Perambulator, Carpenter, 206
Aeolian mode, 9
L'Africaine, Meyerbeer, 143
Afro-American folk music, 204
Agnus Dei of the Mass, 10
Aïda, Verdi, 142
Air, 92
ALBENIZ, ISAAC (1860–1909), 199; piano music of, 156; *Iberian Suite,* 162; 19th-century composers, 166
Alberti bass, 114
ALDHELM, BISHOP (c. 640–709), 23
ALFANO, 197
Algarotti, Count, 127
Alleluia of the Mass, 10
Allemande, 91; in harpsichord music of the 16th century, 57
ALLENDE, HUMBERTO (1885–   ), 202
Also sprach Zarathustra, R. Strauss, 161
Altered chords, 181
Alto Rhapsody, Brahms, 150

Amazonas, Villa-Lobos, 202
Ambitus, 8
Ambrosian chant, 9
America, American; *see also* United States
American Indian music, 204
American Life, Weiss, 207
American Polonaise, Riegger, 206
American Revolution, 113, 167
American symphony orchestras, 204
L'Amfiparnasso, Vecchi, 44
An die ferne Geliebte, Beethoven, 140, 151
Anapaest, 12
Andalusian styles, 199
ANERIO, FELICE (c. 1560–1614), 39
D'ANGLEBERT, HENRI (1635–1691), 93
Anglican chant, 42
Anglican church music, 39, 40, 42, 88
Angularity of melody, 50; in modern music, 183
Anna Magdalena Bach's Music Notebook, Bach, 108
Antar, Rimsky-Korsakov, 162
ANTHEIL, GEORGE (1900–   ), 209
Antiphonal singing, 4, 9; of Venetian school, 39
Apollon Musagètes, Stravinsky, 188
Apollonian cult, 4; in classical ideal, 113
Appassionata spirit, 138
L'Apprenti sorcier, Dukas, 186
L'Après-midi d'un faune, Debussy, 158
Arabesque, 137
ARCADELT, JACQUES (c. 1514–c. 1570), and Italian madrigal, 44; French chansons of, 46
ARCHANGELSKY, ALEXANDER (1846–1924), 190
D'AREZZO, GUIDO, 22
Argentina, 200
Aria, new form in the Baroque, 69; innovation of nuove musiche, 71

99; baroque orchestral music, 101;
19th-century opera, 147; 19th-century
composers, 165–166; the 20th century,
194
English, *see also* England
English discant, 31
English horn in the Baroque, 90; in the
19th century, 137
English suites, Bach, 107
Enharmonic tetrachords, 6
Enigma Variations, Elgar, 158, 162
Ensemble music (instrumental) before
1600, 58; in the Baroque, 97–101; *see
also* Symphony, Chamber music
Entführung aus dem Serail, Die, Mozart,
129, 144
Entr'acte music, 79
Enueg, 12
Episode in sonata-allegro form, 118
"Epitaph of Seikilos," 6
Equal-tempered tuning, 90; in Bach's
Well-Tempered Clavichord, 93
ERBACH, 96
ERKEL, FERENC (1810–1893), 197
Erminia sul Giordano, Rossi, 74
Escenas campesinas chilenas, Allende, 202
Esercizii, D. Scarlatti, 92
ESPOILE, 201
Esquinas, Revueltas, 203
Estampie, 14, 15, 52
Ethos, 4, 6
Etude, 154; in the 19th century, 137
Eugen Onegin, Tschaikovsky, 147
Euridice, Peri-Rinuccini, 72; earliest ex-
tant opera, 73
Euryanthe, von Weber, 145
Evocations, Roussel, 185
Exchange, 25
Exposition in sonata-allegro form, 118
Expressionism, 173

F

Fa-la-la chorus, 45
Fairy Queen, The, Purcell, 79
Faithful, The, Rogers, 207
FALLA, MANUEL DE (1876–1946), 198;
summary of 19th-century composers,
166
Falstaff, Verdi, 142
Familiar style, 32; *see also* Chordal style
Fancy, 53

Fanfare overture, 75
Fantasia, 53; for lute, 55; organ form, 56;
in ensemble music, 58; in baroque
harpsichord music, 93; organ form in
the Baroque, 94; in the 19th century,
137; in 19th-century piano music, 154;
see also Fancy
Fantasy, *see* Fantasia, Fancy
Fantasy on a Theme of Thomas Tallis,
Vaughan Williams, 194
FARMER, JOHN (fl. 1591–1601), 45
FARNABY, GILES (c. 1560–c. 1600), 57
FAURÉ, GABRIEL (1845–1924), *Requiem,*
149; *La bonne chanson,* 151; songs of,
153; piano music of, 156; chamber
music of, 163; summary of 19th-cen-
tury composers, 165
Faust, Gounod, 143
Faust, Spohr, 145
Faust Symphony, Liszt, 150, 160
Fauxbourdon, 31, 32
Favart, 80
Favorita, La, Donizetti, 142
Fedra, Pizzetti, 197
Feen, Die, Wagner, 146
Felsenmühle, Reisinger, 145
Fennimore and Gerda, Delius, 195
FERNANDEZ (1897–   ), 202
Fervaal, D'Indy, 144
FESTA, COSTANZO (d. 1545), 44
FICHER, JACOBO, 201
Fidelio, Beethoven, 140, 145
FIELD, JOHN (1782–1837), 166
Fifth Symphony, Beethoven, 139
Figaro, Mozart, 128, 129
Figuration, 50; in variation form, 54; in
lute music, 55; in English virginal
music, 57; in Scarlatti sonatas, 93; in
baroque string music, 98
Figured bass, 69, 72; innovation of nuove
musiche, 71
Fille du régiment, La, Donizetti, 142
Filling Station, Thomson, 208
Final in plainsong, 8
FINCK, HEINRICH (1445–1527), lied, 47;
Bach's coloration style derived from,
106
Finland, 20th-century, 200
Finta giardiniera, La, Mozart, 129
Fiori musicali, Frescobaldi, 96
Firebird, The, Stravinsky, 177, 188
Fireworks, Stravinsky, 188